THE
Honest Truth
ABOUT
FRAUD

VICTOR E. HARTMAN JD, CPA/CFF, CFE

THE
Honest Truth
ABOUT
FRAUD

A Retired FBI Agent Tells All

A Practitioner's Guide to Fraud

Edited by Dr. Sridhar Ramamoorti

To my Mom

—

She taught me the discipline to fulfill my dreams.

To my wife, Jonna

—

You are the love of my life, and thank you for

your encouragement to pursue my passions.

And to my daughter, Katie

—

Your dedication, talent, and love of life are inspiring.

CONTENTS

FOREWORD

"The credit belongs to the man who is actually in the arena, whose face is marred by dust and sweat and blood; who strives valiantly; who errs, who comes short again and again, because there is no effort without error and shortcoming; but who does actually strive to do the deeds; who knows great enthusiasms, the great devotions; who spends himself in a worthy cause; who at the best knows in the end the triumph of high achievement, and who at the worst, if he fails, at least fails while daring greatly, so that his place shall never be with those cold and timid souls who neither know victory nor defeat." [1]

—DESCRIPTION OF "THE MAN IN THE ARENA"
BY THEODORE ROOSEVELT ON APRIL 23, 1910

President Roosevelt describes my friend, colleague, and author of this book, Mr. Victor E. Hartman—"the man in the arena"—quite well. Vic is also both an attorney and a CPA, the almost ideal combination of professional designations for anyone working at the FBI who is investigating fraud and white-collar crime. Even Lady Fortune smiled on him, for he was stationed in Houston, Texas, when, at the dawn of the twenty-first century, Enron collapsed. He was involved in the initial fact-finding forays by the FBI teams at both Enron and WorldCom to investigate the two large accounting scandals that led to the Sarbanes-Oxley Act of 2002. The quintessential practitioner, Vic Hartman has been there, done that, and pretty much seen everything.

Vic has poured his heart and soul into this book, and he has been quite exhaustive in describing the fraud threat picture. He also coined the term "forensic posture" to describe the position professionals may find themselves in when dealing with any aspect of the fraud life cycle: prevention, detection, investigation, mitigation, and remediation. He has competently captured the highlights of different types of fraud schemes and provided his audience with a practical approach to investigations, including interviewing techniques. His personal examples are compelling. In this book, his incredible background and experience, and his perspective as an antifraud expert come alive, and his passion and enthusiasm for the subject matter are evident throughout. You cannot fail to be impressed. The writing is crisp and matter-of-fact, but also memorable, even contagious!

Over 20 years ago, I recall a senior partner of an accounting firm describing the ideal Big Four firm partner as a "SWAN = smart, workaholic, ambitious, but nice." He went on to add that such a person would look as graceful as a swan on a placid lake (who was paddling unseen like the devil underneath!) Again, the description seems to fit Vic's calm and unflappable demeanor, yet his command and knowledge of the facts and circumstances of each case are so detailed that you just know he has been burning the midnight oil. I have no doubt that if Vic had chosen to be in the private sector instead of the FBI, he would have made a terrific partner in a Big Four firm.

I believe Vic has succeeded in his goal of producing a very different kind of book—one with a broad sweep but sufficiently detailed to afford business professionals of all stripes a solid overview and analysis of fraud and white-collar crime. It is my honor and privilege to have assisted him in assembling this excellent resource for practitioners to learn about fraud and to protect themselves against it.

Dr. Sridhar Ramamoorti
Editor

PREFACE

"Because that's where the money is." [1]

—APOCRYPHAL QUOTE OF LEGENDARY BANK ROBBER WILLIE
SUTTON WHEN ASKED WHY HE ROBBED BANKS

I graduated from the Federal Bureau of Investigation's Academy in Quantico, Virginia, in 1989 with a badge, a gun, and marching orders to investigate savings and loan fraud in Houston, Texas. At the time, the Savings and Loan (S&L) crisis was full-blown, with institutions falling like dominoes and the media reporting on the deluge of crooks who had stolen millions of dollars. Congress, which ironically was as much to blame for the crisis as the crooks, wanted answers. Through legislation known as the Financial Institutions Reform, Recovery, and Enforcement Act of 1989 (FIRREA), Congress funded the FBI and the Department of Justice (DOJ) to hire FBI agents and prosecutors with law, accounting, and regulatory backgrounds to put the S&L scoundrels in jail and recoup America's money.

This is the point in the long history of financial crimes where I began my journey. The country had just gone through a series of prosecutions involving Wall Street insider traders Ivan Boesky, Michael Milken, and the like. The FBI's focus on financial crimes had now moved from securities fraud to bank fraud. Texas developers had purchased banks during a time of rising real estate values. When caught up in a deteriorating real estate environment, these same developers-turned-bank executives made reciprocal loans among themselves to refinance their failing projects in a scheme known as a "daisy chain." Under normal circumstances, a team of FBI agents would be investigating one bank failure, a many-to-one arrangement. But these were no ordinary times. During the S&L crisis in Houston, Dallas, and other cities, one agent was assigned to multiple failures, a one-to-many arrangement.

I had the honor and privilege of being an FBI agent working on behalf of the American public. I knew the job would be challenging. I believed I had the technical credentials to investigate complicated fraud. At the age of 25, I sincerely believed that what I thought I lacked in experience, I would make up for in enthusiasm. That was not exactly the case. There were some critical concepts that I found to be the linchpin for successfully working fraud cases. This was not something taught at the FBI Academy, but it was something I did learn during a career of investigating fraud.

In fact, these practical and useful concepts were the impetus for my writing this book. Let me take a step back and reframe these concepts in the form of a question. Why would an individual make a materially false representation to another individual, company, or governmental entity for the purpose of material gain? Why would the individual do this, knowing he or she could get caught, be forced to pay the money back, suffer great shame, and face the real prospect of federal prison?

Learning the answer to the "why" question would eventually make my work easier and more efficient. Answering the question is at the heart of my journey and is a core theme of this book. Consider these questions: How do I prevent fraud? How do I detect fraud? How do I investigate fraud? What is the current fraud threat picture?

The often-cited quotation of Willie Sutton referenced in the epigraph above is wrong twice over. He did not say it, and it is not true. He actually did not rob banks for the money. In his book, *Where the Money Was*, Sutton reveals his real motive:

Why did I rob banks? Because I enjoyed it. I loved it. I was more alive when I was inside a bank, robbing it, than at any other time in my life. I enjoyed everything about it so much that one or two weeks later I'd be out looking for the next job. But to me the money was the chips, that's all.[2]

Although robbing a bank at gunpoint is not fraud, Sutton's motivation for that serious crime makes my point—it is not always what you think it is. His motivation was clearly not greed. The obvious reason is really not obvious at all. For Willie Sutton, it was all about the emotions that came from fun and excitement. For others, their motivations will probably be something else. Surprisingly, it may not be about greed, the so-called standard explanation.

As a young FBI agent fresh out of the FBI Academy, I was full of piss and vinegar, but I had only mastered the technical skills to fight fraud. As an attorney, I knew the legal elements of each white-collar criminal offense I investigated. I always started with the end in mind. The end is a jury trial in which the government has the burden of proving that the defendant committed each element of the offense beyond a reasonable doubt. As a CPA, I understood the language of business. I could take complex financial documents and explain them to a prosecutor, grand jury, or trial jury.

The piece of the puzzle I was missing was understanding the psychology of the fraudster. My enthusiasm did not fully compensate for this lack of understanding. At that point in my career, I simply had not debriefed enough white-collar defendants to understand them. I was simply lacking the experience of dealing with those who commit fraud—the fraudsters—and the knowledge of why they do it. That does not mean I was not successful. I had all the AICs (arrests, indictments, and convictions) to keep my supervisor happy. I just did not know as much about fraud as I thought I did. I most certainly did not know what motivated individuals to commit fraud. I thought it was all about greed, taking shortcuts, or funding a fancy lifestyle at someone else's expense. Jumping to this conclusion was often wrong. Further, my mistaken assumptions likely caused inefficiencies by my taking unnecessary investigative steps, thereby increasing the costs of my investigations. Later, after understanding the motivation of my targets and their coconspirators, my investigations became much more effective and efficient. I was better able to strategically organize my investigations. Most importantly, my interviews and interrogations were eminently more effective.

I loved every day of my 25-year career with the FBI. My work included investigations into the diverse industries of financial services, health care, and governmental organizations. I served two stints as an attorney representing the FBI. My first role as an attorney was in the Houston Division of the FBI, where I served as Associate Division Counsel, a job that included managing the division's forfeiture team. While in the Houston Division, I was asked to switch to a management role, in which I supervised a bank fraud squad, a public corruption squad, and a health care fraud squad.

The first squad I supervised was a bank fraud squad of agents and task force officers. I was constantly amazed at how many frauds are associated with banks. Although the prevalence of fraudulent mortgages and bad checks were no surprise, the occasional bribery of bank officers was disheartening.

My most challenging role was supervising a public corruption squad. Public corruption cases are often high-profile cases and have lots of over-sight. I truly believe in the need for oversight, especially for corruption cases. However, oversight comes with diverging views on how to proceed with an investigation. Within the field division, there is the Special Agent in Charge and the Chief Division Counsel. Each play a significant role. Then there is the United States Attorney's Office, which prosecutes the cases. A federal prose-cutor never wants to lose a case, especially one involving a high-profile elected official. Accordingly, public corruption cases are often not charged until the conduct becomes so egregious that the prosecutor is confident that a win at trial is almost a certainty. Corruption cases are never straightforward. They usually involve collusion between two parties and no paper trail. On top of that, the defendant's charisma, which probably helped the defendant get elected in the first place, can influence the jury. Then there is Washington D.C. Both FBI Headquarters and the Department of Justice will weigh in on corruption investigations. The fact that these cases ever get prosecuted is somewhat amazing. Invariably, the prosecution is the result of the dogged

FBI street agent who pushes the cases through the system by articulating the hard and undeniable facts uncovered during the investigation.

I also supervised a health care fraud squad, which included the Houston Area Health Care Fraud Task Force composed of six law enforcement agencies and in excess of 50 investigators. Health care is one of the largest sectors of our economy. In terms of the anger I felt as an FBI agent, it was at its highest when I oversaw the Houston Division's health care fraud program. I witnessed firsthand the hundreds of millions of dollars lost because of those who defraud our federal health care programs. I felt this anger because, unlike almost every other type of fraud, there were no victims to cry foul. America was, and is still, asleep at the wheel when it comes to health care fraud. Taxpayers are the victims, and yet, they have no idea of the pervasiveness of the problem or the magnitude of the dollar loss.

While I was assigned to the Houston Division, two major accounting scandals were uncovered: Enron and WorldCom. Enron, a Houston-based company, imploded, and then a year later, WorldCom, located in Jackson, Mississippi, followed with a similar fate. I played leadership roles in the early investigative phases of both of these calamities. The first prosecution related to these cases was actually Arthur Andersen, the auditor for both of these companies. Little did I know at the time that the leadership failures of Enron, WorldCom, and Arthur Andersen would result in the passage of the sweeping legislation known as SOX, the Sarbanes-Oxley Act of 2002. I think it was apropos that a lead sponsor of this legislation, the late Congressman Michael Oxley, was a former FBI agent. He used to joke that many people he met abroad thought his first name was Sarbanes! There are many insights to be gained from studying the root causes of these major frauds that led to the most significant corporate governance reform legislation since the federal securities laws of the 1930s.

My last position with the FBI was as Chief Division Counsel of the Atlanta Division. As an attorney who represented the FBI, I provided legal advice and counsel to FBI executives who were managing all of the FBI's diverse programs. While white-collar crime was always my passion, the FBI had many other priorities that required my attention as legal counsel, including counterterrorism, cybercrime, drugs, organized crime, violent crimes, and foreign counterintelligence.

Even while serving as an attorney, I still wanted to stay involved in the FBI's white-collar crime program. I was honored to be selected to serve on the FBI's elite Corporate Fraud Response Team. This team, which was necessitated by the wave of corporate failures that included Enron and WorldCom, enabled the FBI to quickly respond at any corporate headquarters with a trained cadre of motivated FBI agents and forensic accountants to execute search warrants, interview executives, and start e-mail reviews. For my tough and rugged FBI agent friends who served dutifully on dangerous SWAT (Special Weapons and Tactics) teams, I always tell them I experienced many bloody paper cuts while working on the Corporate Fraud Response Team. There are few other organizations that share the esprit de corps that develops among FBI agents. As with most Type A personalities, there is also a healthy competition among the ranks.

I retired from the FBI after a career spanning a quarter century. I now represent clients needing internal investigations, forensic accounting, fraud mitigation consulting, and assistance with whistle-blower claims. I teach a master's level forensic accounting class at two large universities and regularly speak on the topic of fraud. I believe those in academia also play a significant role in the fight against fraud. First, they are teaching students who are getting ready to enter the workforce, and second, they have produced theoretical models that are of great value. Because of all of these experiences, I am convinced that there is a need for those in charge of companies, not-for-profits, and governmental organizations to better manage the fraud risk they face.

While I truly believe the FBI has done an extraordinary job investigating fraud, it does have resource limitations and perhaps does a poor job of sharing information with the private sector. This knowledge would greatly benefit those responsible for the prevention, detection, and investigation of fraud. That is part of my motivation for writing this book.

Everyone has a role in managing fraud risk. I am confident that my insights will benefit the many professionals who are responsible for overseeing fraud-related issues, including auditors, general counsels, compliance officers, board members, human resource professionals, chief audit executives, heads of security, criminal and civil investigators, regulators, and frontline managers.

Let me end this Preface with one legally required item. Due to my prior employment with the FBI and the examples provided throughout the book, I am required to and did obtain a prepublication review of my manuscript by the FBI. I have only included material that is consistent with FBI policy, and the opinions expressed throughout this book are mine and not those of the FBI.

Vic Hartman
Atlanta, Georgia

INTRODUCTION

I have spent my entire professional life dealing with fraud, including 25 years as an FBI agent and another 5 plus years in private practice. I witnessed fraud from the inside out. I know the players. I have talked to the victims. I have interviewed the witnesses. I have put the fraudsters in prison. I am now on acquaintance terms with some of these reformed felons and make joint presentations with them to various audiences.

The sad truth is that much of the fraud I investigated could have been prevented. Obviously, the victims wanted that outcome. What may perhaps come as a surprise is that many of the fraudsters themselves wished they would have been prevented from committing their acts. The material in this book can help you understand why both fraudster and victim engaged in activities that they may have regretted later.

Fraud has a staggering impact on all of us, including commercial enterprises, not-for-profits, and governmental entities in the United States and around the world. The Association of Certified Fraud Examiners' 2018 *Report to the Nations on Occupational Fraud and Abuse* estimates that organizations, on average, lose about 5 percent of their top-line revenue to fraud from within their organizations. When this figure is multiplied by the gross world product (GWP) of $79.6 trillion, the cost of occupational fraud is nearly $4 trillion dollars.[1]

When I was conducting the research for this book, several categories of fraud caught me by surprise due to the magnitude of the losses associated with them—health care fraud, tax evasion, and theft of intellectual property. I first began calculating the magnitude of health care fraud when I was leading the Houston Area Health Care Fraud Task Force. I now estimate the health care fraud loss to be about a quarter of a trillion dollars. The federal tax gap—the difference between the true tax liability and the amount paid on time—is nearly a half trillion dollars. The theft of intellectual property—technically not fraud—may be in excess of a half trillion dollars. The problem with these numbers is the MEGO (my eyes glaze over) effect. Upon learning these numbers, you did not drop this book, call your congressman or hold a press conference; you probably just yawned and turned the page. Don't worry, you are not alone. But these numbers are alarming, and we should all be concerned about what they represent.

This is a book about fraud. I wrote this book with several audiences in mind. The book is for the casual observer who wants to understand fraud and what can be done to minimize its impact. Another audience includes the many organizations that have been impacted by fraud and whose boards of directors are mandating that something be done so that the horrific event will not happen again. The book is also for the many audiences to whom I speak and who tell me that I should write a book about my experiences. This book is also the textbook for my forensic accounting students, who are learning from a practitioner in the field. Finally, this book is for those forward-looking organizations that assign fraud risk management to a corporate official, such as the chief risk officer or the compliance officer. If you find yourself in any of these roles, this book is for you.

This book is meant to be an easy-to-read reference guide. To try to keep the topics interesting and to show you how the concepts can apply to your organization, I have provided many case examples. While I encourage you to first read Chapter 1, "Fraud Concepts," realistically, you can read any chapter in the order of your interest.

The book is organized into four parts. Part I provides fraud concepts and answers the question, "Why do people commit fraud?" It also defines fraud in the various regulatory, civil, and criminal contexts in which it occurs. Part II provides the fraud threat picture that any organization may face. I have attempted to categorize all frauds, explain the schemes, and where appropriate, discuss prevention strategies. Part III discusses the fraud life cycle from prevention through resolution. Last, Part IV addresses the various professionals who are responsible for dealing with fraud. This last part concludes with various standards and legal requirements that professionals must adhere to when investigating fraud, and it has particular relevance for forensic accountants.

PART I:
Fraud Overview

- Fraud Concepts
- Fraud Defined

CHAPTER 1
Fraud Concepts

"Trusted persons become trust violators when they conceive of themselves as having a financial problem which is non-shareable, are aware this problem can be secretly resolved by violation of the position of financial trust, and are able to apply to their own conduct in that situation verbalizations which enable them to adjust their conceptions of themselves as trusted persons with their conceptions of themselves as users of the entrusted funds or property."

—DR. DONALD R. CRESSEY[1]

I find the most fascinating part of investigating a fraud case is understanding the motivation of the fraudster. Why did Enron CEO (Chief Executive Officer) Ken Lay and WorldCom CEO Bernie Ebbers commit financial statement fraud? Why did congressional lobbyist Jack Abramoff engage in corruption? Why do employees routinely use their company issued P-Cards (purchasing card) or credit card to purchase personal items? These are three distinct types of fraud. As we will explore throughout this book, the motivation behind these frauds usually vary by the type of fraud being committed.

So, why do people commit fraud? Why do we care about why people commit fraud? The answers to these questions will assist us with understanding each component of the fraud life cycle: (1) prevention, (2) detection, (3) investigation, (4) mitigation, and (5) remediation. The fraud life cycle will be explored in more detail in Part III of this book. Fundamentally, understanding what causes someone to commit fraud will be the key to dealing with each facet of fraud from prevention through resolution.

The Fraud Triangle

If knowing the motivation of a fraudster is so important, how can those dealing with fraud gain this insight? What if there were a theoretical model to assist them with answering this question? There is a long lineage of academics who have developed a model, practitioners like me who have validated it, and professional organizations that have adopted it. This theoretical model is the Fraud Triangle. The theory holds that before a person will commit fraud, three elements must be in place: (1) there is an opportunity for it to occur, (2) the person will be under some type of perceived pressure, and (3) the person must be able to rationalize his or her behavior.

The father of the Fraud Triangle is noted sociologist Dr. Donald R. Cressey. The quote at the beginning of this chapter is from Cressey's influential work dating back to the early 1950s, involving his study and interviews of embezzlers.[2] Now, reread the quote and reflect on its significance. The quote summarizes Cressey's work on this subject and is the basis for the three vertices of the Fraud Triangle. The actual descriptive term, "Fraud Triangle," was coined by Dr. Steve Albrecht, who has himself done much research in this area.[3]

The importance of the Fraud Triangle for our purposes lies in the essence of the theory. Just as the "fire triangle" requires the simultaneous existence of heat, fuel, and an oxidizing agent before fire can occur, the Fraud Triangle theory posits that three elements must exist before a fraud can occur. Conversely, if one element of the Fraud Triangle can be knocked out, voilà, fraud may be prevented in an organization. As a caveat, there is a class of frauds for which the Fraud Triangle does not provide an adequate explanation. I will cover this class of frauds below.

Opportunity

The easiest vertex of the Fraud Triangle to understand is opportunity. One simply cannot commit fraud without opportunity. The reason banks lock their cash in vaults is to deny the opportunity for someone to steal it. Likewise, a janitor at a Fortune 500 company cannot commit financial statement fraud because there is no real opportunity. These are conceptually easy to understand. All organizations should have processes, known as "internal controls," for safeguarding assets from cash to inventory. As we will explore in more depth, denying opportunity is only part of the solution for prevention. Laws such as the Sarbanes-Oxley Act of 2002 (SOX) and the Dodd-Frank Act of 2010 can only go so far in preventing fraud by making certain types of actions illegal.

We also must use psychology. Internal controls work because they prevent many frauds. The perception that an internal control is in place is actually just as effective as an actual control. We need to create the perception of detection in our workplaces.

Pressure

The next vertex of the Fraud Triangle is pressure. An employee can experience two types of pressure: (1) pressure from outside the organization and (2) pressure from inside the organization.

I have seen firsthand the many pressures that happen to an individual outside an organization. I call them "life happens" events. These include financial pressures resulting from traumatic health concerns, divorce, bankruptcy, drugs, alcohol, gambling, and other challenges of life.

There are also pressures that occur inside an organization. The obvious one is the pressure to "make the numbers." All of these pressures and an organization's countermeasures will be explored in more detail.

For this vertex of the Fraud Triangle, the concept of "incentive" can be considered along with "pressure." For instance, an employee may be provided a bonus or a higher commission if certain preset goals are met. Thus, incentive-driven behavior is also a type of pressure. If there is one thing we learn from psychology, it is that people respond to incentives.

Rationalization

As you are starting to see, many of the solutions around the fraud problem relate to psychology, and rationalization is certainly at the heart of the psychology of fraud.[4] As part of the human condition, we cannot look ourselves in the mirror and see a fraudster.[5] We simply cannot view ourselves as doing harm to others, and thus our mind has created a defense mechanism known as "rationalization."

By now, you may be asking how your organization is going to stop an employee from rationalizing that his or her fraudulent conduct is somehow permissible. That's a tough one. However, remember the importance of solving this issue, because if we can knock out one element of the Fraud Triangle—in this case, rationalization—we will likely prevent fraud from occurring. What internal control can be put in place to stop rationalization? I will give you a preview of what is to come. The answer lies in creating a soft control, like a positive culture, in the organization.

Case Example

I once interviewed a midlevel procurement manager. Going into the interview, I had strong reason to believe that he had altered a scoring matrix that had been used to calculate the winning bid. I also knew that a bidder was paying bribes to an intermediary, but I did not know which city official was the end recipient of the payments. Further, I also had reason to believe it was not the midlevel manager I was interviewing. So why would he alter the scoring matrix? This was one of those interviews in which I did a lot of homework in advance and listened carefully during the interview. I obtained an admission that he had done it due to pressure from his boss. He wanted an upcoming promotion and thus altered the scoring matrix in order to be a team player. The key to this interview was to develop a theme during the interview based on my theory of the subject's pressures and rationalizations. If the theme resonates with the subject, which it did in this case, the chance of obtaining a confession and cooperation will be substantially increased. This is an example of when knowing the subject's motivation, including pressure and rationalization, will greatly enhance an investigation.

Association of Certified Fraud Examiners

The Association of Certified Fraud Examiners (ACFE) is the world's largest antifraud organization and premier provider of antifraud training and education.[6] The ACFE was founded in 1988 by Dr. Joseph T. Wells and has over 85,000 members worldwide.[7] Wells is also a former FBI agent.

I want to share a very ironic but quite personal story. In 1989, when I was fresh out of the FBI Academy, my supervisor and I traveled from Houston to Austin on a business matter. It was a trip I would make many times as an agent because Austin is the capital of Texas and home to the state's regulatory agencies. My supervisor knew Joe Wells from a time when Joe was still with the FBI, so we paid him a visit. Joe told us about an organization he was creating. He envisioned an organization that would confer a credential to a member who had mastered a certain body of knowledge, followed a code of ethics, and of, course, had paid a membership fee. This body of knowledge would include accounting, law, investigations, and criminology. On our drive home, my supervisor and I evaluated Joe's concept. In the end, we both concluded that the successful launching of ACFE was a long shot and was unlikely to go anywhere. How wrong we were!

Three decades later, I have a different opinion. The ACFE has been a tremendous success and serves its 85,000 members quite well. The "CFE" designation is the mark of excellence for antifraud professionals and is now recognized globally. I have myself been active in the Georgia Chapter of the ACFE, and I have had the honor to serve as its President for four years. Among the ACFE's many contributions are the *Fraud Examiners Manual*, the biannual *Report to the Nations*, its many fraud seminars and conferences, and the Occupational Fraud and Abuse Classification System, fondly referred to as "The Fraud Tree."

The Fraud Tree

The Fraud Tree, shown below, is taken from the 2018 ACFE *Report to the Nations*.[8] The report is free and can be found on the ACFE's website (www. acfe.com). The Fraud Tree is helpful in many regards. For those responsible for internal controls, the Fraud Tree is a visual reference to the many occupational frauds that can occur in an organization. The Fraud Tree also demonstrates that there are three "branches," and this is significant. The three branches of the Fraud Tree are asset misappropriation, corruption, and financial statement fraud. In Part II of this book, I will delve into details of these three categories of fraud. When studying each of these three categories of fraud, there are two questions to consider: Who would likely commit any of these three types of fraud? Why would they commit them?

FIG. 4 Occupational Fraud and Abuse Classification System (the Fraud Tree)

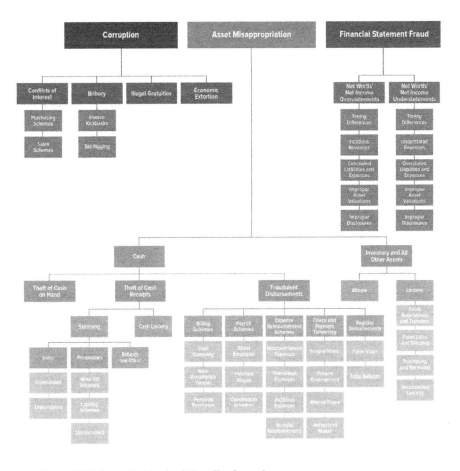

Source: ACFE's Occupational Fraud and Abuse Classification System

Financial Statement Fraud

When considering financial statement fraud in the context of the Fraud Tree, there is a good news–bad news situation. The good news is that, of the three branches of the Fraud Tree, financial statement fraud is the least likely to occur. The bad news is that when it does occur, it results in significantly higher dollar losses to organizations and, in some instances, can result in the demise of the company (e.g., Enron and WorldCom). Who do you suspect is likely to commit most of these frauds? Those in the C-suites, of course, which include the CEO and CFO (Chief Financial Officer). In fact, the *COSO Fraud Studies* of 1998 and 2010 by The Committee of Sponsoring Organizations (COSO) of the Treadway Commission established that in over 80 percent of the cases that COSO studied, the CEO and the CFO had colluded.[9] On May 2011, the Conference Board sponsored a study that found CEOs routinely pressure CFOs to commit financial reporting fraud[10] (e.g., co-founders, Richard Scrushy and Aaron Beam in the case of HealthSouth).

Asset Misappropriation

Asset misappropriation represents a bad news–good news situation. The bad news is that the types of fraud found on this branch occur with the most frequency within an organization. The good news is that on average, these frauds generally result in the smallest losses to the organization. Not surprisingly, these frauds occur more often with lower level-employees.

Corruption

Corruption and conflicts of interest occur both with an intermediate frequency and dollar loss among the three types of fraud found in the Fraud Tree. This type of fraud is generally committed by midlevel to senior level employees. These types of fraud schemes are, however, notoriously difficult to detect, as there is very little in terms of an audit trail.

Nonoccupational Frauds

One of the benefits of the ACFE's Fraud Tree is that at a glance one can see the myriad of frauds an organization might face. By definition, the Fraud Tree is focused on occupational frauds. A significant portion of frauds that victimize individuals and organizations are nonoccupational frauds, which I will discuss in detail in Chapter 7.

Limitations of the Fraud Triangle

The Fraud Triangle, including its three vertices—opportunity, pressure, and rationalization—has great value in understanding why many frauds occur. Its application can greatly help with the prevention, detection, and investigation of fraud. Unfortunately, the Fraud Triangle seems to provide little or no value in understanding an entire category of fraud. What types of fraud would these be? To help us understand these frauds, I will pose two questions:

1. What is the difference between the frauds in the left column and the frauds in the right column below?

• Overstating Inventory	○ Counterfeiting Products
• Revenue Recognition Fraud	○ Ransomware
• Travel Voucher Fraud	○ Insurance Fraud
• Bogus Credit Card Charges	○ Business E-mail Compromise
• Check Forgery by CFO	○ Ponzi Schemes
• Embezzlement	○ Identity Theft
• Point-of-Sale Theft	○ Phishing Schemes
• Phantom Vendor Scheme	○ Penny Stock Pump and Dump Schemes

The frauds on the left are all occupational frauds. Note, however, that the frauds on the right may be occupational frauds depending on whether or not an insider is committing the fraud. While this analysis is true, it is *not* the distinguishing factor that will help us know when the Fraud Triangle has limited application. While you are trying to figure this out, let me give you some more dichotomies to consider.

2. How do the relationships in the two columns below differ?

• Employer and Employee	○ Investment Promoter and Investor
• Family Members in Business	○ E-mail Spammer and E-mail Recipient
• Professor and Student	○ Vendor and Purchaser
• Pastor and Parishioner	○ Check Writer and Check Casher
• Attorney and Client	○ IRS and Taxpayer
• Doctor and Patient	○ Government Program and Beneficiary

- Board of Directors and Shareholders
- C-Suite and Board of Directors

° Insurance Company and Insured

° Contractor and Purchaser

Privity of Trust

The answer to the preceding questions lies at the heart of Cressey's theory—trust! The Fraud Triangle helps us understand the motivation of a trust violator. To be a trust violator, a person must first be in a trust-based relationship which means that the person has to be in "privity of trust." The foundation is based in psychology. Except in the rare circumstance when we are dealing with a psychopath, those in privity of trust have a human connection with each other. A breach of this trust results in a feeling of sadness, embarrassment, and shame by the betrayer. This is why the defense mechanism known as rationalization is so important—after all, one has to be able to "sleep with oneself at night" even after committing a questionable act. When one is in privity of trust, the trust violator must engage in rationalization before and even after committing the fraud.

Conversely, those who are not in privity of trust need not rationalize before committing the fraud, nor do they need to be under any particular pressure. For these fraudsters, I use the term "predators." All a predator needs is an opportunity to exploit a victim. There is an amorphous area between those in privity of trust and the predators. In fact, the bonds of trust can be strong, weak, or nonexistent. Trust can also be evanescent, fleeting or wane over time.

Consider the most costly and pernicious of all occupational frauds: financial statement fraud. The perpetrators of this type of fraud are usually those in C-suites. We generally think that the CEO and CFO are in privity of trust with both their subordinates and their board. Those they lead have great confidence in their ability to take the company forward, provide steady jobs, and ensure that everyone's retirement plan is secure. The board also puts great faith in the C-suite executives who carry out their vision for the company.

What happens if the bond of trust between the board and C-suite executives is broken? What happens if the C-suite culture becomes so toxic that the C-suite executives do not feel they are in privity of trust with either their subordinates or the board? Maybe they begin colluding among themselves. Maybe the board members even become witting or unwitting actors in the collusion. Does this scenario seem too far from real life? In fact, this may have been what happened at Enron. The first fraudulent acts may have been difficult. The C-suite actors were in privity of trust and needed rationalization to cope. This could independently explain how the fraud could occur. In fact, it is very likely that this is how the fraud started. The fraud at Enron, however, lasted several years, included many bad actors, and involved an extremely large number of transactions across various divisions. Another explanation is that the culture had become so toxic that the C-suite executives became predatory.[11]

The Predators

Predatory fraudsters are those fraudsters who are not in privity of trust with their victims. Having no bond of trust, they need neither pressure nor rationalization to commit their fraud. We can simply wad up the Fraud Triangle and throw it out the window, as its precepts are of limited benefit in preventing, detecting, and investigating fraud. The primary way to stop a predatory fraudster is to prevent the opportunity for fraud to occur.

Some frauds can be a hybrid. The fraudster starts out in a trust-based relationship and then becomes predatory. Again, that could have been the case at Enron. However, the classic example is the Ponzi scheme. Every Ponzi scheme I have observed started with the fraudster being in privity of trust with the victims. As the scheme spiraled out of control, the fraudster became a predator—the so-called wolf in sheep's clothing who will pursue anyone who will listen to his or her tale of fortune. During this transformation, I believe that the fraudster's rationalizations for lying to investors was replaced with the raw fear of being detected.

Case Example

I participated on a team that executed a search warrant on a telemarketing fraud. After making entry and securing the shoddy office space, I was amazed at what a telemarketing shop looked like. There were rows of phones on tables, wires crisscrossing the floor, and canned texts written on grease boards for the telephone operators to recite to unwitting victims. After the evidence was collected, I eventually participated in an interview with the ringleader. Despite all of the harm he was doing to his victims, which primarily affected the elderly, he had no remorse. He never met his victims. He never had to witness the harm done to a widow with an empty bank account. He was also not laboring under any apparent financial pressure. This talented ringleader could have run many legitimate businesses, but he chose to run a telemarketing scheme. Lacking privity of trust with his victims, two of the Fraud Triangle's elements—pressure and rationalization—were not really applicable, so he was a remorseless predator.[12]

Some of the chief predatory frauds include:

- Telemarketing Fraud
- Tax Fraud
- Government Program Fraud
- Ponzi Scheme (becomes a predator as the fraud matures)
- Business E-mail Compromise
- Ransomware
- E-mail Spammer
- Con Man Frauds
- Investment Schemes

- Pump and Dump Schemes
- Fraudulent Real Estate Flips

Emotions as Data

Those in charge of fraud prevention for their organization are often assigned to the internal audit function and/or work closely with the CFO. Regardless of where the fraud risk function is assigned, these professionals, often accountants, tend to think of themselves as very level-headed, logically thinking individuals. Further, they may work in a corporate environment that does not encourage discussion, reflection, or evaluation of the underlying feelings and emotions of its employees from the C-suite and lower levels. Why does this matter?

Let's consider the work of organizational psychiatrist Dr. Daven Morrison, who consults with companies in the education of senior leaders and their teams. Dr. Morrison is a thought leader in the Behavioral Forensics Group, LLC, a company specializing in fraud prevention, and he is also one of the authors of the *A.B.C.'s of Behavioral Forensics*,[13] a book that advances the understanding of why people commit fraud. Dr. Morrison instructs us that hardwired emotions and feelings are called *affects*.[14] He explains how these affects are critically important to motivation and constitute the "gateway to action." In other words, without affects there is no action and thus no fraud.[15] Having read his work and having benefited from hearing him present his theories on the topic of fraud to audiences, I like the idea of his leading us to consider emotions or affects as the primary driver of fraud. As he states it, let's use "emotions as data."[16] This might be a strange proposition for an accountant, but it changes the focus from a purely fact-based analysis to an emotion-based analysis.

The following are considered to be the nine innate emotions or affects: [17]

- Enjoyment
- Interest
- Surprise
- Anger
- Fear
- Distress
- Disgust
- Contempt
- Shame

The benefit of considering affects as the driver of fraud is explained by Dr. Morrison as follows:

"With this model, emotions are no longer infinite and subjective but finite, objective, and quite specific (and therefore predictable). Because these affects are common to all human beings, their universal existence helps an investigator of fraud to get past issues of gender, age, culture, and other factors."[18]

Using affects as data is another way to understand why someone commits fraud. Our emotions are formed around our understanding of a situation, regardless of whether our understanding is accurate. Developing a culture in which we have an awareness of emotions provides management with additional information to shape a stronger ethical environment.

From Theory to Practice

I now want to put the theory into motion. I have given thought to the many diverse types of white-collar frauds that I either personally investigated, helped in supervising the fraud investigation, or participated in a fraud investigation debriefing. The most impactful cases for me were the ones in which I personally interacted with the fraudsters.

Most frauds that are prosecuted result in a plea agreement by the defendant. As part of that plea agreement, the defendant (fraudster) is debriefed by the prosecutor and the investigator. The primary purpose of this is for the government to learn the defendant's knowledge of other crimes. This process is known as "flip-and-roll" by those in law enforcement. The government accomplishes the "flip" by having the defendant accept responsibility and plead guilty. The defendant is then expected to "roll" or incriminate others who participated in the criminal offense as well as any other criminal matter the defendant knows about. These debriefings provide amazing insights into the mind of the fraudster.

On occasion, a defendant will exercise his constitutional right to a jury trial. As an aside, this is usually a bad choice by the defendant, since the government rarely loses fraud cases. In the cases that go to trial, a coconspirator will likely cooperate with the government. I have worked with many such individuals.

Cooperators' insights are tremendously helpful. First, because they participated in the fraud, they likely have direct knowledge of the facts and circumstances. Understanding the factors that cause corporate insiders to commit a criminal offense is not only fascinating but also provides indispensable knowledge for professionals who are responsible for fraud prevention, detection, and investigation. Second, the wheels of justice move slowly, and these cases can take months or years to move through the justice system. Accordingly, I spent lengthy periods of time with cooperators reviewing documents, financial statements, bank records, and e-mails, and preparing them for their upcoming testimony.

As with any human interaction, the topic invariably moves from what they did to how it has affected them personally. I learned about these defendants' personal lives, including their hobbies, families, social circles, and colleagues. They faced tremendous embarrassment, shame, and even humiliation. Their names appeared on the front pages of newspapers. If they had any resources left, their defense attorneys probably took their last dime. Divorces and bankruptcies as a result of fraud are also common. Their own children may even disown them. They are also required to testify against former friends and coworkers, knowing that their testimony will help convict them. They are frequently depressed and truly at an all-time low. Listening to these experiences is emotionally draining and quite sad. I can vividly remember having to get a tissue for a cooperator because his tears kept landing on my original government exhibits as we were preparing for trial!

These debriefing sessions provided me with invaluable insight into the mind of a fraudster. I do not believe that academics, theorists, or others who write on the topic can have any better insight than someone who is in a position to ask any question of the one who has actually committed the fraud. Before I get into the details of what I learned, I want to make another observation about the Fraud Tree.

As shown earlier, the Fraud Tree has three branches: asset misappropriation, corruption, and financial statement fraud. These frauds differ significantly in terms of the facts pertaining to the commission of them, concealment of the wrongful conduct, and conversion of the proceeds for personal benefit. Most importantly, the motivation for committing these frauds varies by which of the three types of fraud has been committed. Understanding the differences between these three very distinct types of fraud helps in fraud prevention, detection, and investigation.

Peeling the Onion

I learned invaluable lessons while I was getting to know fraudsters on a personal level. When a person's soul is exposed, there is a lot to see. What I always find fascinating is the motivation for someone to commit fraud. When given the opportunity, I ask the fraudster about his or her motivation. I first ask very direct questions, such as "Why did you commit this fraud?" But that one question is not enough. The answer may actually be quite complicated. The fraudster may not really know all the reasons. I continue asking questions, but I don't ask them all in one sitting. I learn the details over time. Below is a composite of conversations I have had with individuals who pled guilty to committing fraud, usually involving manipulation of financial statements in some way. I call this technique "peeling the onion."[19]

Q: Why did you cause false financial statements to be prepared?

A: To make the numbers.

Q: Why did you need to make the numbers?

A: There was pressure from various sources to include my peers in the C-suite. There was also self-imposed pressure. I was part of an organization, and I wanted to be successful.

Q: Why was the success of the organization so important to you?

A: I was raised to be successful. My parents brought me up that way. I have always been competitive in sports. Most importantly, I am competitive in business. I want to win.

Q: What would happen if you were not successful?

A: I would feel I let my colleagues down. I feel like I am a role-model of sorts to all those around me. I have always wanted to make my parents and family proud.

Q: If you could not accomplish your vision of success, how would that make you feel?

A: Sadness, disappointment, and shame.

As you can see from the discussion, the actual motivation of the fraud seemed to start with "making the numbers," but it was actually an underlying emotion or affect that caused the fraudulent activities. We are all human and complicated. I think Dr. Morrison has it right when he encourages us to consider emotions as data. Although this scenario is relatively common, let's explore other motivators of fraud.

Beyond Greed

When I ask audiences why someone would commit fraud, I invariably hear the answer, "Greed." While I do know that pure greed can be the motivator of fraud, let's consider it as the motivator of last resort. Let's rule out many other causes before we conclude that the answer is greed.

I do understand how one could quickly get to greed as the motivator of fraud. First, there is near universal agreement that fraud is wrong. Accordingly, if fraud is such a bad thing, then one's motivation to commit fraud must also be another universally despised sin—greed. But not so fast, because there are many motivators of fraud other than greed.

Business Need

Many frauds are motivated by a need to save the business. This can occur for a variety of reasons and are not necessarily the fault of company management. The economy could be in a recession, or the company could be in a sector that is experiencing a very bad downward cycle. Consequently, owners of the business may be under tremendous pressure to "make the numbers" for the bankers, regulators, shareholders, or Wall Street analysts who are watching.

The savings and loan (S&L) crisis of the 1980s resulted in liquidity issues for most of the industry. For the many optimistic executives who were involved, they thought they could just fabricate the numbers until the real estate market recovered. While their motivations were a mixed bag between saving their bank and looting their bank, many of the 1,100 convictions during the S&L crisis were related to schemes to inflate regulatory liquidity in an effort to keep regulators from taking over their institutions.[20]

I have often wondered how many fraudulent schemes are successful—I mean successful in the sense that the fraudster got past a troubled period and then stopped the fraud when the business recovered (and thus escaped detection). We will never know the answer to this question because the fraudster was never caught. This concept is akin to Warren Buffett's observation, "Only when the tide goes out do you discover who has been swimming naked."

There are likely a lot of skinny-dippers who suited up before the tide went out.

Ego (Pride and Shame)

Have you ever heard of a corporate executive with an ego? Actually, an executive without a big ego might be the exception rather than the rule. In fact, executives' egos, along with their charisma, likely propelled them to the top of the company and may be a factor in the success of the company they lead. Further, a CEO exhibiting narcissistic traits does not necessarily harm the company and may actually be helpful. If the interest of the executive and the company are congruent, it may be a win–win scenario. The problem, of course, comes when the interest of the narcissistic executive and that of the company are divergent.

Ego-driven frauds can occur in two contrasting scenarios, and I think Enron and WorldCom can best illustrate them for us. Let's consider Enron first. The Enron executives may have felt a hypercompetitive need to be the best in the industry. By all accounts, this certainly was a driving force for Enron CEO Jeff Skilling. In 2001, Enron was ranked number seven on the annual Fortune 500 list.[21] What might this highly watched ranking mean for competitive executives? There are six to go to be number one on the Fortune 500 list! I learned a saying in Texas: "It's not about the money; that's just how we keep score." I have found that to be the case with many wealthy executives. After all, what is another $10 million when you are worth hundreds of millions of dollars? An ego-driven desire to be number one can be a motivation to commit fraud. This is closely related to pride and narcissism.

WorldCom may help explain the other face of ego: the fear of failure and avoidance of shame. WorldCom CEO executive Bernard Ebbers became very wealthy during his leadership of WorldCom. By the year 2000, however, the telecommunications industry, including WorldCom, was in decline. If left to their downward trajectory, the earnings of WorldCom stock would not have met analyst expectations. This was unacceptable to Ebbers for two reasons. Fundamentally, failure was not an option. Also, Ebbers had gone on a buying spree of acquiring interests in ranching, farming, timber, yacht building, hotels, trucking, and sports. These interests were purchased with debt and collateralized with WorldCom stock. A sudden drop in the value of WorldCom's stock would cause Ebbers' creditors to be unsecured. Motivated by fear, Ebbers oversaw what was at the time the world's largest fraud by causing five quarterly bogus accounting entries to be made on WorldCom's books during the period April 2001 to April 2002 totaling almost $4 billion.[22] The fraud would ultimately total $11 billion.

For additional information on personality drivers in the C-suite, read the fascinating article on the "Dark Triad" of personalities—narcissism, Machiavellianism, and psychopathy—in *The CPA Journal* article, "Fraud Risk Models Lack Personality."[23]

Excitement

Excitement can be a great feeling. It keeps our interest. It motivates us to engage in certain activities. We watch sporting events, read mystery novels, and watch action movies all because of excitement. Gambling is another form of excitement. At the turn of a card or the pull of a handle, we learn the fate of a wager. Whether we win or lose, it is the sense of excitement that is appealing. You might also know this type of personality as the adrenaline junky.

One motivation for fraud can be excitement. This too can come in different forms. The excitement may be the challenge of pulling off the fraud or just taking a risk to see if the fraudster can deceive others without getting caught. Again, we can see that it is not so much about the money as it is about the adrenaline rush from engaging in the fraudulent acts.

Another form of this excitement can be found by those in the financial services industry. Take a stockbroker, for example. A stockbroker can easily make stock recommendations for a client that are not appropriate for the client's risk profile. The broker may recommend high-risk trades because the broker enjoys the exhilaration of the potential gains. In effect, this is known as a moral hazard. A moral hazard occurs when one takes more risks because someone else bears the burden of those risks. In this case, if the stock performs well, this is exciting for both the broker and the client. If the stock tanks, the broker does not bear the direct consequences of the loss.

Parity

Everyone wants to feel like they are being treated fairly. Employees can perceive, whether true or imagined, that others in the company are getting perks for which they are not privy. The perception can even be worse when the employees believe they are not being compensated equally for the same work or getting the same bonus as others.

I will give you an example that affects everyone by asking two questions. First, do you believe a significant percentage of Americans cheat on their taxes? Second, do you cheat on your taxes? If you believe other people cheat on their taxes and you do not, doesn't that make you a victim? Why should you subsidize other Americans' tax liability? In fact, if you cheat on your taxes a little bit, you actually are not cheating at all; you may just be breaking even. This is called "achieving parity."

If opportunity and pressure are present, then all an employee needs is rationalization to complete the Fraud Triangle. A perceived lack of parity may be just the rationalization needed for an employee to commit fraud.

Social Compact of Reciprocity

Ingrained in our human psyche is a social agreement that we have with our fellow humans. Whenever someone gives us something, we feel obligated to reciprocate. Dr. Robert Cialdini made similar observations in his national best-selling book, *Influence: The Psychology of Persuasion*.[24] In his book, Cialdini tells us that this social obligation is actually a rule: "The rule says that we should try to repay, in kind, what another person has provided us."[25] Further, this rule has universal acceptance across all cultures.[26]

We see the application of this rule every day. When someone greets us, we return the greeting. When someone extends a hand, inviting a handshake, we shake hands. The rule has tremendous application in sales. Consider a sample food display at a grocery store. When the display of food is unattended by a salesperson, it is easy for a shopper to taste the free sample and walk away without making a purchase. However, when the display is attended by a salesperson, the shopper feels a twinge of conscience to make a purchase. That feeling is an example of the rule at work.

How does this rule affect fraud? More specifically, how does it pertain to corruption and conflicts of interest? When one bestows a benefit on another, there is the desire for the recipient to reciprocate. Knowing this social compact, how can lobbyists, vendors, or contractors ingratiate themselves with a decision maker in government? The problem often starts with them giving the decision maker event tickets, free meals, or trips. The problem is so well understood that most jurisdictions have rules prohibiting the receipt of gifts by government officials. We will explore in Chapter 4 how the social compact of reciprocity can be used to foster corruption in both the government and private sectors.

Slippery Slope

The slippery slope concept is an explanation of how individuals can begin at one point with good intentions and end up at another point with disastrous consequences through incremental changes in their precepts.[27] To share a quote from the book *A.B.C.'s of Behavioral Forensics*, "Did you ever hear of somebody stealing a million dollars and working their way down?"[28] Invariably, it works in reverse.

Case Example

Let me give you a prime example of the slippery slope in action. A publicly traded company is near the end of a quarter. The CEO calls an all-hands-on-deck meeting for the finance and accounting departments. The CEO states that the company is not quite making the numbers that analysts are expecting and wants to know if anything can be done to get the company over the hump. The CEO carefully underscores the importance of adherence to SOX and of following all accounting guidance. Nevertheless, the CEO knows that there could have been mistakes or errors in judgment when closing the books for the quarter. With the CEO's challenge, all of the financial professionals go back and review the numbers. Sure enough, they find some errors as well as necessary adjustments to the accounting estimates, all of which save the day. The CEO openly praises the good work of the individuals who were able to increase the numbers. The same scenario then repeats itself quarter after quarter. Finally, after discovering all of the "errors" and stretching the accounting estimates beyond credulity, the company may easily find that its financial statements are now materially misleading. What went wrong? First, the CEO only asked for errors that worked in the company's favor, not all errors. Further, the CEO rewarded the behavior with praise for those who had accomplished his task.[29]

Status Motivated Frauds: Fear and Greed

Financial status can influence someone to commit fraud, and it comes in two forms. One is fear based, or fear of losing one's status. The other is greed-based, or the desire to enhance one's status. These status-motivated frauds are often what motivate fraudsters to engage in asset misappropriation.

Fear is a tremendous driver of behavior. Consider the manager who has worked her way up the corporate ladder and relies on her salary to pay the mortgage, fund private schools for her children, and mingle in preferred social circles. The fear of losing her job creates an obvious pressure just to maintain the current level of income. Also consider the "life happens" events relating to illness, divorce, bankruptcy, drugs, alcohol, and gambling. All of these fear-based factors can be motivators of fraud.

When I started the discussion of fraud, I encouraged you to first consider motivators other than greed. I did this, not because greed is the least likely cause of fraud, but because you might have failed to consider the many other viable causes of fraud. Considering all of the motivators of fraud will be important in Part III, which discusses the prevention, detection, and investigation of fraud.

Let's now consider greed as a likely candidate for driving someone to commit fraud. I am referring to pure, unadulterated greed, which is related to "keeping up with the Joneses." The motivation may be social pressure to live in the right house or drive the right car. The underlying motivation is status based. These fraudsters' behaviors often become apparent through a change in their lifestyle. When the new wardrobe, fancy sports car, and exotic vacations emerge, they are red flags that greed is at work.

Greed can certainly be a motivator of fraud. I will explain my understanding of greed based on having witnessed many fraudsters who came into extreme wealth due to the success of their fraud. My definition of greed is the accumulation of wealth that is driven by some human emotion and is not need based. In the case of fraud, the accumulation of material things often provides temporary comfort for the stress that the fraudsters have brought on themselves. The Ponzi scheme case example that follows makes this point.

Case Example

I once participated in a Ponzi scheme investigation. In the early phases of the Ponzi scheme, the operator was bringing in millions of dollars while all the while lying to trusted friends, family, and community elites. She also had a penchant for expensive shoes. While many people like their shoes (e.g., Philippines' Imelda Marcos possessed over 3,000 pairs of shoes!), this Ponzi scheme operator carried it to an unbelievable extreme. During a search warrant of her home, she had hundreds of designer shoes still in boxes that clearly had never been worn. Her shoes made front-page news when the U.S. Marshals Service auctioned off her shoe collection, among other assets, to help repay victims for their staggering losses.

Here is what I learned from that case. While fraudsters may appear to be living a stress-free life of luxury, they are really under tremendous pressure. The Ponzi scheme is the classic example because the more fraud the Ponzi scheme operator commits, the more desperate is the operator's need to commit even more fraud in order to keep the scheme from collapsing. Purchasing material things lessens the stress, at least temporarily. Some might know this concept as retail therapy. As the fraud increases, the stress increases, and the need to purchase more designer shoes increases—or a faster sports car, a bigger home, or nicer jet—choose your vice. The lifestyle and accumulation of wealth then becomes greed driven.

CHAPTER 2
Fraud Defined

"The defendant was lying, cheating, and stealing!"

—A COMMONLY MADE ARGUMENT BY PROSECUTORS DURING
CLOSING STATEMENTS.

What is fraud? Since this book is about fraud, I thought it would be an important question to answer. "Lying, cheating, and stealing," is a phrase I have heard echoed from the walls of state and federal courtrooms countless times during closing arguments. Even though this impactful answer gets right to the heart of the matter, this definition is not adequate for our purposes.

In Part III of this book, I will address the fraud life cycle: prevention, detection, investigation, mitigation, and remediation. As we will see, a variety of professionals deal with each of these fraud life cycle components. Depending on their purpose or goal, these professionals will approach fraud from significantly different perspectives. For example, fraud risk managers charged with deterring fraud will approach their work from a different perspective than external auditors conducting audit work to assess if the financial statements are free of material misstatements due to fraud. Internal auditors charged with assessing internal controls will approach their work from a different perspective than FBI agents investigating whether the elements of a crime are present. Likewise, the approach of prosecutors, regulators, and defense attorneys will depend on various legal definitions. Fraud examiners and forensic accountants who assist any of these professionals will need to know the purpose and goals of their clients.

In essence, all of these professionals need to know the "forensic posture" of the case. The forensic posture is the context in which a fraud-related issue presents itself. A professional working with a fraud-related issue will want to know how the fraud presented itself and for what purpose the professional is engaged. The forensic posture will also be crucial for defining fraud, as it will vary by the differing professional standards and laws that apply.

As an FBI agent who investigated fraud, my cases were typically prosecuted in federal court. However, that was not always the case. Many of my cases were declined for federal prosecution and prosecuted in state court. Other cases resulted in a civil action under the federal False Claims Act. When I interviewed or subpoenaed records from other professionals who dealt with any aspect of the fraud, they seemed to have a slightly different understanding of the underlying fraud. The reality is that the definition of fraud will vary, depending on the forensic posture of the case. The discussion of the Ponzi scheme perpetrated by Allen Stanford in the following case example highlights how one major fraud presented multiple forensic postures.

Case Example

In 2004, I was assigned to the U.S. Embassy in Bridgetown, Barbados as an FBI Legal Attaché. Part of my territory included Antigua and Barbuda, an island country east of the Caribbean Sea. I worked on a Foreign Corrupt Practices Act (FCPA) matter involving Ponzi scheme con artist Allen Stanford. FCPA violations are inherently challenging to investigate because in corruption cases, often there is little or no paper trail. Further, I was an FBI agent assigned to a foreign country with little investigative authority. Stanford's activities with Antiguan government officials were suspicious. The FBI made little progress on the Stanford matter until the 2008 collapsing economy began exposing Stanford's fraudulent activity. In 2009, the FBI and the Securities and Exchange Commission (SEC) each charged Stanford with operating a $7 billion Ponzi scheme. If not for Bernie Madoff's outrageous $65 billion Ponzi scheme, Stanford would likely be a household name today.

Stanford's Ponzi scheme, like Enron and WorldCom, are interesting cases to study because of the many forensic postures presented. Once these frauds are exposed, there are numerous plaintiff's attorneys, prosecutors, regulators, creditors, and others pursuing a singular body of evidence on behalf of their clients. While each of these interested parties has a fraud theory they are pursuing, the legal elements for each of these theories will be different.

In the Stanford case, the secrecy of Stanford's finances started to unravel during a paternity suit filed in 2007 by his girlfriend and mother of their two children. Stanford was also married. There were fraud-related issues for the attorneys and forensic accountants to uncover, since Stanford did not want to disclose the magnitude of his wealth in that proceeding. Later, fraud would present itself in a completely different posture when the SEC placed Stanford's collapsed financial empire into receivership. Shortly thereafter, a federal court appointed an examiner to assist the court in discovering the facts. Complex international bankruptcy provisions became an issue, and the authorities in the country of Antigua and Barbuda began initiating their own legal proceedings. Numerous investors, creditors, and other victims filed lawsuits in an attempt to recoup their losses. A board investigation would also be commonly initiated under these circumstances.

Each of these interested parties presented a different forensic posture. For these parties to be successful, their attorneys, forensic accountants, and investigators all needed to understand the differing legal elements for each of the underlying fraud theories they were pursuing.

An often-cited definition of fraud comes to us from *Black's Law Dictionary*:

"A generic term, embracing all multifarious means which human ingenuity can devise, and which are resorted to by one individual to get advantage over another by false suggestions or by suppression of truth and includes all surprise, trick, cunning, dissembling, and any unfair way by which another is cheated."[1]

This is a very colorful definition and can assist the layperson in getting a better understanding of fraud. The language was actually taken from a 1934 Supreme Court of Oklahoma case involving a defendant's claim that the plaintiff had fraudulently induced the defendant to enter into a promissory note agreement.[2] Despite its legal origins, this definition is still inadequate for most of our purposes.

Because fraud occurs in so many different contexts, there are many definitions of fraud. Fraud is a horizontal issue that cuts across many professions. Those in the fraud prevention, detection, and investigation professions, including CPAs, internal auditors, and certified fraud examiners, define fraud for their purposes. External auditors have their definition of fraud, which are focused on financial statements. Government regulators and prosecutors have their own definitions for fraud. The victims of fraud seeking recovery of their losses have to prove that fraud occurred. Although the definitions will naturally vary, the one common element for all of these types of frauds is that the fraudster had the intent to defraud the victim. In fact, *intent* will be the common thread for defining fraud.

Definitions for the Professions:

Public Company Accounting Oversight Board

The Public Company Accounting Oversight Board (PCAOB) is a private-sector not-for-profit corporation created by the Sarbanes-Oxley Act of 2002 (SOX) with oversight by the SEC. The PCAOB's duties include oversight of auditors of public companies. Audits of nonpublic companies are not within the PCAOB's jurisdiction and scope. Although the auditing profession had resisted government oversight, the failures of Enron, WorldCom, and Arthur Andersen brought about this change with the passage of SOX. Prior to the creation of the PCAOB, the auditing profession was self-regulated by the American Institute of Certified Public Accountants (AICPA).

The PCAOB has established standards for registered public accounting firms to follow in the preparation and issuance of auditing reports. One of the standards relating to fraud is AS 2401: Consideration of Fraud in a Financial Statement Audit. Sections .05 and .06 of AS 2401 define fraud as follows:

.05 Fraud is a broad legal concept and auditors do not make legal determinations of whether fraud has occurred. Rather, the auditor's interest specifically relates to acts that result in a material misstatement of the financial statements. The primary factor that distinguishes fraud from error is whether the underlying action that results in the misstatement of the financial statements is intentional or unintentional. For purposes of the section, *fraud* is an intentional act that results in a material misstatement in financial statements that are the subject of an audit.

.06 Two types of misstatements are relevant to the auditor's consideration of fraud—misstatements arising from fraudulent financial reporting and misstatements arising from misappropriation of assets.

- *Misstatements arising from fraudulent financial reporting* are intentional misstatements or omissions of amounts or disclosures in financial statements designed to deceive financial statement users where the effect causes the financial statements not to be presented, in all material respects, in conformity with Generally Accepted Accounting Principles (GAAP). Fraudulent financial reporting may be accomplished by the following:

○ Manipulation, falsification, or alteration of accounting records or supporting documents from which financial statements are prepared

○ Misrepresentation in or intentional omission from the financial statements of events, transactions, or other significant information

○ Intentional misapplication of accounting principles relating to amounts, classification, manner of presentation, or disclosure

• Fraudulent financial reporting need not be the result of a grand plan or conspiracy. It may be that management representatives rationalize the appropriateness of a material misstatement, for example, as an aggressive rather than indefensible interpretation of complex accounting rules, or as a temporary misstatement of financial statements, including interim statements, expected to be corrected later when operational results improve.

• *Misstatements arising from misappropriation of assets* (sometimes referred to as theft or defalcation) involve the theft of an entity's assets where the effect of the theft causes the financial statements not to be presented, in all material respects, in conformity with GAAP. Misappropriation of assets can be accomplished in various ways, including embezzling receipts, stealing assets, or causing an entity to pay for goods or services that have not been received. Misappropriation of assets may be accompanied by false or misleading records or documents, possibly created by circumventing controls. The scope of this section includes only those misappropriations of assets for which the effect of the misappropriation causes the financial statements not to be fairly presented, in all material respects, in conformity with GAAP.

American Institute of Certified Public Accountants

The American Institute of Certified Public Accountants (AICPA) provides standards for auditors who audit nonpublic companies. These standards are very similar to the PCAOB's AS 2401. These auditor's responsibilities relating to fraud in an audit of financial statements can be found in the standard, AU-C Section 240 Consideration of Fraud in a Financial Statement Audit. The AICPA's standard defines fraud differently and can be found in Section .11 of AU-C 240 and provides:

.11 For purposes of GAAS [Generally Accepted Auditing Standards], the following terms have the meanings attributed as follows:

Fraud. An intentional act by one or more individuals among management, those charged with governance, employees, or third parties, involving the use of deception that results in a misstatement in financial statements that are the subject of an audit.

Institute of Internal Auditors

The Institute of Internal Auditors (IIA) is an international professional organization that advances the internal auditing profession. The IIA has a definition for internal auditors:

Fraud. Any illegal act characterized by deceit, concealment, or violation of trust. These acts are not dependent upon the threat of violence or physical force. Frauds are perpetrated by parties and organizations to obtain money, property, or services; to avoid payment or loss of services; or to secure personal or business advantage.[3]

Association of Certified Fraud Examiners

The Association of Certified Fraud Examiners (ACFE), an international organization that is dedicated to antifraud training and education with a focus on occupational fraud defines fraud as:

> Occupational Fraud. The use of one's occupation for personal enrichment through the deliberate misuse or misapplication of the employing organization's resources or assets.[4]

Regulatory Enforcement and Scienter

In the United States, the commercial sector is regulated by state and federal government regulators. Some of the more highly regulated industries include banking, securities, and health care. Each of these industries has government regulators whose mission includes protecting consumers from fraud. Federal, state and local governments often become the victims of fraud through their procurement functions. Once a regulator or a government victim establishes that fraud has occurred, it might seek penalties, interest, disgorgement, or debarment, or impose cease-and-desist orders against the fraudster. A pivotal issue in many enforcement actions is whether the fraudster, which can be an individual or an organization, acted with the requisite intent. When using its civil enforcement powers, the government must establish that the defendant acted with knowledge or intent to deceive, also known as "scienter." Negligence alone is generally insufficient to prove a violation of the applicable statutes, as the government must at least show recklessness, purpose or knowledge. In criminal matters, this purposeful intent to defraud is generally known as *mens rea*. In civil enforcement actions, this intent element is generally known as "scienter."

A prime example of a regulatory enforcement statute is the Securities and Exchange Commission's (SEC) Rule 10b-5. The SEC drafted this rule pursuant to its rule making authority and §10(b) of the Securities Exchange Act of 1934. In 1942, the SEC created Rule 10b-5 in reaction to reports that a company president was making pessimistic statements about company earnings while at the same time buying the company's stock.[5]

SEC Rule 10b-5 states:

> It shall be unlawful for any person, directly or indirectly, by the use of any means or instrumentality of interstate commerce, or of the mails or of any facility of any national securities exchange,
>
> (a) To employ any device, scheme, or artifice to defraud,
>
> (b) To make any untrue statement of a material fact or to omit to state a material fact necessary in order to make the statements made, in the light of the circumstances under which they were made, not misleading, or
>
> (c) To engage in any act, practice, or course of business which operates or would operate as a fraud or deceit upon any person, in connection with the purchase or sale of any security.

When the SEC or a private plaintiff alleges a violation of SEC Rule 10b-5, it will have the burden of proving:

1. Material misinformation
2. Scienter
3. Reliance
4. Causation
5. Damages[6]

Another type of government enforcement action occurs when the United States government itself is victimized by fraud. This frequently occurs in two distinct ways: procurement fraud and program fraud. As the largest purchaser in the world, the United States government is quite often defrauded with false invoices resulting from inferior or nonexistent products or services. The government also hemorrhages money from fraudulent losses from its many beneficiary programs, like Medicaid and Medicare.

Defrauding the federal government is nothing new. President Lincoln oversaw the passage of the False Claims Act (FCA) in 1863 to deal with contractors that sold the Union Army faulty equipment and other goods. The statute is often referred to as "Lincoln's law."[7] The FCA has stood the test of time with its many amendments and is the Department of Justice's best weapon to combat government procurement and program frauds.

The FCA is structured to accomplish the goal of recouping actual losses and exacting substantial penalties. The FCA has its own definition of fraud and states:

(a) Liability for certain acts.

(1) In general.—Subject to paragraph (2), any person who—

(A) knowingly presents, or causes to be presented, a false or fraudulent claim for payment or approval;

(B) knowingly makes, uses, or causes to be made or used, a false record or statement material to a false or fraudulent claim.

(B) DEFINITIONS.—For purposes of this section—

(1) the terms "knowing" and "knowingly"—

(A) mean that a person, with respect to information—

(i)   has actual knowledge of the information;

(ii)   acts in deliberate ignorance of the truth or falsity of the information; or

(iii) acts in reckless disregard of the truth or falsity of the information; and

(B) require no proof of specific intent to defraud.[8]

Penalties under the false claims act can be substantial. The statute provides for a civil penalty of not less than $11,000 and not more than $22,000[9] plus three times the amount of damages the government sustains because of the fraud.[10] Here again, you can see from reviewing the statute that the government must prove scienter, that is, that the defendant had actual knowledge of the false claim.

Civil Actions

The commission of a fraudulent criminal act creates a victim. Whether the victim is an individual, a company or a governmental organization, the victim will likely want to recover the loss from the fraudster. The sad reality for most victims is that the fraudster will have spent, gambled, given away, or hidden the proceeds of the fraud. Accordingly, the victim will have to consider a cost–benefit analysis prior to initiating a lawsuit to recover the proceeds from the fraudster.

Plaintiffs seeking to recover their losses from a fraudster–defendant will generally have to allege and prove five elements to obtain a recovery. While these elements may vary by jurisdiction, the essential elements are:

1. False representation, or willful omission, regarding a material fact by the defendant.
2. Knowing the representation was false.
3. With the intent to induce the plaintiff to act or refrain from acting in reliance on the representation.
4. The plaintiff reasonably relied on the false representation.
5. The defendant's actions were the proximate cause of damages to the plaintiff.

Criminal Statutes

Under English common law, all crimes require an act or omission in addition to a bad state of mind.[11] These two requirements are known as *actus reus*, or guilty act, and *mens rea*, or guilty mind. With some exceptions, both of these elements are found in modern-day federal and state criminal statutes. To hold someone criminally liable without both elements would generally not serve the punitive purposes of criminal law. Not only is the mere thinking of a bad thought difficult to prove, but also a thought alone has not created any harm.

A harmful act without the requisite bad state of mind also does not serve the punitive purpose of criminal law in that it would criminalize an act that was not intended to harm anyone.

Accordingly, the government has the burden of proving *actus reus* and *mens rea* beyond a reasonable doubt. *Actus reus* in fraud cases is generally easy to prove. For example, a defendant will likely have made a false statement or certification. Further, the monetary proceeds of the transaction will likely flow from the victim to the defendant. This first element may be easy to prove. Establishing that the fraudster–defendant acted with the requisite *mens rea* may be difficult to prove. I have investigated cases in which the defendant admitted to doing every act the government charged. The defense was that the defendant did not act with the intent to defraud.

The following statutes are commonly used to prosecute federal fraud-related crimes.

Mail Fraud Statute

The federal statute commonly known as mail fraud, 18 U.S.C. 1341, states:

> Whoever, having devised or intending to devise any scheme or artifice to defraud, or for obtaining money or property by means of false or fraudulent pretenses, representations, or promises . . . places in any post office or authorized depository for mail . . . or . . . any private or commercial interstate carrier . . . shall be fined under this title or imprisoned not more than 20 years, or both.

Wire Fraud Statute

The federal statute commonly known as wire fraud, 18 U.S.C. 1343, states:

> Whoever, having devised or intending to devise any scheme or artifice to defraud, or for obtaining money or property by means of false or fraudulent pretenses, representations, or promises, transmits or causes to be transmitted by means of wire, radio, or television

communication in interstate or foreign commerce, any writings, signs, signals, pictures, or sounds for the purpose of executing such scheme or artifice, shall be fined under this title or imprisoned not more than 20 years, or both.

Honest Services Statute

The honest services statute, 18 U.S.C. 1346, provides that for purposes of both the mail and wire fraud statutes, a "scheme or artifice to defraud" includes "the intangible right of honest services." The parameters of this statute were attenuated in *Skilling v. United States*, 561, U.S. 358 (2010) and is discussed further in Chapter 4. Jeff Skilling was a former CEO of Enron.

The elements of the mail and wire fraud statutes are: (1) use either a mail or wire, (2) devise a scheme to defraud, (3) involving a material deception, (4) intent to deprive another, and (5) loss of property or honest services.

General Conspiracy Statute

Following principles of common law, the drafters of the wire fraud, mail fraud, and conspiracy statutes incorporated the elements of *actus reus* (guilty act) and *mens rea* (guilty mind). Accordingly, the first conspiracy statute shown below requires a defendant to engage in an act and do it with a particular state of mind.

In federal prosecutions involving two or more people, prosecutors often charge conspiracy under 18 U.S.C. 371. In essence, this statute requires the government to prove two or more people conspired to violate any federal offense (*mens rea*) and commit at least one overt act (*actus reus*) in furtherance of the conspiracy.

The federal statute generally used to prosecute conspiracy, 18 U.S.C. 371, states:

If two or more persons conspire either to commit any offense against the United States, or to defraud the United States, or any agency thereof in any manner or for any purpose, and one or more of such persons do any act to effect the object of the conspiracy, each shall be fined under this title or imprisoned not more than five years, or both.

SOX Conspiracy

Due to the calamities of Enron and WorldCom, Congress quickly passed the Sarbanes-Oxley Act of 2002 (SOX). The SOX legislation has its own conspiracy provision for fraud related prosecutions. This SOX conspiracy statute is unique in that it does not require *actus reus* or an act in furtherance of the conspiracy.

> After the passage of the SOX conspiracy statute, a CEO and CFO could agree to make bogus accounting entries for the purpose of misleading Wall Street analysts. At the moment these executives form such an agreement, they will have committed a federal felony. Unlike its sister conspiracy statute (§371), a SOX conspiracy would not require that the officers make an overt act to cause the bogus accounting entries to be made in the company's books and records. The mere agreeing to commit an accounting fraud is enough to violate the statute.

The SOX conspiracy statute is codified at 18 U.S.C. 1349 and states:

> Any person who attempts or conspires to commit any offense under this chapter shall be subject to the same penalties as those prescribed for the offense, the commission of which was the object of the attempt or conspiracy.

Embezzlement

In a nutshell, embezzlement is the misapplication of funds lawfully in one's possession. Many statutes may be used to prosecute this type of fraud. In the United States, we have two separate criminal justice systems: the federal system and those of the various states. Although federal prosecutors have a variety of criminal statutes to choose from, federal indictments involving fraud generally include charges involving the mail, wire, and conspiracy statutes referenced above.

In contrast, each state has its own criminal statutes to prosecute fraud-related offenses. State prosecutors will often use an embezzlement or related statute, and the elements of these crimes will vary by state. Embezzlement related statutes will generally contain the following elements:

1. A trust or fiduciary relationship between the defendant and the victim.

2. The defendant came into possession of the property because of this relationship.

3. The defendant misappropriated or converted the property for the defendant's benefit.

4. The defendant did an act with the intent to deprive the victim of the use of the money.

An example of a common embezzlement scenario is the CFO who endorses a $50,000 company check to himself to purchase a new car. The CFO is a fiduciary of the company, the CFO was entrusted to hold company funds in a checking account, the CFO converted the property for his personal benefit by endorsing a check, and the CFO did this intentionally, knowing the company would be deprived of the money.

The elements of embezzlement are in stark contrast to theft and larceny statutes. These statutes cover acts in which the defendant takes personal property from a victim without the other's consent or permission. An example of theft is the employee who takes a check out of a company's mailroom and deposits it into her account. The key distinction between embezzlement and theft is that the thief never had lawful custody of the property. For our purposes, think in terms of the Fraud Triangle—the embezzler is a trust violator, and the thief is not.

PART II:
Fraud Threat Picture

- Asset Misappropriation
- Corruption and Conflicts of Interest
- Financial Statement Fraud
- Small Organizations: Small Businesses, Local Governments, and Not-for-Profits
- Nonoccupational Fraud
- Cyber Fraud
- Money Laundering and Tax Fraud

CHAPTER 3

Asset Misappropriation

"Of the three primary categories of occupational fraud, asset misappropriations are by far the most common, occurring in 89% of the cases."

—ASSOCIATION OF CERTIFIED FRAUD EXAMINERS, 2018 *REPORT TO THE NATIONS*[1]

A sset misappropriation is by far the most common type of occupational fraud. When this occurs, an employee has either been entrusted with an asset or has the wherewithal to gain access to the asset and then convert it for a wrongful purpose. Those in fraud prevention and investigation routinely deal with these issues. A quick review of the Fraud Tree shows asset misappropriation has more subclassifications than either financial statement fraud or corruption. This is due to the multifarious ways in which this type of fraud can be committed. Asset misappropriation also differs from the other two classifications of fraud because the average dollar loss associated with it is generally lower. You will recall that the motivations for committing fraud discussed in Chapter 1 include:

- Business Need
- Ego (Pride and Shame)
- Excitement
- Parity
- Social Compact of Reciprocity

- Slippery Slope
- Fear
- Greed

Any of these motivations can apply to those who misappropriate assets. In my experience, however, the motivation is more likely fear, greed, or parity based. The "life happens" events relating to divorce, bankruptcy, drugs, alcohol, gambling, and other life challenges may be a factor. This list also includes financial debt, illness, including that of family members, and the threat of a job loss. Greed-based desires to "keep up with the Joneses" can easily be at play. Also, the concept of parity may be a motivator when the employee acts out to correct some type of perceived slight that the employee has experienced. Not surprisingly, fraudsters who misappropriate assets are more often lower-level employees, and their fraud is often made possible due to weak internal controls.

When considering asset misappropriation as a fraud classification, we also need to consider how it differs from corruption (Chapter 4) and financial statement fraud (Chapter 5) in terms of motivation and perpetration. As professionals—managers, accountants, auditors, ethics and compliance officers, forensic accountants, investigators lawyers, and so forth—how they prevent, detect, and investigate these frauds significantly depends on which of the three fraud classifications is being addressed. Knowing which fraud motivators are more closely correlated with the type of fraud being addressed is very helpful. These concepts assist management in prevention strategies. Knowing the potential motivations of a fraud suspect is crucial to investigators who are conducting interviews and interrogations. Prosecutors and defense attorneys can develop motivation-based themes to enhance their arguments.

In this chapter, I will cover the fraud threat picture for asset misappropriation schemes by describing the threats and presenting the best practices for minimizing their occurrence. As you consider each of these frauds, ask yourself these two questions: Is my organization at risk? What can I do to prevent and detect fraud risk within my own organization?

Embezzlement

Embezzlement is really a legal term and not a specific scheme to defraud. However, due to its prevalence—this is by far the most common occupational fraud—I wanted to give this topic special emphasis at the beginning of our discussion of the many types of asset misappropriation schemes. Interestingly, sociologist Donald Cressey was inspired to come up with the Fraud Triangle based on his extensive study of embezzlers, about whom he wrote a book in 1973, *Other People's Money.*

Embezzlement is the misapplication of funds lawfully in one's possession. Embezzlement commonly occurs by an individual with signatory authority over a checking account or who is in possession of a P-Card and simply spends company funds for personal benefit. Fraud is committed in this fashion for two basic reasons: it is so easy to do, and no one is watching. Both check fraud and P-Card schemes are discussed in greater detail later.

Case Example

Forensic accountant Karen Fortune, a partner in the Atlanta-based firm IAG Forensics & Valuation (IAG), investigated a case that typifies an embezzlement scheme. The matter involved an external CFO who worked out of a local accounting firm. This CFO had complete control of the company bank account and accounting system. After establishing an unauthorized bank account, the CFO transferred payroll taxes owed to various states by the company and other company funds to this account. Instead of appropriately remitting the taxes, he paid his CPA firm's expenses, children's college tuition, and daughters' wedding expenses.

After painstakingly tracing funds through checks and wire transfers, forensic accountant Karen Fortune concluded that the CFO had misappropriated over $2 million during the preceding decade. The CFO also took steps to prevent the business owner from receiving warning notices from the taxing authorities, and he produced false financial statements. The embezzlement scheme was discovered by the business owner when the CFO was hospitalized, and his CPA partners began receiving the tax notifications. The case resulted in a settlement from the various parties found to have liability. The CFO and his CPA firm were held accountable. The victim also recovered from a fidelity insurance policy, and the bank was held liable for negligently allowing the CFO to establish an account without the business owner's permission.

Accounts Receivable Fraud

A variety of accounts receivable (A/R) schemes can be perpetrated by a fraudster. The company executive with control over A/R can sell these accounts at a discount and receive a kickback from the purchaser. An employee, with or without the company's knowledge, may also inflate the A/R balance to qualify for loans that otherwise could not be obtained. This scheme could benefit either the company or the employee.

An accounts receivable scheme can also be used to mask theft of inventory. The employee records a fictitious sale with a debit to accounts receivable. The employee then takes the inventory and subsequently writes off the receivable as uncollectable.

A lapping scheme involves an employee altering accounts receivable records. The employee takes the funds intended for a customer's account. A second customer's funds are then applied to the first customer's account. A third customer's funds are then applied to the second customer's account and so on. Like a check-kiting scheme, this is a perpetual scheme that repeats itself until the funds are either repaid or the employee is caught. Detective controls for this scheme include job rotation, mandatory employee vacations, as well as a reconciliation of payments to customers' accounts. If a lapping scheme is suspected, customer confirmation requests can be made to confirm and discover the extent of the fraud.

Case Example

Litigation attorneys Katy Furr and Kevin Stine, shareholders with the law firm Baker Donelson in Atlanta, investigated, litigated, and successfully obtained multi-million dollar judgments against parties associated with a company that had a multi-million dollar asset-based loan with a bank client. The borrower's account receivables served as the primary collateral and borrowing base for a revolving loan over a period of several years, and the borrower failed to repay the loan at maturity after the bank declined to extend the loan again.

During the bank's subsequent investigation, it was revealed that accounts receivables reporting and borrowing base certificates submitted to the bank overstated the borrower's outstanding receivables by more than $9 million. The borrower closed its business shortly afterward, leaving the bank with a multi-million dollar loss. Baker Donelson helped coordinate the subsequent forensic examination of the borrower's operation and collection efforts, including a lawsuit against the obligors in federal court, discovery of hidden bank accounts and third-party asset transfers, and recovery of collateral.

Accounts Payable Fraud

Accounts payable (A/P) fraud can involve improperly paying a vendor. These schemes are relatively common and have the potential to cause significant losses to an organization. They can involve a vendor, an employee, or both. They can also involve corruption and conflicts of interest schemes, described in Chapter 4.

Double payments to vendors are extremely costly and can be done by mistake, by vendors intentionally submitting two invoices and by employees issuing two checks but misapplying one of them. Once an employee discovers that a company's internal controls are weak, a variety of schemes can be perpetrated. A simple scheme is for an employee to just fabricate an invoice and cause the company to make a payment to the employee.

One creative scheme involves an employee who creates a shell company to facilitate the fraud. When the victim (the company where the employee works) receives an invoice from a vendor, the employee creates a fictitious invoice for substantially more than the actual invoice. The employee causes the company to pay the inflated invoice to the employee's shell company. The shell company then pays the vendor the actual amount owed.

Below is a checklist of ways to catch A/P frauds:

- Verify vendors through online searches and the secretary of state.
- Obtain all vendor payment data and put it in an Excel spreadsheet, and then sort by vendors and by dollar amounts to look for duplicate payments.
- Look for invoices that are just below company-set approval limits.
- Look for anomalies in invoice numbers (none, same, or sequential), no tax, wrong date, or illogical purchase of goods or services for the company.
- Compare vendor addresses with employee addresses.
- Compare vendor bank account numbers with employee bank account numbers.
- Review the vendor master file to look for and delete vendors that are no longer being used.

Case Example

Auditors from a local CPA firm in Atlanta uncovered an accounts payable fraud during an audit of a telecom company. As part of their audit program, the auditors tested the substantiation for check payments made to a company's vendor who, as it turned out, also happened to offer credit cards. The auditors noted a string of numbers in the checks' memo lines that did not correspond to the invoices. Through investigative efforts, they discovered the controller used company checks to pay her credit card bills by burying them in the telecom's fiber usage expense accounts. Attached to each check that was used to misapply funds was a duplicate of a legitimate invoice. The forensic team's examination of each check and their search for legitimate substantiation revealed the extent of the controller's scheme. The controller was ultimately found to have embezzled over a million dollars in this accounts payable scheme. In this case, the victim company decided not to seek prosecution, simply settling for partial restitution. The failure to seek prosecution is a relatively common decision and unfortunately sets a bad tone for the victim organization.

Inventory Fraud

Inventory shrinkage can occur through both fraud and theft schemes. Shoplifting and employee theft are particularly common in the retail sector. The stolen goods are often sold through online retail schemes involving Craigslist, eBay, or other Internet outlets.

A "short shipment" scheme involves collusion between a vendor and a company employee. The employee agrees to accept less than the full shipment of goods ordered by the company in exchange for a kickback from the vendor. Inventory schemes can be mitigated with the use of cameras, strong inventory control systems, and the segregation of duties for purchasing and receiving functions.

Purchasing Card Fraud

A P-Card is a term use to describe a purchasing card, a charge card, or a credit card.[2] The use of P-Cards makes financial sense for most organizations due to the significant cost savings involved. Without a P-Card program, the organization uses the traditional and expensive procurement process involving a requisition, a purchase order, and a check payment. An organization that initiates a P-Card program for routine low-cost purchases can greatly reduce its purchasing costs.

P-Card fraud is one of the most common occupational frauds. The irony is that this fraud is also the easiest to prevent. One other key takeaway is that there are always two primary wrongdoers involved: the employee who misused the P-Card to steal and the manager who failed to supervise the employee or to review the expense records. Once P-Cards have been introduced to employees, one problem has been solved but another one has been created. Employees are effectively walking around with petty cash funds in their wallets. Pair this up with the Fraud Triangle—opportunity, pressure, and rationalization—and you get a common occupational fraud.

Unscrupulous employees have been known to put everything on the P-Card, from groceries to adult entertainment. Clever employees will only use the P-Card for dual-purpose expenses—the "gray zone" of expense categories—like gasoline and office supplies, where a business or personal use is difficult to identify. An employee using the P-Card to purchase gift cards is another scheme. Employees may also purchase a restaurant gift card when ordering dinner. Double dipping is a scheme whereby an employee pays for expenses with a P-Card but submits the same claims through an expense reimbursement process. The P-Card can also be used to violate other company policies, like purchasing a phone, tablet, or computer from a vendor of choice. Employees are only limited by their imagination and the internal controls that are present and functioning.

The most common red flag is a manager who is simply too busy to review a subordinate's expense report. Here are some common red flags of P-Card fraud:

- A supervisor who is "too busy" to review subordinates' expense reports.
- Missing or partially complete receipts.
- The receipts provided are the versions that show a total amount and are not itemized.
- Monthly reconciliations are late or are not performed at all.
- An employee is under review for other issues and believes that he or she is about to be terminated.

- An employee rushes the supervisor to approve the expense report.
- The total dollar amount of the expense reports continues to increase.
- An employee says the wrong card was "mistakenly" used for numerous purchases.
- The date of purchase is a nonworking day, like a Saturday, Sunday or a holiday.
- The purpose of the charges is for morale building.

Internal auditors are very comfortable with the concept of hard controls. These include preventive, detective, and corrective controls. An example of a preventive control is to limit P-Card charges through the use of merchant category codes (MCC) restrictions. An MCC is a four-digit number that can enable a P-Card administrator to exclude unwanted purchases (e.g., airlines, professional services, physicians, lawyers, accountants, and utilities) and cash advances. A variation of this control is to use a detective control known as "continuous monitoring" to detect questionable purchases. When a flagged MCC purchase is made, instead of restricting the purchase, a real-time notification can be sent to a manager to assess if the purchase is inappropriate or a false positive. Another type of preventive control is to limit purchases to prespecified dollar limits.

Probably the most effective means of deterring P-Card abuse is a strongly enforced policy with well-defined protocols. This includes firing the employee who engaged in P-Card fraud, taking disciplinary action against the manager who failed to carefully review the bogus charges, and communicating these actions to all employees. Seeking a criminal prosecution of the employee may also be appropriate.

Another control that serves as both a preventive and detective control is to have all P-Card account statements flow through a P-Card administrator. Further, the internal auditing function should audit P-Card statements and the supporting documentation to ensure compliance with policy. A corrective control should include enhancing employee awareness when policy violations do occur. This would also be an appropriate time to educate all employees about policies that are in place.

Case Example

I investigated a fraud at a Fortune 100 company where a vice president gave his password to a trusted administrative assistant for all of his approvals because he was too busy to attend to pesky administrative matters. The assistant began ordering a never-ending number of items from Amazon on her company-issued P-Card. The scheme then escalated into a series of $1,000 gift checks paid for with her P-Card and commercially shipped to her residence. In the end, the scheme exceeded $400,000 before it was caught due to a change of administrative assistants. This case did result in a federal prosecution, a federal prison sentence, and a company executive in need of a significant disciplinary action, all of which were undesirable outcomes that were completely preventable through supervision and monitoring.

Cash Schemes

Cash always presents challenges to organizations due to the ease with which it can be stolen and its fungible nature. There are two basic schemes that involve cash: skimming and larceny.

Skimming is an off-the-books scheme that removes cash before it has entered the accounting system. This scheme is most often done by an employee at the point of sale and includes unrecorded and underreported sales and theft of checks. Another scheme can occur when a salesperson deals directly with a customer in the field (i.e. outside of a retail location), pockets the cash, and the employer is never aware of the transaction. Yet another variation includes placing bogus checks in the register. This enables the register to balance, and the employee hopes management just thinks a bad check was passed.

A red flag that skimming has occurred is that the cost of goods sold increases while sales and accounts receivables remain constant. Placing cameras around point-of-sale areas discourages skimming. Two or more employees should never share the same register. Undercover "customers" can detect schemes when service providers give away products for commissions or tips (e.g., the bartender who gives extra drinks for free).

Larceny involves the theft of cash after it has been recorded in the accounting system. As a result, larceny schemes are easier to detect and are less common than skimming. An employee who shares the duty of both recording a cash deposit and taking the cash to the bank can alter totals on the deposit slip and pocket the difference.

Case Example

Crazy Eddie was a large electronics retailer in the northeastern United States in the 1970s and 1980s. The chain grew in prominence due in large part to the crazy characters portrayed in the company's television commercials, which can still be seen on YouTube. When Crazy Eddie was still in business, a customer's use of cash was much more common. The business was run by the Antar family, which included Sam E. Antar and Eddie Antar. In this case, the Antars skimmed millions of dollars from their own company for the purpose of evading federal income tax. The Antars also used the skimmed cash to pay employees off the books for the purpose of avoiding payment of payroll taxes.

The Antars decided to take the company public in 1984. Due to the size of the skimming scheme, the Antars had to stop the tax fraud and leave the funds in the company so that investors would appreciate the large profit margins and cash flows. The company's troubles increased due to family infighting and other financial frauds. The company ultimately collapsed, and several family members were convicted of federal securities fraud.

Check Schemes

As discussed earlier, the most common check scheme is for an employee with signatory authority to simply embezzle funds by writing a check to himself or herself. However, there are three other schemes, known as a "forged maker," "a forged endorser," and an "altered payee." The forged maker is the simplest of these schemes. Here, an employee can take check stock, make it payable to himself or herself, and forge the maker's signature. Maintaining security of the physical check stock is the control for this scheme.

The forged endorser scheme can occur at any point where an employee (or outsider) can gain access to a check. These could be outgoing checks to vendors or incoming checks from customers. The employee will simply forge the payee's endorsement on the back of the check and deposit the check into a shell company bearing a similar name to the payee or use a check casher.

An altered payee scheme involves a fraudster who gains access to a check and alters the payee's name. In a process known as "washing," it is possible to use chemicals to erase a payee's name on a check and substitute another payee's name. Once the name is changed, the fraudster can deposit the check into an account the fraudster chooses. To accomplish this scheme, the fraudster must first gain possession of the check, often by theft from mailboxes.

Case Example

The very first case I was assigned as an FBI agent, which also was the only case that I almost failed to solve, involved a forged endorsement scheme. I learned more from this case than any other case that I was assigned. The year was 1989, and the country was going through the S&L crisis.

My supervisor assigned me a bank fraud case involving a relatively low dollar loss despite the staggering number of bank failures that needed to be investigated. The purpose was so that I could take a simple case through the entire justice system before tackling the S&L failure cases. I am glad my supervisor had that foresight, as it served me well.

In this case, a Houston bank paid its many vendors with checks to manage properties that it had repossessed through foreclosure—a common problem for banks at the time. However, the vendors began contacting the banks and complained that they had never been paid. The bank knew their checks were getting cashed, so these complaints did not make sense. In a bizarre turn of events and for reasons that were never explained to me, a boyfriend of a bank employee called the bank's security office to advise that he had seen a lot of the bank's checks in his girlfriend's car and that it did not make sense to him. Those were the facts that I was given to start an investigation.

I had two problems. One, my supervisor did not want me to spend too much time on the case due to its likely low dollar loss; I needed to be working on the big S&L failure cases. Two, I couldn't connect the bank's losses to the boyfriend's tip. Here is what I subsequently learned. Talking to a human source is almost always better than any other investigative technique. Human sources are efficient because the investigator can gain information more quickly than the follow-the-money efforts of forensic accountants. In this case, I attempted to record conversations through the use of a body recorder on the boyfriend. These attempts failed because the subject kept wanting to have sex with my informant, requiring him to remove the device. As a last-ditch effort, I asked the subject to take a polygraph test. This turned into a good cop, bad cop ploy. The polygrapher was the good cop, and I was the bad cop. The subject failed the polygraph with flying colors. Although she did not immediately confess, as I had hoped, she later confessed to her boyfriend and then came back to the FBI to make a full confession.

In her confession, she admitted to working in the bank's accounts payable department. When vendor checks were returned to the bank due to the wrong address or wrong dollar amount, she had access to them. With checks in hand, she went on a check-cashing spree at the numerous check-cashing businesses around Houston.

Case Example

I had an informant tell me that he was part of a group that went "flagging" during the week. Of course, I had to ask what flagging meant. The informant told me that they would go through neighborhoods and see flags up on mailboxes. They knew that this meant the mailbox owner was likely paying monthly bills with checks. They stole the checks, "washed" them, and then negotiated them for cash. Since the time that this informant told me about "flagging," I have never raised the flag on my mailbox again. The failure to raise my mailbox flag is not a problem; the mailman comes every day, as I always get junk mail.

Credit Card Refunds

In the credit card refund scheme, the employee simply diverts a valid credit card refund by applying the credit to the employee's personal credit card. In a variation of the scheme, an employee can void a customer credit card refund and then take cash out of the register. When these types of schemes are pervasive, a decline in revenue should become apparent. A way to prevent this is to have a segregation of duties in which a manager approves all credit card refunds.

Payroll Fraud

Payroll fraud involves payroll expenses for services that were not rendered. A common and costly scheme involves nonexistent employees, often known as "ghost employees." This scheme involves putting someone on the payroll or keeping a former employee on the payroll. The latter is more common, since all of the dirty work has been done and no one has to provide a urine sample. Except for the name, the former employee's identifiers can be changed, and the funds are directly deposited into an account controlled by the fraudster. The ease in detecting these schemes depends on how carefully the fraudster planned the fraud. The calculation of a legitimate payroll expense requires that an employee's name be added to the payroll, that wage information for hours worked be collected and calculated, that deductions for taxes, health insurance, and other items be deducted; and that a mode of payment include a check or direct deposit. The failure of any of these items to be present is a red flag for a ghost employee scheme.

The overpayment of wages is another type of payroll fraud. Wage calculations are derived from the hours worked and the rate of pay. The falsification of either of these numbers can result in inflated wages. A similar scheme involves inflated sales commissions. A commissioned salesperson will have an incentive to create fictitious sales, inflate the value of sales, or lump the sales into a particular reporting period. When payroll frauds are substantial, they have the potential to make the company's financial statement materially inaccurate.

Probably the most pervasive form of payroll fraud is employee time theft. A culture in which employees are allowed to arrive late, leave early, and abuse their sick and vacation leave can be very costly. This problem is compounded when employees routinely attend to personnel business while at work.

A more ingenious payroll scheme is for an employee who is in control of payroll taxes to cause the company to overpay federal and/or state income tax, submit an altered Form W-2, and later request a refund. However, the excess amount is not actually withheld from the employee's salary. For example, a payroll tax clerk can intentionally overpay the state for the income tax with-holding by say, $8,000. The employee then creates a bogus W-2 showing the excessive withholding amount. Later, the employee completes the scheme by requesting a refund from the state when filing her annual income tax return.

Another type of payroll-related fraud was demonstrated in the Crazy Eddie case, in which employees were paid off the books to avoid payroll taxes.

CHAPTER 4

Corruption and Conflicts of Interest

"The Rule for Reciprocation—The rule says that we should try to repay, in kind, what another person has provided us. . . . By virtue of the reciprocity rule, then, we are obligated to the future repayment of favors, gifts, invitations, and the like."

—ROBERT B. CIALDINI, *INFLUENCE: THE PSYCHOLOGY OF PERSUASION*

This chapter will delve into corruption and conflicts of interest. Conceptually, these terms can be confusing because they mean different things to different people, so I will carefully define them throughout this chapter. Corruption and conflicts of interest may be terms defined by a company policy as well as by state and federal criminal law. Determining if a policy or law relating to corruption or conflicts of interest have been violated can be challenging. As you will see, even the United States Supreme Court has wrestled with these issues over the decades.

Of the three fraud classifications—corruption, asset misappropriation, and financial statement fraud—corruption is generally the most difficult to prevent, detect, and investigate. The difficulty is due to the personal relationships among the actors. Corruption often involves collusion between an outside vendor and an inside employee. There may not be a paper trail, and if there is one, it is difficult to find or follow. The influence could be difficult-to-trace benefits like meals, gifts, trips, or cash.

Corruption occurs with an intermediate frequency when compared to the other two classifications of fraud: more frequently than financial statement fraud but less frequently than asset misappropriation. Corruption also results in an intermediate dollar loss between those two classifications of fraud. Most significantly, it is also the most underreported type of fraud. The victims of most frauds eventually learn of its occurrence because they suffer a direct monetary loss. In the corruption context, the victims rarely even know that wrongful conduct has occurred.

Public corruption involves a public official—elected or appointed—who has abused the office for personal gain. In public corruption schemes, the taxpayers are the ultimate victims, but they often are not able to prevent or detect its occurrence.

Public corruption is the FBI's top criminal investigative priority. It is also the most challenging and difficult violation that the FBI investigates. The FBI's rationale for placing such a high priority on this criminal violation is clearly stated on its webpage: "Public corruption poses a fundamental threat to our national security and way of life."[1] Our democracy is run and controlled by federal, state, and local officials who are either elected or appointed. Corruption has the potential, among other things, to make our nation's borders less secure, increase the cost of our government services and programs, improperly influence ordinances and zoning rules, change jury verdicts, or cause law enforcement to turn a blind eye to crime.

As an FBI agent who observed many criminal trials, I found three types of professionals whom juries really have a hard time convicting: doctors, police officers, and politicians. In the case of doctors and police officers, these are professionals whom we as a society should be able to trust, and many jurors have a hard time believing that these professionals can do wrong. You may be shocked to find politicians in this group of hard-to-convict defendants, but remember, the defendant–politician got elected by a majority of the voters.

A jury will likely be composed of many of those same voters who elected the politician. Voters tend to be supportive of a person they helped elect.

I also think the literature on corruption is significantly lacking. I attribute this to the lack of tangible evidence that can be researched, evaluated, and reported to stakeholders, who could benefit from that knowledge. This is in direct contrast to asset misappropriation and financial statement fraud, about which much has been written. Asset misappropriation is well understood because of the frequency of its occurrence and the paper trail involved. Financial statement fraud is also well understood due to the publicity surrounding it, the investigations by boards, and the scholarly work of academics. Corruption, however, is not well understood, the paper trail is often limited, and few people get to fully debrief and hear directly from the corrupt actors, if they are even caught.

Public corruption prosecutions often involve a conspiracy between a government insider wielding power and a business outsider trying to obtain something of value. Either of these two classes of defendants—the insider or the outsider—may plead guilty and cooperate. I have worked with these individuals during the weeks and months of trial preparation. The insights and information they disclose as to how and why they got involved in a public corruption scheme is simply invaluable. These insights are rarely provided to elected officials, boards, internal auditors, academics, or others who could benefit from this knowledge when seeking to create corruption-resistant organizations. What happens in reality is that after these disgraced public officials and businesspeople cooperate with law enforcement and serve a prison sentence, they are rarely heard from again. Nevertheless, their stories are enlightening. Newly elected or appointed public officials can clearly benefit from hearing about the missteps of others that led to corruption. Their message should be delivered in a "scared straight for public officials" venue. Law enforcement, especially the FBI, can do a better job of educating the public.

Definitions

Corruption: Involves the wrongful use of influence to procure a benefit for the actor or another person, contrary to a duty or the rights of others.[2]

Conflict of Interest: Occurs when an employee or agent—someone who is authorized to act on behalf of a principal—has an undisclosed personal economic interest in a matter that could influence that employee's or agent's professional role.[3] By definition, once the employee or agent fully discloses the conflict and the principal approves it, with or without safeguards, there is no longer a conflict of interest.

Bribery: Providing something of value to a person in a position of trust in an attempt to corruptly influence an official action or business decision.

Kickback: A form of bribe between a seller and a buyer of goods or services in which the buyer receives an undisclosed percentage or other payment in exchange for the seller receiving favorable treatment.

Let me give you some examples that will flesh out some of the distinctions between these concepts. Take, for example, a purchasing agent who works for a company that routinely purchases widgets. This employee also owns a company that sells those same widgets, and the employee does not disclose her ownership interest in the company to her employer. This employee then causes the employer to purchase widgets from her company. This is clearly a conflict of interest because the purchasing agent's interests are on both sides of the transaction. The employer should have a well-written conflict of interest policy that prohibits this conduct.

Now take the example of an employee who knowingly accepts an inflated invoice from a vendor and causes the employer to pay the fraudulent invoice in full. As part of the scheme, the vendor provides a kickback for a portion of the payment to the employee. This is an example of a kickback.

These two examples demonstrate conduct that may be violations of state criminal commercial bribery statutes. If the employee is a state employee, the conduct almost certainly violates state law. In both examples, if the employee were a federal employee, the conduct might violate federal bribery, conflicts of interest, and related statutes.

A civil remedy is usually available to a business that is a victim under various legal theories that include common law fraud, breach of fiduciary duty, as well as the civil adaptation of the Racketeer Influenced and Corrupt Organizations Act (RICO) statutes present in at least 33 states.

Case Example

The city of Houston had a large corruption scandal involving several council members. One of the council members had an alleged history of accepting bribes in exchange for his official duties. This case turned into the strongest public corruption case I have ever observed. The evidence presented at trial included a video of an undercover FBI agent, posing as a businessman, paying a council member a cash bribe in exchange for his council vote. The lengthy recording showed the council member counting the cash and telling the undercover agent that unlike other council members who say they do good things for the community, this council member said he does good things for himself. This was absolutely the most compelling evidence I have ever seen in a corruption case and clearly demonstrated the defendant's corrupt intent, or *mens rea*. The trial ended, however, in a hung jury!

Corruption is simply different than other types of crimes. The underlying conduct inherently involves relationships among human beings. Despite a court's clear instructions on the law or the strength of the facts, how a juror evaluates these relationships will vary by age, sex, race, religion, politics, and other factors.

Public Corruption

The term "public corruption" is an amorphous concept often used by citizens to help explain their disdain for a politician, government official, or those abusing a government program. As an FBI public corruption supervisor for many years, I heard this term bandied about when someone wanted to complain to me about a public official. The complainant believed there was public corruption occurring but often could not provide facts with any degree of specificity. For the government to obtain a conviction of a public official, the jury must find specific facts that violate each element of a criminal statute beyond a reasonable doubt. All of this is against a potential backdrop that the public official may be well liked in the community. Trust me when I tell you, this is tough! Accordingly, I have found that prosecutors have an unwritten rule that public corruption cases require a higher degree of certainty (despite the legal standard being the same) before they will file charges.

Public corruption cases are better prosecuted in the federal system (as opposed to the state system) for a variety of reasons. There are fewer politics involved if federal prosecutors handle these cases. A county district attorney who prosecutes a local public official will inherently have to deal with the defense's argument that the prosecution is for political purposes. The argument is based on the fact that the district attorney is an elected official. These cases are also resource-intensive. Many cases require an undercover operation so that investigators can capture evidence of a crime in progress. Absent the public official making incriminating statements on a surreptitiously recorded tape, juries will often not convict a public official. In reality, only the FBI has the resources and expertise to investigate many of these cases.

Public corruption cases are better investigated and prosecuted in the federal system regardless of whether the public official is a state or federal official. Unfortunately, federal law draws a significant distinction between state and federal officials. Congress has given federal prosecutors specific statutes to prosecute federal officials to include: (1) federal bribery, 18 U.S.C. 201(b);

(2) gratuities prohibition, 18 U.S.C 201(c); and (3) theft statutes, 18 U.S.C. 641, 654.

Those statutes work well because they are designed to prosecute corrupt federal officials. There are not really any federal statutes specifically designed to prosecute state and local officials. When prosecuting these officials, federal prosecutors must make creative use of other federal statutes, which include: (1) honest services mail and wire fraud, 18 U.S.C. 1341, 1343, and 1346; (2) Racketeer Influenced Corrupt and Organizations Act, 18 U.S.C. 1961; (3) extortion, 18 U.S.C. 1951, (4) federal program bribery, 18 U.S.C. 666; and (5) the Travel Act, 18 U.S.C. 1952.

In the United States, state and local officials greatly outnumber federal officials, and not surprisingly, the prosecutions of those state and local officials outnumber federal officials. As you will see, there is a long history of legal challenges that federal prosecutors have faced when prosecuting state and local officials with the federal statutes. Why doesn't someone fix this glaring problem? Who could do that? Here is another interesting question: Of the three branches of government (executive, legislative, and judiciary)—which one do you think is the most hostile toward giving federal prosecutors the laws they need to prosecute state and local officials? If you are like me, the answer will surprise you. The discussion that follows will reveal the answer.

Let's review a brief history of the body of law that prosecutors most often use to combat corruption-related offenses for state and local government officials. I referenced the mail, wire, and honest services fraud statutes in Chapter 2. The mail fraud statute was first passed by Congress in 1872, and the wire fraud statute followed much later in 1952. These statutes capture most fraudulent schemes in which the defendant used the mail (or commercial carrier) or a wire (e.g., communication devices to include a landline telephone, computer, cell phone, or fax machine). As we explore the use of these statutes, also consider the underlying conduct at issue: (1) fraud, (2) corruption, and (3) conflicts of interest. Further, consider whether the conduct in question is done by a public or a private official.

The mail and wire fraud statutes, i.e. federal law, have a long and sustained use for prosecuting cases involving the loss of property. A prime example would be a Ponzi scheme in which the victim relied on false information and wire transferred $50,000 to the fraudster. This is unequivocally an appropriate case in which the mail and/or wire fraud statutes could be used to prosecute someone who unlawfully obtained property from a victim.

Now, let's consider a contractor who pays a $10,000 bribe to a city council member to gain support for a contract. Is this a scheme to defraud? Has anyone lost a property interest? Here, prosecutors creatively developed the theory that the citizens have been deprived of the "intangible right of honest services" by a government employee. Under this theory, federal prosecutors have successfully used the mail fraud and wire fraud statutes to prosecute bribery and kickback cases. The prosecutors then used the honest services theory to prosecute state and local government officials for undisclosed conflicts of interest. Federal prosecutors continued to stretch the statute to prosecute not only government officials but also private corporate officials for bribery, kickbacks, and conflicts of interest. This theory continued in popularity until the United States Supreme Court decided *McNally v. United States*, 483 U.S. 350 (1987).

The *McNally* case involved a kickback scheme related to Kentucky's purchase of workers' compensation insurance. In exchange for kickbacks, the Kentucky Chairman of the Democratic Party decided which insurance companies would provide the state with workers' compensation insurance. In total, there were $851,000 in kickbacks paid to various entities. Charles McNally was a front man for one of the entities that the chairman controlled, and McNally was paid $75,500 for his efforts. McNally argued that his conduct could not constitute honest services fraud because he had no fiduciary duty to the citizens of Kentucky. The Supreme Court agreed and even went further. The Court held that the mail and wire fraud statutes could only be used to prosecute losses of money and property and not the intangible right of honest services. The Court stated that "If Congress desires to go further, it must speak more clearly than it has."[4]

Congress acted quickly. It passed the "intangible right of honest services" statute (18 U.S.C. 1346) in 1988, which was within one year of the *McNally* decision. This statute effectively overruled *McNally*, codified the honest services theory that federal prosecutors had used for decades, and placed prosecutors right back where they were before the *McNally* decision. Now, unimpeded, prosecutors continued to prosecute public and private individuals who had harmed others through corruption and undisclosed conflicts of interest schemes.

However, this all changed when former Enron CEO Jeff Skilling appealed his conviction to the United States Supreme Court, arguing that the government's use of the "intangible right of honest services" provision of 18 U.S.C. 1346 was unconstitutionally vague. *See Skilling v. United States*, 561 U.S. 358 (2010). The government charged Skilling with wire fraud for violating his duty to provide honest services when he defrauded Enron's shareholders by misrepresenting the company's fiscal health, thereby artificially inflating its stock price. The Supreme Court agreed with Skilling and found that the government's use of the honest services provision was too broad. The Court limited the government's use of the honest services fraud theory by providing some clearer guidelines. Under current law, honest services prosecutions are limited to only bribery and kickback schemes. Also important, the Court allowed federal prosecutors to continue charging both public and private officials for this conduct.

After the *Skilling* decision, the law involving the prosecution of corruption and conflicts of interest for both public and private officials became clearer. Although this was certainly not what law enforcement wanted to hear, it was at least clearer. For public corruption prosecutions, one issue that remained unresolved was what constituted an "official act" for purposes of bribery. When a public official receives something of value, that is, a bribe, what corresponding official act will trigger honest services fraud? What is the *quo* in *quid pro quo*? This Latin term means "a reciprocal exchange," or literally, something (*quid*) for something else (*quo*).

The prosecutions of former Governor of Virginia Robert McDonnell and his wife, Maureen McDonnell, provide some guidance as to what constitutes an official act.[5] The McDonnells were both charged with bribery-related offenses, including honest services fraud. Wealthy Virginia businessman Jonnie Williams was the CEO of Star Scientific, a company that sold a dietary supplement from a compound found in tobacco. Williams wanted to obtain FDA approval for the dietary supplement, thereby making the rights to this product significantly more valuable. To accomplish this, expensive clinical trials were needed. Williams sought the assistance of Governor McDonnell and his wife Maureen. The McDonnells were both vulnerable as they had significant debt.

The courting of the McDonnells by Williams was extensive and included lavish gifts and loans totaling $175,000. Williams provided the following gifts and loans to the McDonnells: (1) use of Williams' plane to assist with an election, (2) $20,000 worth of designer clothes for Maureen McDonnell during a shopping trip, (3) a $50,000 loan to assist the McDonnells with their struggling rental properties at Virginia Beach, (4) a $15,000 gift to help pay for the McDonnells' daughter's wedding, (5) a Rolex watch for Governor McDonnell, (6) a $20,000 loan, (7) golf trips for Governor McDonnell and his children, (8) a $10,000 wedding gift to the McDonnells' daughter, and (9) use of Williams' vacation home and Ferrari.

Also interesting was the fact that Maureen McDonnell bought 6,000 shares of stock in Williams' company, Star Scientific. She then sold the stock in December of that same year only to repurchase the shares in January. The purpose of selling and repurchasing the shares was to avoid an end-of-year reporting requirement for elected officials or immediate family members to report stock held in excess of $10,000.

The government alleged that Governor McDonnell had committed the following "official acts":

During the time the McDonnells received these gifts and loans worth $175,000, the government showed at trial that Governor

McDonnell was doing the following things for Williams: (1) arranging meetings for Williams with Virginia government officials; (2) hosting and attending events at the governor's mansion, designed to encourage Virginia university researchers to initiate clinical studies and to promote Star Scientific's products to doctors for referral to their patients; (3) contacting other government officials in the governor's office as part of an effort to encourage Virginia state research universities to initiate clinical studies; (4) promoting Star Scientific's products and facilitating its relationships with Virginia government officials by allowing Williams to invite individuals important to Star Scientific's business to exclusive events at the governor's mansion; and (5) recommending that senior government officials in the governor's office meet with Star Scientific executives to discuss ways that the company's products could lower health care costs.[6]

The question for the Supreme Court was whether or not Governor McDonnell's actions constituted "official acts" for purposes of violating the honest services fraud law. The Supreme Court unanimously vacated Governor McDonnell's conviction, holding that the governor's activities such as holding meetings, attending parties, and telephoning authorities were not "official acts." Those actions were in contrast with the governor's powers, which included signing or vetoing laws, appointing individuals to fill vacancies, and issuing pardons, among other powers. The Department of Justice declined to retry the case. The Supreme Court ended its opinion with the following observation:

> There is no doubt that this case is distasteful; it may be worse than that. But our concern is not with tawdry tales of Ferraris, Rolexes, and ball gowns. It is instead with the broader legal implications of the Government's boundless interpretation of the federal bribery statute. A more limited interpretation of the term "official act" leaves ample room for prosecuting corruption, while comporting with the text of the statute and the precedent of this Court.[7]

McDonnell v. United States is the law of the land. Now, there must be a direct connection between the bribe and an "official act." Absent a clear use of the officeholder's powers, *McDonnell* tells us that there is no official act and thus no *quo*.

Consider a U.S. Secretary of State who hosts meetings with foreign dignitaries at or near the same time those officials donate millions of dollars to a large not-for-profit foundation bearing the secretary's husband's last name. In a post-*McDonnell* era, that factual pattern would likely not be in violation of the honest services fraud statute.

Of the three branches of government, the United States Supreme Court has been the most prodefendant branch. Prosecutors have asked for strong laws, Congress has provided them, and the Supreme Court has curtailed them.

Procurement Corruption

I have spent a considerable portion of my professional career both in the FBI and the private sector addressing the prevention, detection, and investigation of procurement corruption. All governments must procure goods and services as part of their service to constituents, and these expenditures likely encompass a large portion of their budgets. The providers of these goods and services are naturally eager to obtain lucrative government contracts. The problem arises when either a contractor is willing to engage in illegal conduct to win these contracts or a government official solicits a payment to steer a contract.

The prevention, detection, and investigation of procurement corruption are extremely difficult endeavors due to corruption's collusive nature. Despite this limitation, I have learned that in government procurement, especially local governments, there are three key government stakeholders who may be involved in any procurement corruption. These stakeholders either originate the fraud or become complicit when approached by an unscrupulous vendor. These three stakeholders are: (1) elected officials, (2) procurement officers, and (3) subject matter experts.

Inherent in our democratic process, elected officials are effectively placed in a conflict of interest when they run for office. Vendors and contractors specializing in government work will often contribute to elected officials' campaigns. My observation may be a little cynical, but I don't think these vendors are doing it out of the goodness of their hearts; I believe they are doing it with the expectation of receiving favorable treatment in their interactions with government officials. I can assure you that after an election, a high probability exists that these same vendors who contributed to the officials' campaigns are now making phone calls, office visits, and lunch engagements where they are promoting their firm. Nothing is inherently wrong with officials accepting those overtures.

Elected officials do cross a line, though, when they begin promoting one vendor over another. Once ingratiated with a vendor, an elected official can be motivated to discuss a vendor's proposal with a government's user department personnel and/or the government's procurement officials. During these discussions, the elected official may make a subtle comment, such as "XYZ Company sure seems like a highly qualified company." Or, the comment can be very direct: "I need you to be a team player and ensure that XYZ Company gets this contract!" The scenario becomes blatantly illegal when the elected official receives a bribe in exchange for these acts.

A procurement officer is another category of government official who can play a significant role in shepherding a procurement through the process. These officials write solicitations, establish bid deadlines, communicate with vendors, accept sealed bids, evaluate bidders, assess if a bidder is responsive and responsible per the terms of the solicitation, and make other judgment calls throughout the process. These and a whole host of other functions require integrity of all the procurement officials involved.

The last category of government officials involved in the procurement process is the subject matter experts. These officials usually reside in the government's user departments and provide expertise for complex procurements like a road, bridge, fire station, technology solution, on-call architectural service, and a myriad of other complex purchases. Without subject matter experts to assist in drafting these solicitations and evaluating bidders' responses, a governmental organization could not effectively handle these procurements. However, just like elected officials and procurement officers, subject matter experts are also at risk of being compromised. Due to their technical expertise, they can easily steer a contract by writing a solicitation specification in such a way that only one vendor qualifies. Furthermore, when sitting on a committee that evaluates multiple bidders, a subject matter expert's authoritative opinion can easily persuade an entire committee to select a particular vendor.

Case Example

The forensic accounting team at IAG Forensics & Valuation investigated a procurement officer for a large organization. Through his position, the procurement officer was able to create new vendors in the organization's procurement system. He established his own company to do business with the organization. Thereafter, his company provided staffing for various large sporting events, concessions, security, and other services. He even used employees of the organization as his staff. Through interviews of personnel, IAG discovered that the procurement officer's conflicts of interest were widely known except by his superiors. Due to his position, he could circumvent the procurement policies by underbidding competitors, and his position enabled him to gain access to an available labor pool. Although the organization was not found to have suffered a loss through any excessive pricing, the procurement officer did engage in obvious conflicts of interest and violated important procurement policies. In this case, the procurement officer was disciplined, internal controls were strengthened, and training was enhanced.

Procurement Terms and Fraudulent Schemes

Bid Suppression or Bid Rotation: Bidders conspire to take turns bidding on contracts so that they do not competitively bid against each other. In a variation of the scheme, a bidder submits a high bid knowing the bidder will not win.

Bid Tailoring: A government insider writes bid specifications tailored to a specific bidder. Another version of the scheme is to write the specifications so vague that bidders will either not respond or will not be able to adequately address the government's needs in their proposals.

Emergency Contract: A contract that is awarded outside the normal bidding policy due to a time constraint involving an emergency. A lack of competitive bidding and transparency puts these contracts at higher risk for corruption.

Insider Information: Government information not disclosed in the bid solicitation, and the content of competing vendor's bid information before it becomes public.

Need Recognition: Vendors' outreach efforts to government officials to educate about the benefits of a particular product or service.

Sole Source Contract: A contract that cannot be competitively bid because there is realistically only one vendor that can provide the service or good.

Split Purchase: A government official splits a purchase into two or more smaller purchases for the purpose of evading an authorization threshold.

Unbalanced bid: For a solicitation involving multiple line items, a bidder may price some unit items very high and price some units very low, making the overall bid extremely competitive. A bidder might do this for one of three reasons: (1) It may be part of a front-loading scheme where the artificially high items are completed in the first part of the project, (2) A bidder may know there will be change orders requiring the high-priced items, and (3)

The bidder may know that the low-priced items may not actually be needed in the contract.

Conflicts of Interest

A conflict of interest occurs when an agent takes an interest in a matter that is adverse to the principal and is not disclosed. This can occur in professional relationships, like the attorney–client, CPA–client, or realtor–client relationship. Conflicts of interest also commonly arise in the corporate setting between the company and its employees. This occurs when an employee has an undisclosed economic interest in a transaction that adversely affects the company.

Most conflicts of interest fall into one of two categories: a purchasing scheme or a selling scheme. In a purchasing scheme, the employee has an undisclosed interest in a company that is selling a product or a service to her employer. Due to the conflict, the employee may negotiate a high sales price that harms the employer. In a more egregious purchasing scheme, the employee could just submit completely false or inflated invoices. A selling scheme involves the reverse scenario in which the conflicted employee has an undisclosed interest in the company purchasing a product or a service. Here, the conflicted employee may negotiate too low a sales price to the company in which she has an undisclosed interest. In a more egregious version of this scheme, the employee may write off the account receivable or just simply not attempt collection of payment from the company in which the employee has an undisclosed interest.

In contrast to the preceding examples, conflicts of interest can be entirely unintentional. Take, for example, the executive of a construction company who sits on a board of directors for a large charity. The charity needs a new building and begins soliciting construction companies. Through no fault of his own, the construction executive can immediately find himself in the middle of a conflict of interest. What the executive does next will be pivotal. The right thing to do is to *disclose* the conflict of interest. The disinterested board members of the charity can then make decisions going forward as well as place certain safeguards around the executive to mitigate the conflict. Should the executive not disclose the conflict of interest and participate in a business transaction, the executive could be in legal jeopardy. A plaintiff harmed by someone engaged in an undisclosed conflict of interest may have civil remedies based on various legal theories, including common law fraud or a breach of any of the following duties: fiduciary duty, duty of due care, or duty of loyalty.

Gratuities and Gifts

A gratuity is something of value that is generally provided after the delivery of goods or services. A gift is anything of value given before, during, or after a transaction but is not specifically negotiated. Both a gratuity and a gift can be a conflict of interest. They can also be relatively innocuous, violate a code of conduct, result in civil liability, or be a violation of criminal law. Examples of gifts can include a fruit basket given during the holiday season by a long-time vendor, electronic tablets given to managers, or expensive vacations given to key decision makers.

For government employees, state law will vary on how gratuities are handled. Federal employees are covered by a criminal gratuities statute, 18 U.S.C. 201(c). This statute differs from the bribery statute because the language of the statute does not require proof of a *quid pro quo* or a corrupt intent to influence an official act. Like the corruption statutes discussed earlier, the federal gratuities statute has been met with resistance by juries, the courts, and the United States Supreme Court.

Consider a series of prosecutions that resulted from two companies that provided gifts to Secretary of Agriculture Michael Espy. Espy was prosecuted under the federal gratuity statute for his receipt of gifts, sports tickets, lodging, and airfare by companies regulated by the Department of Agriculture. A jury acquitted Espy. In a related prosecution, a company that provided the gratuities to Espy appealed its conviction to the United States Supreme Court.

The Court reversed the conviction, construing that the statute required a link between the gift and an official act.

The government will rarely be able to establish that there is a connection between a gift and an official act. The very essence of a gift is that it is a socially acceptable gesture that does not overtly suggest that a reciprocal act is expected. The Department of Agriculture, like all federal agencies, has rules against receiving gifts in excess of certain minimal thresholds. The obvious purpose of these rules is to prevent the corrupting influence that gifts can have over decision makers. I believe that these gifts, which are seemingly innocuous to some, are extremely harmful. Clearly, Secretary Espy violated his own department's rules. He received substantial gifts from companies that his department regulated. Those who receive gifts under these circumstances are likely unaware or at least unwilling to admit the deleterious effect on their decision making. Just as bad, this conduct sets a corrupt tone from the top as department employees observe that important ethical rules are being violated by high-level government leaders.

International Corruption

Many Americans tend to think our corporations are plagued with corruption. There is obviously some merit to this belief because both the DOJ and the SEC do constantly charge U.S. corporate officials with corruption-related conduct. This trend is also likely to continue. However, American executives who do business overseas are exposed to a level of corruption that is not generally seen in the United States.

Transparency International is a respected international nongovernmental organization with a mission that includes exposing and preventing corruption. Transparency International produces an annual Transparency International Corruption Perception Index that ranks the perception of corruption in more than 180 countries as determined by opinion surveys and expert assessments. Below is a chart that is an excerpt taken from the Transparency International's 2017 report. The scores are like golf scores—the lower the better. For the year

2017, notable countries include: United States at 16, China at 77, Russia at 135, and Somalia at 180.

Transparency International Corruption Perception Index 2017 Rankings

#	Country	#	Country	#	Country	#	Country
1	New Zealand	46	Georgia	91	Albania	135	Honduras
2	Denmark	46	Malta	91	Bosnia and Herzegovina	135	Kyrgyzstan
3	Finland	48	Cabo Verde	91	Guyana	135	Laos
3	Norway	48	Rwanda	91	Sri Lanka	135	Mexico
3	Switzerland	48	Saint Lucia	91	Timor-Leste	135	Papua New Guinea
6	Singapore	51	Korea, South	96	Brazil	135	Paraguay
6	Sweden	52	Grenada	96	Colombia	**135**	**Russia**
8	Canada	53	Namibia	96	Indonesia	143	Bangladesh
8	Luxembourg	54	Italy	96	Panama	143	Guatemala
8	Netherlands	54	Mauritius	96	Peru	143	Kenya
8	United Kingdom	54	Slovakia	96	Thailand	143	Lebanon
12	Germany	57	Croatia	96	Zambia	143	Mauritania
13	Australia	57	Saudi Arabia	103	Bahrain	148	Comoros
13	Hong Kong	59	Greece	103	Côte D'Ivoire	148	Guinea
13	Iceland	59	Jordan	103	Mongolia	148	Nigeria
16	Austria	59	Romania	103	Tanzania	151	Nicaragua
16	Belgium	62	Cuba	107	Armenia	151	Uganda
16	**United States of America**	62	Malaysia	107	Ethiopia	153	Cameroon
19	Ireland	64	Montenegro	107	Macedonia	153	Mozambique
20	Japan	64	Sao Tome and Principe	107	Vietnam	155	Madagascar
21	Estonia	66	Hungary	111	Philippines	156	Central African Rep
21	United Arab Emirates	66	Senegal	112	Algeria	157	Burundi
23	France	68	Belarus	112	Bolivia	157	Haiti
23	Uruguay	68	Jamaica	112	El Salvador	157	Uzbekistan
25	Barbados	68	Oman	112	Maldives	157	Zimbabwe
26	Bhutan	71	Bulgaria	112	Niger	161	Cambodia
26	Chile	71	South Africa	117	Ecuador	161	Congo
28	Bahamas	71	Vanuatu	117	Egypt	161	Dem. Rep. of Congo
29	Portugal	74	Burkina Faso	117	Gabon	161	Tajikistan
29	Qatar	74	Lesotho	117	Pakistan	165	Chad
29	Taiwan	74	Tunisia	117	Togo	165	Eritrea
32	Brunei Darussalam	**77**	**China**	122	Azerbaijan	167	Angola
32	Israel	77	Serbia	122	Djibouti	167	Turkmenistan
34	Botswana	77	Suriname	122	Kazakhstan	169	Iraq
34	Slovenia	77	Trinidad and Tobago	122	Liberia	169	Venezuela
36	Poland	81	Ghana	122	Malawi	171	Korea, North
36	Seychelles	81	India	122	Mali	171	Equatorial Guinea
38	Costa Rica	81	Morocco	122	Nepal	171	Guinea Bissau
38	Lithuania	81	Turkey	122	Moldova	171	Libya
40	Latvia	85	Argentina	130	Gambia	175	Sudan
40	Saint Vincent & Grenadines	85	Benin	130	Iran	175	Yemen
42	Cyprus	85	Kosovo	130	Myanmar	177	Afghanistan
42	Czech Republic	85	Kuwait	130	Sierra Leone	178	Syria
42	Dominica	85	Solomon Islands	130	Ukraine	179	South Sudan
42	Spain	85	Swaziland	135	Dominican Republic	**180**	**Somalia**

Source: Transparency International[8]

The primary U.S. law to prevent international corruption is the Foreign Corrupt Practices Act (FCPA) of 1977.[9] The FCPA was passed in response to several SEC investigations in the 1970s, including the Watergate scandal, revealing widespread bribery of foreign officials by U.S. companies. The purpose of the law was to combat the payment of bribes and kickbacks by U.S. companies and employees. Despite its passage in 1977, the SEC and DOJ did not bring significant actions against violators until after the turn of the century, starting with the Bush administration and significantly expanded during the Obama administration.

The FCPA's enforcement provisions are designed to work in two different ways: (1) criminal—the antibribery provisions prohibit payments to foreign officials to obtain or retain business,[10] and (2) civil—the accounting provisions require that publicly traded companies make and keep accurate books and records,[11] and maintain an adequate system of internal accounting controls.[12]

The challenge any company faces when doing business with corrupt foreign countries is that some country officials are so corrupt that without the payment of a bribe, the company may not be able to get licenses to operate in markets, obtain government contracts, or sell products or services to the foreign government. We should question the wisdom of the FCPA. Is U.S. law so restrictive that it effectively prohibits American businesses from competing overseas? What greater good is created by disadvantaging American companies competing in foreign markets? These were questions I asked in the late 1990s when I supervised a public corruption squad charged with ramping up FCPA investigations. Twenty years later, I think the SEC's and DOJ's prosecuting efforts have very positively shaped the international-commercial landscape by exposing corruption, improving the lives of those in many foreign countries, and leading other countries to enact and enforce similar laws.

Let's consider how the bribery provisions of the FCPA work. The elements of the bribery provisions are: (1) A U.S. person or business, (2) corruptly offers or provides anything of value, (3) to a foreign official, and (4) to obtain or retain business.[13]

Take, for example, a U.S. pharmaceutical company that wants to have its drugs dispensed in a Chinese hospital network. A pharmaceutical representative agrees to pay a percentage of all drug sales to a Chinese government official in exchange for that government official agreeing to execute the contract, that is, a kickback arrangement. This violates the bribery provision of the FCPA, since it involves a U.S. company making a corrupt payment to a foreign official to obtain or retain business.

This entire arrangement should raise several red flags. China is an at-risk country because it ranks 77th on the Transparency International Corruption Perception Index in 2017, and further, China is a communist regime. As a communist country, hospitals are generally state-owned or operated by the government, and the doctors and other employees are government officials. The pharmaceutical industry is also at risk for corruption due to sales practices in which representatives are compensated by exerting influence over doctors to prescribe specific drugs.

Now let's consider the accounting provision of the FCPA that is also known as the "books and records provision." If a U.S. company were to pay a $10,000 bribe to an official from the hypothetical country of "Corruptistan," what would the correct accounting entry be for the bribe on the U.S. company's books and records? The accounting treatment would include a journal entry showing a debit to an expense account and a credit to cash as follows:

	Debit	Credit	Notation
Bribe Payments	$10,000		Bribe to Corruptistan Official
Cash		$10,000	

Do you think any financial officer would ever make this entry on a publicly traded company's books? No, of course not. A company that allowed this entry to appear on its books would clearly be acknowledging it has violated the FCPA. Accordingly, the company's books would invariably contain a false or misleading entry to describe the payment as something other than a bribe in order to conceal the payment. The DOJ and SEC's publication, *FCPA: A Resource Guide to the U.S. Foreign Corrupt Practices Act*,[14] provides common examples of how bribes have been mischaracterized on a company's books to include:

- Commissions or Royalties
- Consulting Fees
- Sales and Marketing Expenses
- Scientific Incentives or Studies
- Travel and Entertainment Expenses
- Rebates or Discounts
- After-Sales Service Fees
- Miscellaneous Expenses

- Miscellaneous Expenses
- Petty Cash Withdrawals
- Free Goods
- Intercompany Accounts
- Supplier/Vendor Payments
- Write-offs
- "Customs Intervention" Payments

In an effort to disguise the bribe payment, the journal might look like this:

	Debit	Credit	Notation
Entertainment Expense	$10,000		Division Holiday Function
Cash		$10,000	

Proving that a U.S. company or an individual paid a cash bribe to a foreign official in a foreign country is very difficult for either the FBI or the SEC to establish. Thus, the FCPA's accounting provisions are a creative way of enforcing punishment for corrupt payments to foreign officials, like when the federal government was unable to convict Al Capone for murder and extortion but was able to prosecute him for tax evasion.

Once the FBI or the SEC gathers information that bribes have been paid, often through a whistleblower, a civil or criminal enforcement action can be made much easier through the FCPA's books and records provision. Proving that a journal entry is false or disguised is much easier than showing that a foreign official has received a cash payment. For example, company officials could be interviewed to establish that there was no division holiday function. The FCPA also has an "internal controls" provision. This provision requires that a company have internal controls to provide reasonable assurances that transactions are executed in accordance with management's authorizations, among other requirements.[15]

Companies engaging in international business are legally responsible for the acts of their agents. A company may need to outsource many of its functions through third-party consultants, agents, or partners, and those companies that do outsource these functions can be held legally responsible for their agents' unlawful acts. To assist in minimizing this risk, a company needs to have a strong right-to-audit clause in all of its agreements with those acting on behalf of the company. They should also exercise these rights and ensure that the company's funds are not being used to violate the FCPA's provisions.

Now let's consider the FCPA's civil and criminal enforcement authorities for both the bribery and accounting provisions. The FCPA's bribery provision covers U.S. companies (public and private) and U.S. citizens. The FCPA's accounting provisions only cover publicly traded companies and those individuals who aid and abet (usually financial insiders) them. Civil enforcement of the FCPA's provisions are brought by the SEC for a publicly traded company. Criminal enforcement of the FCPA's provisions are brought by the DOJ. In those rare instances in which the SEC does not have civil enforcement authority over the individual or company, the DOJ will enforce the law.

The FCPA has at least three defenses. The FCPA will not be violated if the payment was lawful under the written laws of the foreign country.[16] I have never seen this used as a successful defense because foreign countries do not have laws that make it legal to bribe their officials. A second defense is used if the expense or payment is a reasonable and bona fide expenditure related to promotion, demonstration, or explanation of a company's product or services (e.g., a foreign official's travel to the United States).[17] This exception can be tricky, since expenses can go from reasonable to unreasonable very quickly. On the one hand, it may be reasonable to pay for travel of a foreign official to visit a company's production plant. On the other hand, it is unreasonable to bring the official's entire family to Disney World for a three-week stay.

The third defense is known as a "facilitation payment,"[18] and this provision also has a significant application. A facilitation payment exception applies when a small payment is made in connection with a routine governmental action involving nondiscretionary acts. Examples of a facilitation payment could include gratuities to a clerk for processing visas and obtaining utilities like phone and water services. This exception does not apply to a government official's discretionary acts like a decision to award a contract.

Case Example
Hypothetical: Facilitating Payments[19]

Company A is a large multinational mining company with operations in a Foreign Country, where it recently identified a significant new ore deposit. It has ready buyers for the new ore but has limited capacity to get it to market. In order to increase the size and speed of its ore export, Company A will need to build a new road from its facility to the port that can accommodate larger trucks. Company A retains an agent in Foreign Country to assist it in obtaining the required permits, including an environmental permit, to build the road. The agent informs Company A's vice president for international operations that he plans to make a one-time small cash payment to a clerk in the relevant government office to ensure that the clerk files and stamps the permit applications expeditiously, as the agent has experienced delays of three months when he has not made this "grease" payment. The clerk has no discretion about whether to file and stamp the permit applications once the requisite filing fee has been paid. The vice president authorizes the payment.

A few months later, the agent tells the vice president he has run into a problem obtaining a necessary environmental permit. It turns out the planned road construction would adversely impact an environmentally sensitive and protected local wetland. While the problem could be overcome by rerouting the road, such rerouting would cost Company A $1 million more and would slow down construction by six months. It would also increase the transit time for the ore and reduce the number of monthly shipments. The agent tells the vice president he is good friends with the director of Foreign Country's Department of Natural Resources and it would only take a modest cash payment to the director and the "problem would go away." The vice president authorizes the payment, and the agent makes it. After receiving the payment, the director issues the permit, and Company A constructs its new road through the wetlands.

Was the payment to the clerk a violation of the FCPA?

No. Under these circumstances, the payment to the clerk would qualify as a facilitating payment, since it is a one-time, small payment to obtain a routine, non-discretionary governmental service that Company A is entitled to receive (i.e., the stamping and filing of the permit application). However, while the payment may qualify as an exception to the FCPA's anti-bribery provisions, it may violate other laws, both in Foreign Country and elsewhere. In addition, if the payment is not accurately recorded, it could violate the FCPA's books and records provision.

Was the payment to the director a violation of the FCPA?

Yes. The payment to the director of the Department of Natural Resources was in clear violation of the FCPA, because it was designed to corruptly influence a foreign official into improperly approving a permit. The issuance of the environmental permit was a discretionary act, and Indeed, Company A should not have received it. Company A, its vice president, and the local agent may all be prosecuted for authorizing and paying the bribe.

Worldwide enforcement of antibribery laws has significantly increased in recent years. The United Kingdom passed the U.K. Bribery Act of 2010, which is actually more expansive than the U.S. FCPA's provisions, because it prohibits all bribery, not just bribes to foreign officials, and it prohibits facilitation payments. A growing body of literature exists for those who are trying to build compliance programs and better understand the law. Following are some of these resources:

- The DOJ and SEC's 2012 Resource Guide—*FCPA: A Resource Guide to the U.S. Foreign Corrupt Practices Act*

- U.K. Ministry of Justice's *The Bribery Act 2010 Resource Guidance*

- *The Anti-Corruption Handbook: How to Protect Your Business in the Global Marketplace* by William P. Olsen, 2010 (John Wiley & Sons)

- Organisation for Economic Co-operation and Development's *Good Practice Guidance on Internal Controls, Ethics, and Compliance*

- International Organization for Standardization's *ISO 37001 Antibribery management systems*

Root Causes of Corruption

I have learned the root causes of corruption from those who engaged in it. I will share observations I have gained from debriefing corrupt contractors, lobbyists, and government officials, and juxtapose those insights with the literature from psychologists and ethicists to assist us in explaining why corruption occurs. The essence of what I have learned is that corruption is a gradual process between individuals. Even though the United States Supreme Court overturned his conviction, the Governor McDonnell example illustrates precisely how corruption occurs. The quintessential example is the contractor who bribes an elected official. The information that follows includes excerpts from the article, "Public Corruption: Causes, Consequences & Countermeasures."[20]

Individuals caught up in a corruption prosecution always seem to question how they found themselves in such a mess. In my experience, governmental officials come to office to do the right thing for the right reason. What happens? I think there is a symbiotic relationship between the contractor and the government official. I call it "the social compact of reciprocity." It is an unwritten rule that seems to be encoded in our DNA.

After years of working on corruption cases, I have observed common behaviors from those working on the outside of government and from those working inside government. Following are compilations of debriefings from various outside vendors and lobbyists that form a common theme:

When the politician saw me coming, he knew he was getting something. The first encounter may just be me giving my business card, but I always made sure his hand was out and I could see his palm. The next encounter might be a pen or book, but he was going to walk away with something that he knew was from my firm. This gift giving escalates to meals and entertainment. Eventually, the relationship looks more like a friendship than a business transaction. Trips to the family home, an outing to Vegas, or a quick trip on the corporate jet, it's all about giving the official something. What you're developing is the "ace in the hole." You never know when you need to call on it, but you know it is there. And when you do call in your chit, this is when it gets beautiful. You both know you just straight-up own him. You can now ply him with envelopes of cash, and everyone pretends like nothing is happening.[21]

Those attempting to gain access will have different modus operandi, but effectively they all exploit the social compact of reciprocity. Conversely, it is enlightening to understand the thought process of those officials charged with corruption. Many have a difficult time admitting they did anything wrong. For those officials who pleaded guilty and cooperated, their story goes something like this:

> I have always done what is in the best interest of my constituents. I work very hard at this job and have done a lot of good. This job is difficult. A lot of campaign rules exist, and I don't always pay attention to details. Sure, people gave me money, but I assumed it was essentially campaign contributions. And yes, we go to a lot of dinners, but that's how business is done in the real world. As for the gifts and trips, it was relatively insignificant, and we always accomplished a lot of good on those trips. We may have met in the political world, but we are really good friends. In hindsight, I can see this looks bad. When my wife asked me why I always paid in cash and where was the money coming from, it finally hit me: I had somehow sold my office.[22]

Psychologist Dr. Robert B. Cialdini adeptly captured the rule of reciprocity in his book, *Influence: The Psychology of Persuasion*. The rule says that we should try to repay, in kind, what another person has given us. By virtue of the reciprocity rule, then, we are obligated to the future repayment of favors, gifts, invitations, and the like.

Jack Abramoff, arguably the most corrupt lobbyist in U.S. history, was the master of this craft until FBI agents arrested him. At the height of Abramoff's corruption machine, he was giving out an unimaginable number of skybox tickets, pricey restaurant meals, and golf junkets to government officials in Washington, D.C. He even established his own high-end restaurant near Capitol Hill, called "Signatures," where he regularly treated elected and appointed federal officials and their staffers.[23] The ingenuity and efficiency of this setup was that he could sit at his favorite table and peddle influence on a large scale. When Abramoff's government friends tried to pay for their high-priced meals, Abramoff told them their money was no good at Signatures.

What was Abramoff trying to accomplish? He simply wanted access for his clients. When he placed a phone call to Capitol Hill, he wanted someone to answer the phone so that he could pitch an idea to a decision maker. If congressmen or senators received a few nice meals at Signatures, the least they could do was to answer the phone.

The free lunch is the "gateway drug" to corruption. Abramoff epitomized it. When I debriefed government officials who were caught up in a scandal, they could always recall their first free meal. The frequency of free meals invariably increased and then turned into more substantial gifts and benefits.

"Ethical erosion" is characterized by a series of small, sometimes unnoticed acts that erode ethical behavior, with each act providing a foundation for even further erosion.[24] However, when the slow, deliberative but nevertheless ethically corrosive process is happening to elected officials or corporate executives, they are unaware of what is taking place, or they may have a misplaced confidence in their internal, psychological defenses. In reality, before they realize what is occurring, it's already too late, the trap has been sprung, and the unsuspecting victim has walked right into it.[25]

Prevention and Detection

Corruption and conflicts of interest are significantly different than the other two categories of fraud: asset misappropriation and financial statement fraud. The root causes are different, and the manner in which these fraudulent schemes are executed are radically different. Accordingly, we must adapt our responses for preventing and detecting these schemes accordingly.

An organization's internal controls over its cash, assets, and processes, even when strong, are unlikely to have a material effect in deterring corruption. Those types of "hard controls" are very familiar to management who design them and to internal auditors who test them. In contrast, I believe the key to corruption prevention is the development of strong "soft controls."

Soft controls pertain to an organization's culture. These controls involve the understanding, development, shaping, and then testing of the culture of an organization. Hard and soft controls are covered in depth in Chapter 10.

Corruption prevention includes strong organizational policies that should be found in the employee handbook, conflicts of interest policy, anti-fraud policy, and/or a code of conduct. Corruption and conflicts of interest should be clearly proscribed. The rules governing the receipt of gifts and gratuities should be very tight. I personally like the idea of a zero-tolerance policy in which the rule is that no one is allowed to receive meals and other gifts. At a bare minimum, there should be no gifts or meals from those who do business with the organization. These concepts should be taught during employee onboarding and should be routinely reinforced thereafter. More stringent rules should be adopted for board members, officers, and higher-risk employees. On an annual basis, these employees should be required to read the organization's conflicts of interest policy, provide written disclosures for all potential conflicts of interest, and certify in writing that their disclosures are accurate.

This annual disclosure of any conflicts of interest by high-risk employees is crucial, since it serves as a preventive, detective, and corrective control. Here, employees would at least be required to reflect on the organization's policy and thereafter disclose all potential conflicts of interest. Organizations should, although they rarely do, audit these disclosures. Open-source information like that available from a secretary of state is a rich source of information for discovering undisclosed conflicts of interest. Fee-for-service providers can also assist in providing beneficial information for auditing conflicts of interest.

An employee's signed certification also has significant legal ramifications. For the employee who wrongfully fails to disclose a conflict of interest, an organization will be in a much better position to bring a lawsuit for a breach of a fiduciary duty, the duty of care, and the duty of loyalty. The employee's certification of knowledge of the rules and any resulting failure to disclose any conflicts of interest will be key evidence in any legal proceeding. In the government sector, a false certification can expose the employee to criminal prosecution. This is a strong deterrent for all government employees.

A red flag for nondisclosure of a conflict of interest is the employee late filer. This employee faces the dilemma of wanting to hide the conflict of interest as well as of not wanting to file a false document. The employee procrastinates and either files the annual certification late or not at all. Either of these circumstances is a red flag that a conflict of interest is at play. An organization with a weak compliance program can easily allow for a certification to slip through the cracks. Delinquent filers are high-risk employees, and their disclosure forms should be audited.

All policy and ethics violations, even the small ones, should be strictly enforced, as this will minimize the occurrence of larger violations. Social scientists James Wilson and George Kelling wrote an article in the March 1982 issue of *The Atlantic Monthly* entitled "Broken Windows." In this article, they argued that the monitoring and enforcement of smaller violations of the rules will create an atmosphere of law and order, thereby preventing more serious offenses.

CHAPTER 5
Financial Statement Fraud

"We have to make the numbers."

—WORLDCOM CEO BERNIE EBBERS INSTRUCTING CEO SCOTT
SULLIVAN TO COMMIT FINANCIAL STATEMENT FRAUD.[1]

On the early morning of July 3, 2002, my home phone rang in Houston, Texas. I was off work that day, as it preceded a holiday, and I was looking forward to a long, pleasant holiday weekend. The voice on the other end of the phone was an FBI agent assigned to the Corporate Fraud Unit at FBI Headquarters in Washington, D.C. I knew him well, as I used to be his boss when he was assigned to my public corruption squad in Houston. I knew him well enough to ask why he was calling my home phone so early on my day off. What I heard next was, "Listen up, you're heading to Jackson, Mississippi, as part of the management team leading the WorldCom investigation, and you need to get there immediately." So much for my long holiday weekend.

The phone call summoning me to the WorldCom headquarters was unusual. White-collar crimes, despite their potential egregiousness, have a five-year statute of limitations and invariably take a long time to investigate. While these investigations are very important, white-collar crimes do not ordinarily dictate a dire sense of urgency—it's not like an armed robber is holding bank employees hostage. However, these were no ordinary times. Enron was in bankruptcy and under investigation by the Enron Task Force. Enron and WorldCom's auditor, Arthur Andersen, was convicted of obstruction of justice in a Houston federal court on June 15, 2002. At the time, a long list of U.S. corporations were under investigation by the FBI, and the list was growing. Now there was a sense of urgency at the highest levels of government. The FBI's role was to shine a light on corporate fraud, "perp-walk" the corrupt executives right to prison (think deterrence) and help end the crisis.

By the time WorldCom imploded, the conduct of corporate America had truly put our financial markets at risk. The United States is a capitalist country. Our free markets desperately depend on accurate and transparent financial information that can be trusted and relied upon. The increasing number of publicly traded corporations brought down by accounting scandals caused investors to question whether they could continue to rely on audited financial statements filed with the SEC.

Realizing our free markets were under attack, on July 9, 2002, President George W. Bush signed Executive Order No. 13271: *Establishment of the Corporate Fraud Task Force*. This multiagency task force helped agencies share intelligence and focus their resources on an increasing number of corporate bad actors. In direct response to the Enron, Arthur Andersen, and WorldCom failures, the U.S. Congress, led by former FBI agent and Congressman Michael Oxley, and the Senate, led by Senator Paul Sarbanes, quickly passed the Sarbanes-Oxley Act of 2002 (SOX), and President Bush signed into law on July 30, 2002.

With the passage of SOX, the policing of corporate America by an independent, self-regulated auditing profession came to an end. There was a new sheriff in town, and it was the Public Company Accounting Oversight Board (PCAOB). Under the new post-SOX regime, the PCAOB oversees the auditors, and the auditors continue to police the corporations.

The FBI dispatched me to Jackson, Mississippi, to serve in a leadership role in the WorldCom investigation, in part because of my involvement in the Enron investigation. I had previously played a leadership role in the early phase of the Enron investigation. When large corporate collapses occur, several things need to happen. From an FBI management perspective, investigative needs have to be assessed and then married with the right resources. From an investigative perspective, the fraudulent schemes needed to be evaluated so that a strategy can be formulated, including which witnesses to interview and which documents to gather, subpoena, or obtain by a search warrant.

At the time of its failure, Enron was the largest fraud in history. Shortly thereafter, the Enron fraud was eclipsed by WorldCom. In case you are keeping score, Bernie Madoff's $65 billion Ponzi scheme is now the largest fraud in U.S. history.[2]

Despite the epic frauds at Enron and WorldCom, the frauds were actually significantly different. The Enron fraud was a multiyear, multidefendant, and multitransactional fraud that reached across several Enron divisions. Accordingly, it was a very complicated federal prosecution. Some common themes in the Enron fraud were lying to market analysts to drive up the stock price, bogus revenue recognition schemes, hiding debt in special-purpose entities (SPEs), and insider trading.

In contrast, the WorldCom case involved a simple accounting fraud. Prosecutors charged the defendants with causing top-side accounting journal entries to be made at the end of seven consecutive quarters for the purpose of meeting analysts' expectations. Expecting the demand for digital services in the telecommunications market to expand eightfold each year, WorldCom management went to third-party network providers and leased what is known as telephone-line capacity costing billions of dollars in order to meet this anticipated consumer growth. When growth did not materialize, WorldCom was stuck with enormous lease costs with no corresponding revenue. At the direction of CEO Bernie Ebbers, the accounting staff debited balance sheet accounts relating to "Property, Plant & Equipment" and credited an income statement account, "Line Expense." The net effect was to improperly capitalize expenses, thereby inflating the balance sheet and increasing revenue on the income statement. This fraud continued for seven consecutive quarters until it was discovered by WorldCom's internal auditor.

I knew that the Enron, Arthur Andersen, and WorldCom investigations were big cases when I was involved with them because they were making headlines in all of the national news outlets. Only with the passage of time, however, have I come to appreciate their broader implications. The shortcomings of these companies have dramatically reshaped corporate America. In the final analysis, these failures were human failures.

Fraudulent financial reporting involves both acts of commission or intentional misstatements, and acts of omission or disclosures in financial statements that leave out key facts to deceive the users of those financial statements. The users of financial statement information include bank officers, investors, financial analysts, and other stakeholders. For a publicly traded company, the fraud can include false reporting of a company's performance in quarterly and annual disclosures via SEC Forms 10-Q and 10-K.

In Chapter 1, "Fraud Concepts," I covered many of the motivations that drive this fraudulent conduct. The motivation for financial statement fraud is usually different than the motivation for asset misappropriation and corruption. Some of these financial statement frauds directly benefit the fraudster through commissions, bonuses, and stock options. For other frauds, the connection is not as clear. Instead, the motivation for these financial statement frauds may be ego-driven forces like pride (we outperform our competition) or shame (we can't lose). Financial statement fraud is usually committed or directed by the highest-level officials in an organization and often on behalf of the organization as opposed to against it. As a category of fraud, financial statement fraud occurs with the least degree of frequency. Unfortunately, when it does occur, the losses can be staggering and may even result in the demise of the company.

This chapter explores how corporate executives commit financial statement fraud and what we can do to prevent and detect these schemes. Finally, when a scheme is detected, we need to know the ethical and legal rules that govern reporting to external stakeholders, like the SEC and DOJ.

Company executives deal with real economic pressures. These executives are responsible for all of the components that drive a company's stock price, most importantly earnings. These pressures can lead to income statement fraud (increase revenue or decrease expenses) or balance sheet fraud (increase assets or decrease liabilities). How will corporate executives "make the numbers?" What schemes will they use? When reviewing these schemes, we will observe that fraudulent financial reporting will generally fall into one of three categories:

- Manipulation, falsification (including forgery), or alteration of accounting records or supporting documentation from which the financial statements are prepared
- Misrepresentation in, or intentional omission from, the financial statements of events, transactions, or other significant information
- Intentional misapplication of accounting principles relating to amounts, classification, manner of presentation, or disclosure[3]

The Schemes

Any discussion of financial statement fraud should begin with revenue recognition schemes, as these are by far the most common. The obvious reason for the prevalence of these schemes is that Wall Street analysts want to see earnings grow, and corporate executives want to ensure that their company meets these expectations. The risk associated with improper revenue recognition is so well recognized that the auditor's standard for assessing fraud in a financial statement audit has a presumption that this risk might exist.[4] Further, if auditors were to conclude that this presumption did not exist, this finding would have to be well documented in the work papers.[5]

Revenue Recognition Schemes

The following are typical revenue recognition schemes:

- Recording fictitious sales
- Overstating gross sales by understating returns, discounts, and allowances

- Recording sham sales such as round-trip trades and related-party transactions

- Recording revenue recognition in which the incidents of sale have not occurred, such as consignment sales, sales with special conditions, or products shipped for evaluation purposes

- Holding the books open for sales made after the end of a reporting period or accelerating shipments

Side Agreements

A variety of revenue recognition schemes can be placed under the category of side agreements. The SEC Staff Accounting Bulletin No. 101 requires evidence of a definitive sales agreement. The purpose of this documentation is to ensure that a company can properly follow revenue recognition standards and auditors can have auditing evidence. Side agreements between management or sales personnel and a customer can result in improper accounting treatment of a transaction. Side agreements can include asset misappropriation schemes by sales personnel to inflate their commissions, liberal return policies, allowing customers to cancel orders, or a change in payment terms. Side agreements are difficult to detect because they are not disclosed. Detection may require examination of contract terms with actual delivery and payment evidence. Interviews with management and sales personnel can be crucial to discovering side agreements.

Channel Stuffing

Channel stuffing is a practice by a company to induce its customers to purchase extra products by offering deep discounts, extended payment terms, or other concessions. This is often done at the end of an accounting reporting period to increase sales. The practice can be entirely legitimate if all of the terms of the sale are disclosed and are given the correct accounting treatment. For public companies, SEC Staff Accounting Bulletin No. 101 requires: (1) persuasive evidence that an arrangement exists, (2) delivery has occurred or services have been rendered, (3) the seller's price to the buyer is fixed or determinable, and (4) collectability is reasonably assured. The practice is illegitimate when a company recognizes revenue in contravention of these requirements. Red flags of channel stuffing include: (1) side agreements, (2) undisclosed liberal return policies, (3) increased shipping costs at the end of a reporting period, and (4) deep discounts. As an example, Sunbeam Products Inc. and its CEO, Albert Dunlap, were charged by the SEC for pushing its products to retailers in a massive accounting scheme that led to false financial statements.

Bill-and-Hold

Bill-and-hold is another scheme in which revenue is improperly recognized. Here, a seller of goods has an incentive to recognize revenue even while products are still being produced or are sitting in inventory awaiting purchase. Accordingly, the revenue recognition standards require that the reason for the bill-and-hold arrangement must be real, the product must be identified as belonging to a specific customer, the product is ready for delivery, and the seller cannot use the product or sell it to another customer.[6] Red flags that a bill-and-hold scheme may be at play are shipping dates at the end of a period, missing shipping information, and increased warehouse costs.

Construction Contract Accounting

The construction industry is ripe for accounting abuse due to the subjectivity required when applying the accounting treatment. Generally Accepted Accounting Principles (GAAP) require that contract revenue be accounted for under the percentage-of-completion method or the completed-contract method. Further, the percentage-of-completion method can only be used when management can reasonably estimate the progress toward the construction contract.[7] However, in these circumstances, management has considerable flexibility and discretion in "making up" the numbers. This method can easily be used to inflate earnings. Management can make aggressive estimates that result in early revenue recognition by underestimating the costs of completion or overestimating the percentage completed to date.

Software Sales

Software sales can raise complicated accounting issues due to multiple-element revenue arrangements. A company that sells software products and services may actually be selling three distinct type of software solutions: (1) software product, (2) maintenance agreement, and (3) services. Each of these three items may be on different timetables in terms of the incidents of sales being completed, resulting in corresponding time lags for revenue recognition. A company that wants to inflate earnings can misallocate the income streams from these three categories. This improper accounting treatment can result in the company's financial statements being misleading.[8]

Round-Tripping

This scheme involves the sale of a product or service between two companies for which there is no economic substance. I have seen this in two difference contexts. The most common is to inflate sales volume. This can increase a market participant's standing in the industry. The transaction will effectively be a wash or a net loss when transaction costs are considered. If the two transactions are straddled across a reporting period, it can inflate revenue for the first reporting period. In the case of El Paso Corp., an energy trader, Todd Geiger, was indicted for making round-trip natural gas trades to inflate an industry price-index. These market-moving trades enabled El Paso to profit from market manipulation.

"Cookie Jar" Reserves

GAAP requires that companies report revenues and expenses in the same accounting period. In very profitable periods, management may want to defer their company's profits to a future reporting period when the company's performance is not as stellar. This is one way to create income smoothing because investors prefer even levels of net income. Cookie jar reserves can be accomplished by a company overstating such reserves as acquisition costs, bad debt, litigation estimates, or taxes. In late 2000 and early 2001, Enron generated as much as $1.5 billion in profits during the California energy crisis. Enron would have been extremely embarrassed if the public knew of its tremendous profits during a time when the citizens of California were experiencing rolling brownouts due to market manipulations. Enron created a bogus reserve account to hide its profits.

Big Bath

A company may have an incentive to lower net income or even to show a loss. This can occur when Wall Street already is aware of bad news, a new acquisition is creating a decline in revenues, or a new CEO is coming on board. Here again, a company may overstate reserves such as acquisition costs, bad debt, litigation estimates, or taxes. The company can then bounce back the next year, thereby giving the appearance of a successful management team.

Understated/Omitted Liabilities

The misrepresentation of liabilities can be associated with any of the liability accounts on the balance sheet. The following are common examples:

- Accounts Payable (A/P). A/P can be understated in a variety of ways: (1) failure to report the liability in the accounting system, (2) reporting an A/P after a year end, (3) overstating a purchase discount or return, and (4) reversing a valid A/P.

- Unrecorded Obligations. Companies that issue warranties and returns can intentionally underestimate the associated liability.

- Contingent Liabilities. GAAP requires that a contingent liability be recorded on the balance sheet as a liability if the likelihood of a loss is probable.[9] Such a liability may be intentionally understated.

- Debt Forgiveness. Remove a valid debt from the books by debiting a note payable and crediting a revenue account.

- Recognizing Unearned Revenue. Recognizing an advance payment as revenue before the performance of the service or the delivery of the goods.

- Understate Accrued Liabilities. Accrued liabilities can be understated or not recorded at all and may include payables involving interest, utilities, salaries, payroll taxes, and rent.

Inventory Schemes

GAAP requires that inventory be reported at the lower of either cost or market value. A company may inflate inventory for a variety of reasons that include enhancing the value of collateral for a loan or, as discussed below, inflating net income. Conversely, a sole proprietor may actually reverse the scheme to lower net income for tax purposes.

A variety of inventory techniques can be used to increase net income. To understand these schemes, we need to know the relationship of the accounts related to inventory (asset) and the accounts related to cost of goods sold (expense), and how all of these accounts flow through the balance sheet and income statement from year to year. As you can see from reviewing the two charts below, if the inventory at the end of the period is overstated, the cost of goods sold is understated and net income is overstated by an equal amount. During year 1 of the scheme, net income will be inflated. However, unless the fraud is continued into year two, net income will now actually decrease by an equal amount. This scheme is like a Ponzi scheme or an accounts receivable lapping scheme: once it gets started, company management needs to continue it. For this reason, you might think that intelligent corporate executives would not engage in this type of fraud, but this type of inventory scheme has occurred at Rite Aid Corporation, Phar-Mor, and Miniscribe, among others.

Chart 1

Cost of Goods Sold	
Beginning Inventory	30
+ Purchases	80
– Returns to Vendors	–5
– Obsolescence-Shrinkage	–5
= Goods for Sale	100
– Ending Inventory	–40
= Cost of Goods Sold	60

Chart 2

Income Statement	
Gross Sales	100
– Sales Returns	– 5
– Sales Discounts	– 5
= Net Sales	90
– Cost of Goods Sold	–60
= Net Income	30

Due to the number of accounts involved, net income can be inflated in various ways. For example, cost of goods sold can be understated by overstating ending inventory or understating purchases. This can also be accomplished by overstating purchase returns to vendors or overstating obsolescence and shrinkage. Overstating the ending inventory should be the most suspect method, as it has the advantages of both increasing net income and inflating assets on the balance sheet.

Case Example

Miniscribe was a publicly traded company that manufactured computer hard disk drives. The CEO and the Chairman of the Board were prosecuted for orchestrating financial statement fraud involving an inventory overstatement scheme.

In year one of the scheme, management inflated the inventory by approximately $4 million. These bogus numbers were reported in their 10-K and 10-Q SEC forms and also enabled the firm to raise $97 million in debt. In year two of the scheme, the inventory was inflated by $15 million. In year three of the scheme, the company was showing a loss of $40 million, at which time the scheme collapsed when various board members learned of the growing inventory gap and formed a committee to investigate the issue.[10]

Expense Reduction Schemes

Another way to increase net income is to improperly lower expenses. Many of these schemes require the judgment of management. If management discretion is exercised within a reasonable margin of error, it is difficult for an auditor or forensic accountant to argue to the contrary. Conversely, red flags that these schemes are being used to improperly increase net income may include a change of accounting without justification, poor documentation of an accounting policy and the reason for any deviation, and a significant change in an account from one year to the next. A variety of expense reduction schemes can be used to inflate revenue. In each of these schemes, if expenses are inappropriately moved to a future year, the net effect is inflated profit in the current year.

- Depreciation and Amortization. Management can increase the estimated life of an asset, which lowers the annual depreciation and amortization cost.
- Advertising Costs. These costs should be expensed as incurred unless demonstrable evidence exists to show that advertising costs will enhance revenue in a future period.
- Start-up Costs. These are to be expensed in the year incurred and not mischaracterized in an effort to capitalize the costs.

- Software Development Costs. GAAP requires that costs associated with computer software be expensed when incurred until technological feasibility has been established for the product, at which time the expenses are capitalized. The assessment of when technological feasibility has been met is up to management's discretion.[11]

- Research and Development Costs. GAAP requires that R&D costs be expensed as incurred. However, assets like material, equipment, and facilities that have alternative uses can be capitalized. Again, this is subject to management's discretion.

Inadequate Disclosures

A publicly traded company's annual financial report contains a wealth of information other than the numbers disclosed in the financial statements. Fraud occurs when required disclosures are intentionally misleading or omitted. Contingent liabilities must be disclosed if the likelihood of loss is reasonably possible.[12] These risks are known by management, and in the case of litigation risk, they may also be known by legal counsel.

SOX and its implementing regulations require management to certify its quarterly and annual reports filed with the SEC. A company can also misrepresent the nature of its products or services in news reports or on its website. The "Management Discussion and Analysis" (MD&A) section of the annual report can be misleading or contain material omissions. A lot of information can be gleaned from the footnotes to the financial statements of publicly traded companies; in fact, these are regarded as integral to the presentation of financial statements. Probably the most common type of omission-related fraud is the failure to disclose related-party transactions, as these are likely part of a revenue recognition scheme. Of course, when a company is engaged in fraud, it is unlikely to disclose critical information, and if it does disclose critical information, it may be cryptic. For example, the SEC charged former top executives of Tyco International Ltd. for failing to disclose millions of dollars of low-interest and interest-free loans they had obtained from the company.

Asset Misappropriation

The asset misappropriation schemes described in Chapter 2 generally will not rise to the level of financial statement fraud because they many not meet materiality thresholds. The materiality threshold is met when the judgment of someone relying on the financial statement might be influenced. However, some misappropriation of assets schemes are so egregious that the accounts on the financial statements are, in fact, materially misleading. Tyco International Ltd. is a prime example of this; the executives' looting of the company had a material effect on the financial statements.

Prevention

Fraud prevention is discussed in more detail in Chapter 10. An additional discussion is warranted here due to some of the unique characteristics associated with financial statement fraud. The magnitude of the potential loss to investors and other victims of this type of fraud necessitates a corresponding amount of controls to mitigate the risks. From a macro perspective, these controls include distinct institutional safeguards that are aptly known as the "six pillars of financial statement oversight." These oversight entities have overlapping functions and, when working effectively, may prevent many of the schemes discussed in this chapter.

Six Pillars of Financial Statement Oversight

1. Board of Directors
2. Audit Committee
3. Executive Management
4. Internal Auditors
5. External Auditor
6. Oversight Bodies (SEC, PCAOB, AICPA, NYSE (New York Stock Exchange), NASD (National Association of Securities Dealers), DOJ)

Sarbanes-Oxley Act of 2002

The failures of Enron, WorldCom, and Arthur Andersen ushered in the passage of the SOX legislation in 2002. Many of SOX's provisions were designed to prevent future conduct of the type that was uncovered during the investigation of the calamities associated with these three companies. Following is a brief summary of SOX's 11 sections, including provisions related to fraud prevention.

Title I—Public Company Accounting Oversight Board: Establishes the PCAOB to regulate the auditing profession and requires auditors to maintain work papers for seven years.

Title II—Auditor Independence: Establishes auditor independence rules, including limiting the nonauditing services that the auditor can provide a client, which include forensic accounting services.

Title III—Corporate Responsibility: Establishes certain audit committee requirements, including procedures for the receipt of anonymous complaints, that is, a hotline; requires the CEO and CFO to certify the accuracy of financial statements; provides for SEC enforcement authority if an officer or director improperly influences the external auditor; and requires attorneys to report up-the-ladder, but not outside the company.

Title IV—Enhanced Financial Disclosures: Requires disclosures of off-balance sheet transactions, prohibits loans to officers, and requires real-time disclosures of material changes to the company's financial condition. Most significantly, §404 requires the establishment of internal controls over financial reporting by management and the test of the controls by the external auditor.

Title V—Analyst Conflict of Interest: Establishes conflict of interest rules for securities analysts.

Title VI—Commission Resources and Authority: Establishes various administrative rules pertaining to the SEC.

Title VII—Studies and Reports: Requires reports relating to accounting firms, credit rating agencies, enforcement actions, and investment banks.

Title VIII—Corporate and Criminal Fraud Accountability: Establishes record-keeping requirements, whistleblower protections, a specific securities fraud statute, and penalty enhancements to other criminal statutes.

Title IX—White-Collar Crime Penalty Enhancements: Enhances criminal penalties for mail and wire fraud statutes, creates a "SOX conspiracy" that does not require a specific act in furtherance of the conspiracy or *actus reus*, and creates a criminal provision for a CEO or CFO who knowingly certifies financial reports that are inaccurate.

Title X—Corporate Tax Returns: Requires the CEO to sign the federal income tax return.

Title XI—Corporate Fraud Accountability: Enhances the obstruction of justice statute that deals with witness tampering, destruction of records, or impeding a federal investigation.

Yates Memo

United States Deputy Attorney Generals have a long tradition of writing a "memo" shortly after taking office that relate to white-collar crime enforcement policy. Deputy Attorney General Sally Quillian Yates is no different, and she penned the "Yates Memo" in September of 2015. These so-called memos become DOJ policy and are incorporated into the U.S. Attorneys' Manual that federal prosecutors are required to follow.

As a result of the 2007–2008 financial crisis, including the subprime mortgage bubble, the Lehman Bros. collapse, and questionable banking practices, many observers were left with the perception that the DOJ did not aggressively prosecute those responsible. For a discussion of the difficulties associated with prosecuting those involved in the financial crisis, see the "Nash Conspiracy" section below. I believe Deputy Attorney General Yates's motivation for writing her 2015 memo was in direct response to the public backlash for DOJ's failure to prosecute more individuals. Regardless of her motivation, DOJ's policy for holding individual corporate wrongdoers accountable can be summarized as follows:

1. In order to be eligible for any cooperation credit, corporations must provide to the DOJ all relevant facts about the individuals involved in corporate misconduct.

2. Both criminal and civil corporate investigations should focus on individuals from the inception of the investigation.

3. Criminal and civil attorneys handling corporate investigations should be in routine communication with one another.

4. Absent extraordinary circumstances, no corporate resolution will provide protection from criminal or civil liability for any individuals.

5. Corporate cases should not be resolved without a clear plan to resolve related individual cases before the statute of limitations expires, and declinations as to individuals in such cases must be memorialized.

6. Civil attorneys should consistently focus on individuals as well as the company and evaluate whether to bring a lawsuit against an individual based on considerations beyond that individual's ability to pay.

Nash Conspiracy

Johns Forbes Nash, Jr. was a Princeton University Nobel Laureate in Economics, but he was more popularly known as the paranoid-schizophrenic genius featured in the 2001 movie, *A Beautiful Mind*, starring Russell Crowe. This section explains the government's limitations in prosecuting individuals involved in the 2008 financial crisis using Professor Nash's game theory.

Professor Nash's greatest contribution to economic game theory, which studies strategic behavior of interacting opponents, has come to be called the Nash equilibrium. The Nash equilibrium holds true for a noncooperative game involving two or more players. Each player is assumed to have knowledge of the strategies of all of the other players, and each player acts rationally. The outcome of the game is determined by the set of strategies of each player and their corresponding payoffs. The Nash equilibrium is attained when no player has anything to gain by changing his or her own strategy.

In short, the Nash equilibrium is a game theory concept in which the optimal outcome of a game is one in which no player has an incentive to deviate from his or her chosen strategy even after knowing the choice of all of the other players. For our purposes, an ancillary principle of the Nash equilibrium is the players do not have to communicate with each other. Let's apply the Nash equilibrium to the U.S. mortgage crisis.

By way of summarizing the U.S. mortgage fraud crisis, an entire market of mortgages was originated all too often with "bad paper," that is, false or misleading documents and support. Congressional policy to create affordable home ownership, under the Community Reinvestment Act, may be considered the first step in this process. With the acquiescence of Fannie Mae and Freddie Mac, the race to provide home ownership to everyone started. Mortgage brokers sold mortgages to buyers of homes with the inability to repay the mortgages due to predatory lending, ignorance, and oftentimes fraud. After origination, the mortgages were usually resold in the secondary market to participants who undoubtedly had knowledge of the quality of the paper. These mortgages were then rated by the big, but rather conflicted, credit rating agencies and resold on Wall Street as exotic financial instruments with names like residential mortgage-backed securities (RMBS) and collateralized debt obligations (CDOs), even synthetic CDOs. Ultimately, the only nonparticipant in all of this wheeling and dealing, the U.S. taxpayer, bailed out the entire market.

An essential key to this mortgage-lending crisis was the market's belief that Fannie Mae and Freddie Mac guaranteed these mortgages even if they, as guarantors, became insolvent, which it turned out was a valid strategy. At this point, let's introduce the economic concept of a moral hazard into each participant's strategy. A moral hazard occurs when someone takes more risks because someone else bears the burden of those risks if the strategy fails and losses are incurred. In a mortgage fraud crisis such as the one in 2008, each player is passing the bad paper simply because it's profitable whenever the risk taking pays off. Each participant is working under the assumption that someone else bears the risk of loss should a mortgage, portfolio, or tranche become impaired.

Can Nash's insights into game theory shed some light on the U.S. mortgage fraud crisis? My argument is that each market participant stood in the Nash equilibrium. The game was noncooperative and involved numerous market participants. They all understood the others' strategies and acted in their own self-interest. No party had to communicate with another.

The Nash equilibrium also provides insight into another question that has frustrated U.S. taxpayers: Why haven't more bankers gone to jail? Part of the answer lies in the requirement for the prosecutor to prove *mens rea* or criminal intent beyond a reasonable doubt. In the case of the mortgage fraud crisis, those standing in the Nash equilibrium were, by definition, noncooperative. Proving a well-orchestrated criminal conspiracy by individual defendants is challenging because the market participants are not communicating game-playing strategies with each other. Further, each participant plays a single, isolated role (e.g., consider the separation of mortgage initiation, mortgage-servicing functions, and selling RMBS and CDOs on Wall Street). The market participants are also presumed to have knowledge of the criminal and regulatory rules enforced by the DOJ, SEC, and banking regulators, and thus constrain their behavior to provide the perception that they are operating within legally permissible boundaries. However, proving that any one individual or defendant violated these rules by knowingly transferring impaired mortgages onto the next participant has proven challenging for prosecutors.

In an attempt to hold sophisticated market participants criminally liable for their individual roles, can a prosecutor charge a "Nash Conspiracy?" Each defendant would be charged with a Nash Conspiracy, imputing knowledge of the noncooperative game strategy on each defendant. The object of the conspiracy is a moral hazard whereby all defendants are taking unreasonable risks, creating "systemic risk" to the entire U.S. economy but knowing full well that the U.S. taxpayers could ultimately bear the burden of loss (in the so-called too big to fail bailouts).

Although it is not as vindicatory as seeing an executive in handcuffs, the SEC and DOJ have had much success extracting large settlements from financial institutions as opposed to individual defendants. In these civil lawsuits, the government has a lesser burden of proof in establishing that the corporate entity acted with the requisite level of intentional wrongdoing, known as scienter. Although regulators were probably not thinking in Nashian terms, the essence of these civil suits was to hold institutions accountable for their market participation in the mortgage fraud crisis.

Detection

Many professionals hold job responsibilities that include the detection of financial statement fraud. External auditors have a duty to find it when it is material to the financial statements. Internal auditors want to know of all frauds, regardless of materiality. Forensic accountants are called in when fraud is suspected. External bodies charged with oversight also have an interest to include the SEC, PCAOB, AICPA, NYSE, NASD, DOJ, and FBI. As I will discuss in more detail in Chapter 11 regarding fraud detection, employee insiders are the most likely individuals to identify fraud, and when these insiders are not handled appropriately, they may become external whistleblowers.

Detection of financial statement fraud is difficult because it is usually perpetrated by executive management that can override internal controls. Despite these challenges, we can learn best practices for detecting fraud from those professionals charged with finding it.

External Auditors

External auditors have a strong incentive to find fraud material to the financial statements because it is their professional duty, and they can be held liable for negligence when they do not find it. Since external auditors are charged with finding fraud, reviewing their professional standards is a good place to see how they do it. Let's first look at the big picture and then zero in on the professional standards.

External auditors conduct their work in two stages: (1) testing account balances and (2) assessing internal controls. The audit requires that certain professional standards be followed to obtain reasonable assurance about whether the financial statements are free of material misstatement. The purpose of the audit is for the external auditor to reach a professional opinion about whether the financial statements present fairly, in all material respects, the financial position of the auditee in conformity with U.S. generally accepted accounting principles.

To reach this opinion, the external auditor must consider fraud in a financial statement audit. In the case of publicly traded companies, the external auditor (registered public accounting firms) must follow the standard of the Public Company Accounting Oversight Board

Audit Standard 2401, *Consideration of Fraud in a Financial Statement Audit.* In the case of nonpublicly traded companies, the external auditor must follow the standard of the American Institute of Public Accountants, AU-C 240. The standards for both the PCAOB and the AICPA are similar. The key elements of these standards are as follows:

- The auditor is responsible for obtaining reasonable assurance that the financial statements are free from material misstatement due to fraud.
- The standards provide a definition of *fraud.*
- The auditor must maintain professional skepticism throughout the audit.
- The critical part of these standards is that the engagement team must engage in brainstorming about how the entity's financial statements might be susceptible to material misstatement due to fraud and how management could perpetrate and conceal it.

- Risk assessment procedures and auditing procedures responsive to identified risks are required.

- The auditor must discuss the fraud risk with management and others within the entity.

- There is a presumption of a fraud risk associated with revenue recognition.

External auditors must conduct their work so that they can gain reasonable assurance that material misstatements will be detected. Accordingly, the definition for *materiality* is important:

> Materiality is the magnitude of an omission or misstatement of accounting information that, in light of surrounding circumstances, makes it probable that the judgment of a reasonable person relying on the information would have been changed or influenced by the omission or misstatement.[13]

External auditors have a risk model to assist in evaluation of audit risk:

$$AR = f(IR, CR, DR)[14]$$

Audit Risk: The risk that an auditor may give an unqualified opinion on financial statements that are materially misstated.[15]

Inherent Risk: The susceptibility of transactions being recorded in error or being influenced by management's fraudulent activities.[16]

Control Risk: The risk that a material misstatement could occur but would not be prevented or quickly detected by an organization's controls.[17]

Detection Risk: The risk that the auditor will fail to detect a material misstatement that exists in an account balance. The auditor controls detection risk after specifying an audit risk and assessing inherent and control risks.[18]

Internal Auditors

The most famous internal auditor is undoubtedly Cynthia Cooper, the former Vice President of Internal Audit for WorldCom. Cooper led an internal auditor team that approached its job with curiosity and professional skepticism, which in turn led them to discover highly suspect accounting entries. Their findings were presented to WorldCom's audit committee on June 22, 2002. Based on their findings, the CFO and controller were dismissed and WorldCom restated earnings by $3.8 billion. In reality, WorldCom's fate had already been sealed due to the downturn of the telecommunications industry. Cooper's efforts effectively unmasked the fraud and allowed the board to stop the hemorrhaging by putting the company into a Chapter 11 bankruptcy on July 21, 2002.

The FBI often learns of fraud from the victims, and WorldCom was no different. However, most victims do not know the magnitude of the fraud or exactly how it was perpetrated. In this regard, WorldCom was significantly different than Enron. In the Enron investigation, key insiders did not cooperate. The FBI was forced to use the time-tested and time-consuming "flip and roll" technique as the FBI worked its way up to the CEO and CFO of Enron. In the WorldCom case, Cynthia Cooper's presentation to the WorldCom's board was basically a road map for investigators and prosecutors. While much investigative work still remained for FBI agents, Cooper's audit work advanced the criminal investigation light years from where the investigation would have been without it. For an intriguing read into the details of Cooper's uncovering of the WorldCom fraud, I highly recommend her book, *Extraordinary Circumstances*.

Internal auditors play a role in fraud prevention and detection. Internal auditors detect fraud about 15 percent of the time, right after tipsters, which discover them about 40 percent of the time.[19] The internal auditing profession is growing in both importance and stature. The Institute of Internal Auditors (IIA) is the worldwide standard setter for the auditing profession. The IIA defines *internal auditing* as follows:

Internal auditing is an independent, objective assurance and consulting activity designed to add value and improve an organization's operations. It helps an organization accomplish its objectives by bringing a systematic, disciplined approach to evaluate and improve the effectiveness of risk management, control, and governance processes.[20]

SOX §302 and 404 place certain requirements on both the audit committee and senior management. These increased responsibilities, especially the internal controls over financial reporting, require a robust and independent audit function. For publicly traded companies, the chief audit executive invariably reports to the board's audit committee. In order to create independence, the chief audit executive should always report to those in charge of governance.

The relevant standards of the IIA as they relate to fraud risk management are as follows:

1210.A2—Internal auditors must have sufficient knowledge to evaluate the risk of fraud and the manner in which it is managed by the organization but are not expected to have the expertise of a person whose primary responsibility is detecting and investigating fraud.

1220.A1—Internal auditors must exercise due professional care by considering the:

- Extent of work needed to achieve the engagement's objectives
- Relative complexity, materiality, or significance of matters to which assurance procedures are applied
- Adequacy and effectiveness of governance, risk management, and control processes
- Probability of significant errors, fraud, or noncompliance
- Cost of assurance in relation to potential benefits

2060—The chief audit executive must report periodically to senior management and the board on the internal audit activity's purpose, authority, responsibility, and performance relative to its plan and on its conformance with the Code of Ethics and the Standards. Reporting must also include significant risk and control issues, including fraud risks, governance issues, and other matters that require the attention of senior management and/or the board.

2120.A2—The internal audit activity must evaluate the potential for the occurrence of fraud and how the organization manages fraud risk.

Ethics and Legal Privilege

Hopefully, you find yourself working in a fraud-resistant organization where the internal controls are high, the culture is strong, and significant fraud does not occur. Unfortunately, that is not always the case. What happens when fraud is discovered? We will discuss this issue later, in Part III, "The Fraud Life Cycle." However, when a company's financial statements are materially misleading due to fraud, an external auditor may have an affirmative duty to report the fraud outside the organization or an ethical duty of confidentiality not to disclose anything. How others should respond upon learning this information will depend on whether they are an attorney, a CPA, an internal auditor, or another professional and whether the company or client is public, private, or subject to a government audit. To add another level of complication, how the professional responds may also depend on the state in which the professional resides and whether the matter is in federal or state court. Let's first review the ethics rules and laws for some of the professions that can be impacted.

Ethics Codes

The American Bar Association's Rule 1.6—Confidentiality of Information states that a lawyer shall not reveal information relating to the representation of a client unless the client gives informed consent.

The American Institute of Certified Public Accountants Code of Professional Conduct Rule 1.700.001—Confidential Client Information Rule states that a member in public practice shall not disclose any confidential client information without the specific consent of the client. One of the exceptions provides that the rule does not apply to a validly issued and enforceable subpoena or summons, or to prohibit a member's compliance with applicable laws and government regulations.

The Institute of Internal Auditors' Code of Ethics Rule 3.2 provides that a member shall not use information for any personal gain or in any manner that would be contrary to the law or detrimental to the legitimate and ethical objectives of the organization.

The Association of Certified Fraud Examiners' Code of Ethics provides that an ACFE member shall not reveal any confidential information obtained during a professional engagement without proper authorization.

Law of Privilege

The attorney–client privilege allows the client to keep confidential those communications with an attorney. The privilege protects communications between an attorney and a client for the purpose of securing legal advice. The privilege does not apply to communications in which third parties are present. The communication also does not apply if the client and attorney are acting in the furtherance of a crime, known as the "crime-fraud exception." The attorney–client privilege is the most sacrosanct privilege in American jurisprudence. The privilege allows a client to provide full and frank disclosures to the attorney without fear of disclosure. Nevertheless, during the passage of SOX, there was a discussion about requiring attorneys to report potential fraudulent conduct to the SEC. The final rule requires attorneys to report up to the chief legal officer or the CEO, and if their response is not appropriate, to report to the audit committee or the board, but not outside the organization.[21]

When attorneys and CPAs uncover financial statement fraud, ethics rules, state laws, and federal securities laws will dictate what these professionals should do with their discovery. The rules for attorneys are clear: they never disclose their findings outside the client organization.

The law for CPAs is a little more complicated. The outcome may also depend on whether the financial statement fraud involves a public or a private company. The Private Securities Litigation Reform Act of 1995 places certain requirements on the external auditor of publicly traded companies. Pursuant to this federal law, the external auditor has an affirmative duty to design procedures to detect illegal acts that would have a material effect on the financial statements of the company. If this type of illegal act is found, the auditor then has a duty to report the findings to the board. If the board does not take remedial action, the auditor must put the board on notice of its obligation to notify the SEC of the auditor's findings. If the company still fails to notify the SEC within one business day, the auditor must notify the SEC. Since federal law preempts state law, the CPA (more precisely, the external auditor known as a registered public accounting firm) will have to make this disclosure regarding its client despite ethical rules or a state CPA–client privilege to the contrary.

For financial statement fraud that does not involve a publicly traded company, the plight of the CPA is not as clear-cut since the law of privilege varies by state. Of course, the ethics rules require nondisclosure by the CPA. However, this can put the CPA in a dilemma when knowledge of a fraud is discovered, and third parties might be severely harmed. The majority of states do not recognize the CPA–client privilege. I will familiarize you with Georgia law since that is the state where both my law and CPA licenses are held. A fascinating Georgia court case will help us sort out some of the nuances relating to the CPA–client privilege for those states that recognize the privilege.

Georgia is one of the minority of states that statutorily recognizes the CPA–client privilege.[22] The purpose of the privilege is to encourage a client to be forthright and candid with information to a CPA without fear of the CPA disclosing confidential information to third parties.

Case Example

Let's examine *Roberts v. Chaple*, 187 Ga. App 123 (1988), a case touching on various aspects of Georgia's CPA–client privilege. In the *Roberts* case, a CPA had a long-time client and had prepared tax returns for him personally and for the companies in which the client was an officer.

Before going further, we need to understand how the law of privilege is applied in federal courts. Federal courts have their own body of law relating to privilege.[23] Federal courts do not recognize the CPA–client privilege, with one exception. If the matter at issue pertains to state law as opposed to federal law (e.g., a negligence issue involving an automobile accident where state law will control the issue), then the federal court will also look to state law on the issue of privilege. Otherwise, the federal court will not recognize the CPA–client privilege. For example, when a court is hearing a matter about U.S. federal tax law, the court will not recognize the CPA–client privilege.

In the *Roberts* case, an Internal Revenue Service (IRS) agent, without a subpoena, requested information from the CPA about the client and his companies. The CPA provided the information to the IRS agent. Armed with damaging client information provided by the CPA, the IRS proceeded on an enforcement action against the client in federal court. The client was obviously very upset that his CPA had disclosed confidential information to the client's detriment. The client then sued his CPA in state court and attempted to block the use of the information in federal court. How did the state and federal courts rule? In the Georgia court, the action against the CPA was allowed to proceed because the CPA clearly had violated his legal duty of confidentiality to his client under Georgia's CPA–client privilege law. In federal court, however, the client lost, and the harmful information was allowed to be used against the client. The rationale was that the matter before the federal court involved a federal tax issue, and therefore, the court would not recognize Georgia's CPA–client privilege.

This case has several learning points, as it demonstrates the application of federal and state law regarding privilege. A key fact in this case was that the IRS agent did not have a validly issued subpoena. Had the CPA been served with a subpoena, the CPA would have been legally obligated to comply and would have been saved from liability.

For CPAs governed by the AICPA rules, the guidance on this issue is AU-C Section 250—Consideration of Laws and Regulations in an Audit of Financial Statements. For those CPAs governed by the PCAOB, the guidance is AS 2405—Illegal Act by Clients. Both of these provisions recognize that the discovery of fraud by the CPA presents thorny legal issues and recommend that the CPA seek the advice of legal counsel. The application of these and other rules pertaining to successor auditors can also be of assistance. A CPA–auditor who no longer wants to be affiliated with the client can resign. The successor auditor can and should make inquiries of the predecessor auditor with the consent of the client. If a client will not consent to a successor auditor communicating with a predecessor auditor, this should raise a big red flag that criminal or unethical conduct is at play.

Tax Practitioner–Taxpayer Privilege

Pursuant to 26 U.S.C. §7525, federal law recognizes privileged communications between a federally authorized tax practitioner and a taxpayer, much like the attorney–client privilege. However, this privilege does not apply to criminal matters or matters involving tax shelters.

Financial Statement Analysis

Financial statements are a snapshot of an organization's financial health at a particular point in time. When they are analyzed singularly, a forensic accountant is unlikely to uncover fraud. To make the information useful, several things need to occur. The numbers need to be converted to percentages so that the information can be better understood. Several years of statements need to be obtained to look for trends over a period of time. Further, a thorough understanding of the company, its business, and the industry in which it operates is needed. With this information, analytical procedures can be used to isolate anomalies. The investigation of the causes of these anomalies is what may actually lead to the detection of fraud.

Before we proceed with further discussion of financial statement analysis, let me address a caveat. The academic literature has extensive discussions of how financial analysis can be deployed to detect fraud. Academics have analyzed the major accounting frauds that have occurred during the last two decades and have identified red flags of fraud for these companies. Why didn't they tell us this before the fraud was discovered? An after-the-fact analysis appears brilliant as it reverse-engineers the fraud, resulting in an answer that is already known.

Bethany McLean is a talented journalist, author, and former Goldman Sachs financial analyst. In her March 2001 article in *Fortune* magazine, "Is Enron Overpriced?," she foreshadowed the collapse of Enron. McLean observed that Enron's debt was on the rise and its cash flow was on the decline. This high-level information helped her question the financial health of Enron, but it came nowhere near predicting that the company was riddled with fraud. In fact, her other findings were more telling. She could not really understand how Enron even made money. Financial disclosures in the financial statements were inadequate, and when CEO Jeff Skilling and CFO Andy Fastow were pressed on the issue, they spoke in esoteric gobbledygook, making it impossible for analysts to understand the true financial condition of the company. This is, of course, exactly what they wanted. Further, much of Enron's debt was hidden in off-balance sheet transactions, and the disclosures in the financial statement footnotes were inadequate.

The FBI only initiates a fraud investigation after it has learned that there is a basis for believing that a federal crime has occurred. During my time with the FBI, I did not become aware of any fraud case that was initiated as the result of financial statement analysis done by someone looking for fraud. Cases were much more likely to be opened once the company began imploding or a whistleblower came forward. This material on financial statement analysis is presented for a variety of reasons. Financial statement fraud can cause significant harm, and any tool that can aid in early detection of it should be considered. Internal and external auditors may use these techniques to uncover fraud that is actually never made public. For example, a company that restates its financial statements may be doing so because an external auditor used financial statement analysis that detected material misstatements.

Financial statements present a certain picture of the company. A more pragmatic use of financial analysis is to critically consider the picture painted by the financials in light on nonfinancial performance measures. Why is a company's bottom line improving when the industry in which it is operating has been showing declining profit margins? Why is the company's warehouse lease expense decreasing when its inventory on hand is increasing year after year? During the trial of former HealthSouth CEO Richard Scrushy, federal prosecutors argued that Scrushy must have known something was wrong with the company's financial statements. The prosecution argued that Scrushy must have known that twice during the seven-year fraud revenues and assets had increased even though the number of HealthSouth facilities had decreased.[24]

Despite the limitations of financial statement analysis, including vertical analysis, horizontal analysis, and ratio analysis discussed below, it can at least be attempted to discover an anomaly. Further, these techniques may be of benefit to forensic accountants who are engaged to address matters involving business interruption, breach of contract, antitrust, and damage calculations.[25]

Vertical analysis

Vertical analysis is a technique for analyzing the components of an income statement or balance sheet. This is done by converting the numbers to a percentage of a specified base value. This technique is also known as "common sizing." On the income statement, net sales is the base value and is expressed as 100 percent. On the balance sheet, total assets and total liabilities are the base values and are each expressed as 100 percent. All of the components of the financial statements are then expressed as a percentage of the base value. This technique enables an analyst to compare items within the financial statements more easily as well as to compare them with peer companies of different sizes.

Horizontal analysis

Horizontal analysis is similar to vertical analysis. The financial statements are first analyzed, using the technique of common sizing, by converting them to percentages. These percentages are then compared over a span of years. This allows an analyst to quickly discover sizeable changes in account balances from year to year. If a significant change is noted, the issue should be reviewed to understand the reason for the change.

Ratio analysis

Ratio analysis is a quantitative way of measuring the relationship between two amounts on financial statements. These ratios are often used by a financial analyst to measure the performance or financial health of a company. As fraud investigators, we can use these same ratios to identify red flags of fraud. These ratios can be compared from year-to-year to identify anomalies. Investigating the cause of an anomaly may lead to the discovery of fraud. Ratios that can be used for this purpose are shown below:

Current Ratio: $$\dfrac{\text{Current Assets}}{\text{Current Liabilities}}$$

Quick Ratio: $$\dfrac{\text{Cash + Securities + Receivables}}{\text{Current Liabilities}}$$

Debt to Equity: $$\dfrac{\text{Total Liabilities}}{\text{Total Equity}}$$

Profit Margin: $$\dfrac{\text{Net Income}}{\text{Net Sales}}$$

Receivable Turnover: $$\dfrac{\text{Net Sale on Account}}{\text{Average Net Receivables}}$$

Collection Ratio: $$\dfrac{365}{\text{Receivable Turnover}}$$

Inventory Turnover: $$\dfrac{\text{Cost of Goods Sold}}{\text{Average Inventory}}$$

Average Number of Days Inventory is in Stock: $$\dfrac{365}{\text{Inventory Turnover}}$$

Asset Turnover: $$\dfrac{\text{Net Sales}}{\text{Average Assets}}$$

CHAPTER 6

Small Organizations: Small Businesses, Local Governments, and Not-for-Profits

"While the City was suffering, the defendant was living her dreams."

—ASSISTANT U.S. ATTORNEY JOSEPH PEDERSEN THE FEDERAL SENTENCING OF RITA CRUNDWELL FOR HER $53.7 THEFT FROM THE SMALL TOWN OF DIXON, ILLINOIS.

Small organizations can include a small business, a local government, or a not-for-profit organization. These organizations often share two common traits: (1) employees generally work in a trust-based environment, and (2) internal controls are often weak. Unfortunately, these organizations also share two other common features: (1) they are more likely to be victimized by fraud, and (2) the average dollar amount of the fraud will likely be higher. The Association of Certified Fraud Examiners' 2018 *Report to the Nations* shows that organizations with less than 100 employees are victims in 28 percent of frauds and experience an average dollar loss of $200,000. An interesting contrast is that organizations with over 10,000 employees suffer 24 percent of frauds, with an average dollar loss of $132,000. Of course, the impact of these frauds is disproportionately more devastating to the small organization and often results in severe hardship to the victims.

For our purposes, small organizations are those with 100 or fewer employ-ees. As organizations get larger, they naturally have more resources to prevent and detect fraud. This certainly does not mean small organizations have to be defenseless because they do not. The problem invariably is that small organizations do not appreciate their fraud risk until it is too late. Those in charge of governance place too much reliance on trust and do not establish effective internal controls. In this chapter, we will discuss the types of frauds that small organizations may experience and the appropriate internal controls that can reduce their susceptibility to fraud. Further, small organizations can also act as predators and themselves commit fraud.

Case Example

Dixon, Illinois is a small municipality with under 16,000 residents and was the childhood home of Ronald Reagan. This is not exactly where you would expect to find the largest municipal fraud in history. According to the federal indictment, controller and treasurer Rita Crundwell defrauded the city of Dixon out of $53.7 million from 1990 until her arrest by FBI agents in 2012.[1]

On December 18, 1990, Crundwell opened a bank account in the name of the city of Dixon styled "RSCDA," and she was the only signatory on the account. The RSCDA (Reserve Sewer Capital Development Account), despite its official-sounding name, was a bogus account used to misapply funds for Crundwell's personal benefit. She caused taxpayer funds to be accumulated in the city's Capital Development Fund account. She then wrote checks off this account made payable to "Treasurer" and deposited them into the RSCDA account. Further, she created fictitious invoices purporting to be from the state of Illinois to mislead the city's auditor into thinking that the funds were being used for a legitimate purpose. For more than two decades, she proceeded to move funds from Dixon's Capital Development Fund account and other accounts into the RSCDA account that she controlled.

The fraud was uncovered when Crundwell was on vacation and the city clerk intercepted the RSCDA bank statements. The clerk realized the bank account statements were unusual and brought them to the mayor's attention, who alerted the FBI. Crundwell led a lavish lifestyle that included showing horses, managing a large Quarter Horse operation, and purchasing expensive automobiles.

Crundwell's lavish lifestyle was in plain view of city officials and the external auditor. The amount of loss was clearly material to the financial statements. Because Crundwell controlled Dixon's finances, bank accounts, and prepared the financial statements, she was able to both perpetrate and conceal the fraud. Due to the negligence of the city of Dixon's auditors and its bank, the city recovered $40 million of its losses from those two defendants as part of litigation. The FBI's forfeiture efforts brought in another $10.3 million.[2] This case represents one of the rare instances in which the victim recovered much of the losses that it had sustained.

This case also has several teaching points. Trust is not an internal control. Simple segregation of duties and oversight would likely have prevented this fraud. A lavish lifestyle—"living beyond one's means"— at least should have been a red flag. Job rotations and mandatory vacations are appropriate internal controls whenever feasible.

Segregation of Duties

Segregation of duties is the touchstone for preventing the opportunity to commit fraud in an organization. To evaluate a segregation of duties issue, you should understand which individual(s) are performing the following **ABCR** duties:

- **A**uthorization of Transactions
- **B**ookkeeping
- **C**ustody of Assets
- **R**econciliation of Accounts

If two or more of the above duties are performed by the same person, the organization has a segregation of duties issue. Further, this type of issue is very common in small businesses due to the limited number of personnel handling the organization's finances, and because, by necessity, the organization needs "to do more with less." When this occurs, the organization needs to establish a compensating control. One compensating control is to have someone obtain the bank statements directly from the bank or to have access to them online. This should be the organization's owner, the city mayor, or the executive director, as the case may be. The review of bank statements must be done each month, and others in the organization should be made aware that this review occurs routinely. This single step will go a long way to preventing fraud. If two or more of the **ABCR** duties are performed by a single person, then another person needs to review the work. When segregation of duties is not practical, compensating controls may include the following:

- Independent review of bank statements
- Restricted access to the bank account
- Second review of transactions
- Surprise checks and audits
- Internal and/or external audit
- Whistleblower program
- Follow-up of suspicious transactions and other red flags

Small organizations can experience any of the frauds described in Chapter 3, Asset Misappropriation. However, small organizations are particularly at risk for embezzlement-related schemes due to a lack of segregation of duties. Red flags in small organization include the following:

- Missing bank account statements
- Unexplained lifestyle or wealth
- Customer, employee, and vendor complaints
- Records are in disarray
- Undocumented transactions
- Cash flow issues
- Unexplained decrease in revenue
- Inventory shortage

When fraud does occur, small organizations often encounter another problem. The fraudster may have a connection to the organization other than through employment. The fraudster may be a relative of the owner, the founder of the not-for-profit, or an elected official. In these circumstances, those in charge of governance may have a difficult time prosecuting the fraudster. Not only is this bad policy, but also it sets a bad tone for the organization. On the other hand, some very difficult decisions have to be made. For example, a small business is very unlikely to prosecute the owner's relative.

Small Business Fraud

As an FBI agent, I normally worked on large cases because this is the type of work the FBI is charged with investigating. Now that I am in private practice, I work on many cases that the FBI would traditionally not pursue or prosecute due to the low dollar threshold. Unfortunately, when I say low dollar threshold, a dollar amount less than a million dollars is low by FBI standards, whereas for the rest of America, that is a considerable amount of money.

These frauds often involve one of the partners who founded the small business, and these frauds are quite prevalent—so much so that I have been quite shocked at the number of calls I receive in which one member of a limited liability company (LLC) has been defrauded by another member through an embezzlement scheme. When I receive these calls now, I can usually finish the sentences of the victim and provide a narrative of what must have happened. The business is successful, profit margins are excellent, and the financial manager's conduct is suspect. The victim realizes that bank balances are low and the profit and loss statements do not reflect the seemingly robust business. I instinctively ask for the bank account statements and credit card statements, because these items may readily identify the problem.

I am always rather saddened by these frauds. As part of my investigation, I will typically interview the financial manager who abused his trust by embezzling funds and will attempt to obtain a confession. Regardless of the outcome, the members' successful business has now suffered a giant, perhaps irrecoverable blow. As noted earlier, trust is not an internal control. Small businesses must implement compensating controls when segregation of duties is not possible or practical, given the circumstances.

Small business owners are not just victims of fraud; they can also be predatory fraudsters. I have seen small business owners engage in at least two type of frauds. One pertains to financing. A small business owner is faced with many challenges, including cash flow or liquidity issues. The small business owner will often need to obtain financing even if the business is not credit worthy. Schemes to enhance its financial strength may involve misleading its CPA through window-dressing its financials. A bank may be willing to make a loan on unaudited financial statements, known as a "compilation." For a compilation of financial statements, the CPA relies on the information provided by the client and merely compiles the information into financial statements. Here, it is easy for the client to enhance the income statement by falsifying revenue and providing the bogus numbers to the CPA for preparation of the compilation. The small business owner can also provide false tax returns to a bank. Either of these scenarios can potentially result in federal bank fraud charges.

A more aggressive small business fraud involves what is known as a "bust-out scheme."

The scheme can be committed in different ways. As an example, the fraudster-business owner establishes what appears to be a viable business. The owner then obtains a line of credit. The funds may actually be used to further the business for a period of time. Sometimes large inventories are accumulated. As the business appears to prosper, the line of credit is increased. However, instead of repaying the loan, the revenues of the company are misapplied for the owner's benefit. The inventories may be sold outside the business, with the proceeds going to the fraudster. Ultimately, the fraudster defaults on the line of credit and may even declare bankruptcy.

Local Government Fraud

Local governments are like any other small business. They are trust-based organizations that may have weak internal controls. Public corruption is covered in detail in Chapter 4, including a discussion of bribery and kickbacks involving public officials. Like all small businesses, the ability to perpetrate and conceal an embezzlement scheme may be relatively easy for government officials.

I investigated a Georgia County Commissioner who misused her P-Card. During the investigation, I reviewed the work product of the internal auditor who routinely audited all P-Card holders' expenditures. When the auditor asked for the Commissioner's P-Card statement and receipts, the Commissioner feigned poor record keeping. Think big red flag! The internal auditor was also faced with the reality that the Commissioner was an elected official and was really only accountable to the voters. Of course, the voters cannot audit the Commissioner's use of her P-Card for personal expenses, so this lack of oversight enabled the Commissioner to both perpetrate and conceal the fraud. Subsequent to this case, the Georgia General Assembly created the Office of Independent Internal Audit for Georgia County and gave the auditor subpoena power.

You might not think a governmental entity would engage in financial statement fraud due to a general lack of incentives for financial managers and those charged with governance. However, this type of fraud has increased in recent years. One reason for this increase is that governmental entities have intentionally understated pension liabilities in order to obtain more favorable financing terms. The SEC maintains a list of enforcement actions against the participants in the $3.8 trillion municipal securities market on its website.[3]

Not-for-profit Fraud

The culture of not-for-profits is inherently trust-based where volunteers and employees are focused on a charitable mission. Like any small organization, a not-for-profit may have poor internal controls. Donations are provided to the not-for-profit on a nonreciprocal basis, meaning the proper use of these donations is left to the good will of the not-for-profit, where there may be less accountability. When frauds do occur, those in charge of governance may be hesitant to prosecute for fear that negative publicity will harm fund-raising activities.

Those in charge of running a not-for-profit organization are like any other business executive: they want to be successful in their mission. A common matrix to measure the performance of a not-for-profit is the ratio of its fund-raising activities to total expenses. For example, if 20 percent of the revenues are used for fund-raising activities and 80 percent are used for program activities, the not-for-profit may be viewed favorably. The incentive to drive down the fund-raising activities expenses on the Statement of Activities (i.e., an income statement for a not-for-profit) can lead to financial statement fraud by the not-for-profit.

To assist donors or other potential users of a not-for-profit's financial statements, the accounting rules require that the not-for-profit's expenses be distinguished between two categories: (1) fund-raising activities and (2) program activities. Technical guidance on accounting for costs of not-for-profit organizations is provided by the Financial Accounting Standards Board and the American Institute of Certified Public Accountants.[4]

At least five different methods can be used by not-for-profit organizations to artificially enhance a program expense ratio:[5]

- Netting the results of special fund-raising events and activities
- Exaggerating the values of noncash gifts received and made
- Improperly reporting contributions raised on behalf of other not-for-profits
- Misapplying the accounting rules applicable to "joint" activities that purport to serve both programmatic and fund-raising objectives
- Outright misclassification of fund-raising or management expenses as program expenses

Not-for-profits are required to file IRS Form 990, and it is a public document. Form 990 discloses key financial data for not-for-profits. However, not-for-profits are generally not required to disclose their financial statements. Also, all not-for-profits' Form 990 can be readily found on GuideStar's webpage: www.guidestar.org. Because of the ease of obtaining information from IRS Form 990, that data is often used to calculate the fund-raising activity ratio. Unfortunately, the tax preparer for the organization may not be well versed in not-for-profit accounting rules and can easily miscategorize fund-raising activities and program activities, either unintentionally or intentionally. The requirements for reporting financial information for publicly traded companies is the reverse of those requirements for not-for-profits. For publicly traded companies, audited financial statements can be found on the SEC's EDGAR database; however, federal tax returns are not required to be reported.

CHAPTER 7
Nonoccupational Fraud

"There is nothing new under the sun.
It has all been done before."

—SHERLOCK HOLMES IN
A STUDY IN SCARLET, BY SIR ARTHUR CONAN DOYLE

This chapter addresses the numerous and diverse nonoccupational frauds. These frauds are in stark contrast to the occupational frauds involving asset misappropriation, corruption, and financial statement fraud. Occupational frauds generally involve insiders who are in a trust-based relationship with their victims, which I call "privity of trust." Before these fraudsters become trust violators, the precepts of the Fraud Triangle must be present: opportunity, pressure, and rationalization. Accordingly, when privity of trust is present, those in charge of governance can develop internal controls to address each of the three vertices of the Fraud Triangle to minimize fraud in their organization.

Fraudsters committing nonoccupational fraud, however, are generally not acting in an occupational capacity. Rather, these fraudsters are mostly outsiders preying on individuals and organizations. Another significant distinction is that these fraudsters are generally not in privity of trust with their victims. Since these fraudsters are not in privity of trust, *pressure* and *rationalization* (two vertices of the Fraud Triangle) often play no role in their motivation. I call these fraudsters "the predators." The only real way to prevent this type of fraud is to simply deny these fraudsters the *opportunity* to commit the fraud.

The lack of privity of trust is not a uniform rule for nonoccupational frauds. Some predators may work with an insider as a coconspirator. An example would be a corrupt vendor who pays a bribe to a government purchasing manager. On occasion, a company insider may become so angry with his or her employer (the bonds of trust have become broken) that the employee may sabotage the company. For example, an insider might deploy ransomware in the company's computer network. This chapter will focus on nonoccupational predatory frauds. These frauds can be broken down into the following categories:

- Scams and Con Artists
- Securities Fraud
- Government Fraud
- Insurance Fraud
- Financial Institution Fraud
- Bankruptcy, Matrimonial, and Business Divorce Fraud
- Theft of Intellectual Property and Information

Scams and Con Artists

Many of the scams discussed in this section have been around for decades or longer. These scams are constantly repackaged to conform to technologies or customs of the time. However, just because these frauds are commonplace does not mean that the victims will not fall prey to fraudsters of these types of fraud.

For a colorful history of "confidence men" scams, see David W. Maurer, *The Big Con: The Story of the Confidence Man*. Maurer was a distinguished student of criminal argot, and in addition to his masterwork on confidence men, which contains a long chapter on the con man's lingo, he wrote enduring books and essays on the language of dice gamblers, prostitutes, drug addicts, moonshiners, pickpockets, faro bankers, and three-card Monte players. The 1973 film *The Sting*, directed by George Roy Hill for Universal Pictures, is based on *The Big Con*.

Nigerian 419 Letter

You may have received an e-mail from an alleged Nigerian government official who has come into a large sum of money. The "official" wants to move the money into your bank account, for which you will be rewarded with a large sum of money for your assistance. As the scam progresses, the "official" may ask that an advance fee be paid to assist with taxes and the transfer of funds. The intended victim may also be asked for various identifiers, like name, social security number, or bank account number. Although the scams vary, the purpose may be to obtain an advance fee, which will never be returned, or to obtain personal identifiers as a part of an identity theft scam. These frauds are known as "Nigerian 419 scams," which is named after the part of the Nigerian code that criminalizes them. The Nigerian Criminal Code Act, Part 6, Chapter 38, Section 419 states the following:

> Any person who by any false pretense, and with intent to defraud, obtains from any other person anything capable of being stolen, or induces any other person to deliver to any person anything capable of being stolen, is guilty of a felony.

When I was an FBI bank fraud supervisor in Houston, Texas, I saw several of these letters every week because the victims called the FBI asking what to do. All squads across the bureau kept these letters in a "Nigerian Letter Zero File." Invariably, that file would be the largest file in the squad. Before the popularity of e-mail, these letters would arrive in intended victims' mailboxes. Now the fraudsters save postage and e-mail the "Nigerian Letter" in bulk to victims around the world.

Ironically, the most famous victim of the Nigerian 419 scam is probably Mark Whitacre of Archer-Daniels-Midland Co. (ADM) "price-fixing" fame; he served as an FBI informant and subsequently served nine years in prison for committing fraud while he was at ADM. The story is recounted in the movie *The Informant,* in which Whitacre is played by actor Matt Damon. In an unrelated fraud, Whitacre and top executives at ADM suffered $660,000 in losses when they fell prey to a Nigerian scam, but they charged the losses to ADM.[1]

Advance Fee Schemes

An advance fee scheme typically involves promising a victim a loan or other item of value, but the fraudster requires that an advance fee be paid. Upon payment of the advance fee, the victim may be required to pay other fees. Ultimately, either the victim gets tired of paying fees or the fraudster disappears, and the victim is left without a loan or whatever was promised.

Telemarketing Frauds

Telemarketing fraud is an insidious ploy that plays on an individual's emotions and vulnerabilities, and the elderly are often the victim. These scams can be as creative as the telemarketer's devious mind will allow. Common schemes are magazine sweepstakes and prize-winning scams that require the victim to pay something in advance, akin to the advance fee scheme. The pitch may be that the victim has won a car, but the payment of taxes and shipping fees must be paid in advance.

Case Example

Many perpetrators of telemarketing scams operate in foreign countries where it is more difficult to investigate and extradite the fraudsters. When I was an FBI bank fraud supervisor, I received a call from a bank security officer advising that an elderly customer of the bank was obtaining large money orders with proceeds from her account and mailing them to someone in Canada. The customer had just left the bank with a money order in the amount of $80,000. The bank had reason to believe that the payee of the money order was a telemarketing fraudster but could not dissuade the customer from purchasing the money order. I telephoned the customer and tried to convince her not to mail the check. This phone call was extraordinarily sad, as the customer explained to me how nice the people whom she had talked to on the phone had been to her and how much money she had already mailed to Canada. Knowing it was in her best interest, I continued to be really firm with her, even suggesting that she could be a coconspirator for aiding in the illegal conduct.

Unfortunately, nothing was working. I soon discovered that she lived near the FBI office, and I put the call on hold. I instructed a fellow agent to get to her house as quickly as possible and do whatever he could to stop her from mailing another check to Canada. While I was on the phone, I heard the agent arrive at her front door. During the conversation, the customer showed the agent the check. Per my instruction, the agent obtained the check and tore it to pieces. That was probably not a textbook solution for the problem, but I did not see any viable alternatives. I was envisioning someone's grandmother becoming destitute at the hands of an unscrupulous telemarketer.

Disaster Relief Scams

As technology changes, the Internet can be a tool to commit frauds that once were done over the telephone. Playing on the victim's emotions, fraudsters lie in wait for national or international disasters. These fraudsters know that natural disasters pull at the heartstrings of those watching the devastating results in the safety of their homes. Through social media, websites, e-mails, and texts promotions, the fraudsters may cause people to quickly donate monies before they properly vet the bogus charity.

Romance Scams

Online dating sites have caused another type of fraud to explode—romance scams. Due to technology, a scammer can be anywhere in the world and set lures for the unwary in search of a romantic connection. The victims are typically older divorced and widowed women who place trust in someone they met on the Internet. After several exchanges of e-mails and phone calls, it does not take long for the fraudster to begin making requests for money. According to the FBI, in 2016, it received almost 15,000 complaints about losses exceeding $230 million in connection with romance scams.[2] I suspect these numbers are highly underreported, as victims are embarrassed to complain when they learn they have been defrauded in a romance scam.

Securities Fraud

Securities fraud can include a variety of frauds involving the purchase or sale of a security. Accordingly, a transaction that involves a "security" can trigger a host of state and federal security regulations. So, what is a security? The Securities Act of 1933 §2(a)(1) and the *Securities Exchange Act of 1934* §3(a)(10) have almost identical definitions of a "security." These definitions include recognizable financial instruments, including notes, stocks, bonds, transferable shares, debentures, and a security futures. The federal securities acts also use generic concepts to capture the essence of a security and include the terms "evidence of indebtedness," "investment contracts," and "certificate of interests in profit-sharing agreements."

The term "investment contract" has been defined by the United States Supreme Court in the landmark case, *SEC v. W. J. Howey Co.*, 328 U.S. 293 (1946), in which it established a four-pronged test. An investment contract is "a contract, transaction or scheme where [1] a person invests money, [2] in a common enterprise and [3] is led to expect profits, [4] solely from the efforts of others."

Once a matter is deemed a security, it becomes subject to various state and federal security rules, including registration requirements and regulations. A security is also subject to the antifraud provision of §10(b) of the Securities

Exchange Act of 1934 and its implementing regulation, known as Rule 10b-5. Rule 10b-5 was described in detail in Chapter 2, "Fraud Defined." Rule 10b-5 contains civil and administrative provisions that are enforced by the SEC and criminal sanctions that are enforced by the DOJ. Rule 10b-5 has been interpreted to permit private causes of actions that have proliferated.

When DOJ prosecutors charge a defendant with a violation of Rule 10b-5 for securities-related offenses, they are likely to include mail and wire fraud violations in their indictments. While the elements of all of these criminal statutes vary, they share a common element that the defendant engaged in a scheme or artifice to defraud. For example, Bernie Madoff was charged with violations of Rule 10b-5 and mail and wire fraud for his execution of the world's largest fraud.[3]

Ponzi Schemes

A Ponzi scheme is a fraud in which the fraudster promotes a bogus investment opportunity to lure investors. The fraudster pays purported profits to earlier investors with proceeds from newer investors. Because the fraudster is repaying investors with their principal plus a fictitious profit, the scheme is only viable if it can attract new investors. The fraudster will likely have made the sustainability of the scheme more challenging to herself by promising high rates of return. The scheme quickly gets out of hand, and the fraudster desperately seeks new investors to keep it alive and going. At this point, the fraudster is hopelessly trapped because the scheme must eventually collapse as the supply of new investors dwindles.

In my experience, most Ponzi scheme fraudsters initially start a business or an investment opportunity with the intent of creating a viable opportunity for investors. Then two things occur: the underlying business or investment struggles due to unforeseen circumstances, and the fraudsters learn that their charisma allows them to keep raising investor funds. Other factors compound the problem. These Ponzi scheme fraudsters often begin enhancing their lifestyle due to a flood of funds with no internal controls. Combine these factors with an exaggerated sense of confidence that these fraudsters possess, and you have the classic Ponzi scheme.

Studying Charles Ponzi's scheme is instructive because it lays bare the *modus operandi* of these type of investment frauds. Attorney and Charles Ponzi historian Mark Knutson has captured the fascinating details of Charles Ponzi in his research.[4] Charles Ponzi had collected $9.5 million from 10,000 investors by selling promissory notes paying 50 percent in 45 days.[5] Ponzi advised that guaranteed high rates of return were possible because of an ingenious weakness he purportedly found in the international postal system.

Ponzi became aware of the internationally accepted postal reply coupon. This allowed the sender of a letter to include a reply coupon. The recipient could exchange the coupon for postage in the recipient's country, thereby enabling the recipient to reply without incurring postage. By international convention, the cost of the reply coupon was fixed. However, shortly after World War I, some currencies became devalued relative to others. Ponzi claims to have created an arbitrage opportunity due to the fixed costs of the reply coupon compared to differing valuations of currencies. Ponzi claimed, "The same amount of American money will buy more value in coupons in Bulgaria than in the United States."[6] Ponzi's purported investment would work as follows: (1) send money to Italy, (2) convert the money to Italian lire, (3) purchase international postal reply coupons, (4) ship the coupons to the United States, (5) use the coupons to purchase stamps, (6) sell the stamps for cash. By sending $1 to Italy, Ponzi could theoretically generate $3.3 worth of stamps in Boston.[7]

To investors, the investment opportunity seemed as if Ponzi had found a loophole to exploit. The charismatic Ponzi widely published and promoted his investment opportunity. Ponzi's operation expanded dramatically, and at one point he was taking in $1 million a week.[8] Eventually, federal, state, and county officials took notice and began investigating. The telltale signs of fraud in Charles Ponzi's scheme can be found in most Ponzi schemes and include the following:

- The investment is either not disclosed or confusing.

- The fraudster is charismatic.

- High rates of return are promised.

- Consistent rates of return create a false sense of security.

- Investors are told there is little or no risk.

- Unregistered investments are typically utilized.

A quick way to spot a Ponzi scheme is to learn if the promoter is stating that the investment has no risk. In the United States, only a treasury bond or a certificate of deposit has no risk. Other than these U.S.-government-backed investments, anyone promoting an investment with no risk is most likely misstating the investment and may be promoting a Ponzi scheme.

A pyramid scheme has similarities to a Ponzi scheme, but it can also be a legal business structure. A pyramid scheme is structured so that the initial promoter recruits other investors who are required to recruit additional investors. If a real profit is being recognized from the sale of an underlying product, these structures can be entirely legal, and in this context, are known as multilevel marketing agreements. In contrast, when the sustainability of the pyramid is only the result of finding additional investors and is not from sales of a product, the structure is likely to be illegal. By definition, a pyramid scheme requires recruiting new participants as the scheme grows. A Ponzi scheme could theoretically involve a single investor who keeps contributing an increasing amount of money. Furthermore, and most importantly, in a Ponzi scheme, there is no legitimate underlying business or investment.

Insider Trading

Insider trading is a fraud perpetrated by someone inside a publicly traded company who has knowledge of material, nonpublic information obtained through the insider's corporate position and uses that information to buy or sell the company's stock. The exact parameters of what constitute insider trading continues to evolve as the interpretation of the controlling regulation, SEC Rule 10b-5, is a matter of federal common law. The law prohibiting an insider from profiting from insider information is clear. The law governing outsiders has been less clear.

Trading securities by certain outsiders is also clearly prohibited. For example, Company A is conducting business with Company B in a transaction that will have an effect on Company B's stock. Company A's officials, who are actually outsiders, are likewise prohibited from trading on this market-moving information. This prohibition also applies to a range of outsiders, like accountants, lawyers, and investment bankers, who because of their relationships are required to keep the information they receive in confidence.[9] The rule has also been held to apply to a financial printer who has access to corporate documents relating to takeover bids.[10]

The liability of a "tippee," or one who receives insider information from the tipper, has continued to evolve in recent years. The standard for tippee liability is controlled by the United States Supreme Court's decision in *Dirks v. SEC*.[11] Dirks was a securities analyst who closely followed the insurance industry. Dirks learned of a massive fraud and impending failure of an insurance company from a former company insider and tipper named Secrist. Dirks, the tippee, passed this information on to his clients, who dumped their holdings before the information became public. The question before the Supreme Court is whether Dirks has liability for passing on insider information. The Court found an element of a tippee's liability is that the tipper must have breached a fiduciary duty. Furthermore, this breach will only be found if the insider obtained a personal benefit. Here, the court found that tipper Secrist did not personally gain from this information. The standard for tippee liability is that the tipper must receive a personal benefit for breaching a fiduciary duty and the tippee must have knowledge of the tipper's breach. Dirks was held to have no liability because the tipper did not personally benefit.

One issue that remained after the *Dirks* case was what constitutes a personal benefit. What if an insider provides information to a family member but does not receive any pecuniary benefit? The Supreme Court resolved this issue in *Salman v. United States* (2016),[12] holding that the benefit a tipper-family member receives in connection with a breach of fiduciary duty need not be pecuniary and a jury can infer that the tipper personally benefited from making a gift of confidential information.

Front Running

Another fraud scheme that violates SEC Rule 10b-5 is known as "front running." This is a form of insider trading that usually is done by someone in a brokerage firm who has access to privileged information about an impending trade of a client. If the insider believes the client's purchase or sale of a security will move the market, a purchase or sale of the security can be made ahead of the client for a profit. This front runner will likely make trades using a spouse, a friend, or a nominee's account in hopes of avoiding detection.

Pump and Dump

A pump and dump scheme involves a fraudster purchasing stock in a company and then spreading false, but positive, information to investors, thereby pumping up the value of the stock. Once the fraudster's stock has significantly risen, the fraudster sells or dumps the stock and walks away with a profit. This fraud is more commonly done with penny stocks or microcap stocks where the stock is thinly traded. In a more aggressive variation of this scheme, the fraud promoters will either form a new company or purchase an existing company for the purpose of executing a pump and dump scheme. A "short and distort" scheme works in the opposite manner as a pump and dump scheme. Here, a fraudster first short-sells a stock. The fraudster then spreads false, but negative, information about a company, causing the stock's price to drop. Next, the fraudster covers the short position, thereby yielding a profit equaling the amount the stock has dropped in value.

Backdating Stock Options

Stock options backdating refers to a practice of changing the date on which a stock option was granted to a date on which the stock was trading lower than it was on the grant date. This is usually, but not necessarily, a prior date. The grant date is the date the option was provided to the owner. The strike price is the price at which the owner can exercise the option and is fixed at the time the option is granted. For example, a board grants the CEO 1,000 stock options on June 1, 2019 to purchase the company's stock at the market price on the date of the grant but only after the strike price has been reached. The stock closes at a price of $50 on June 1, 2019, and the strike price is set at $55. Accordingly, the CEO can exercise the options at any time the stock trades at $55 or higher. If the stock price closes at $60 a share on June 1, 2020, the CEO could profit $10 a share by exercising the options. Now assume the company backdates the option to June 1, 2018, a date on which the stock closed at $40 a share. By simply backdating the option by one year, the CEO is now "in the money" by $20 a share instead of $10 a share.

Stock options backdating is not necessarily illegal. If the company makes full disclosures of the practice, the effects are reflected in earnings, and the proper tax treatment is provided, the practice can be appropriate. However, this is not likely to be the case. In fact, prosecutions of those engaged in stock options backdating became the crime *du jour* in 2006, shortly after a study by two professors showed a high number of cases in which companies granted stock options to executives shortly before the company's stock rose sharply.[13] The case of former United Health CEO, Dr. William McGuire, involved one of the largest stock options settlements by the SEC. The case also involved the first settlement under the "clawback" provision of the Sarbanes-Oxley Act in which McGuire agreed to pay $468 million, including a $7 million civil penalty, for causing the company to grant him backdated in-the-money stock options to himself.[14]

Government Fraud

The United States federal government is victimized by both procurement fraud and program fraud. As the largest purchaser of goods and services in the world, the federal government is an easy target for procurement fraud.[15] Procurement fraud occurs when vendors target federal agencies with a variety of frauds that include billing for services or goods not provided or rendered, double-billing, and delivery of substandard goods or services. When the fraud is done by a government insider, it can also be a form of corruption.

The federal government also hemorrhages from losses associated with program fraud. Program fraud is a type of fraud in which a government's program funds that are meant for beneficiaries are misapplied by either the service providers or the beneficiaries themselves. The prime examples of program fraud are Medicare and Medicaid schemes due to the substantial losses incurred by these programs. Other programs include federally insured loans and mortgages, highway funds, agricultural subsidies, student loans, federal grants, and disaster assistance. State and local governments are also victimized by procurement and program frauds. Many federal programs pass funds to state agencies for the management of the programs. Frauds involving these programs can affect both federal and state governments.

Health Care Fraud

During my time managing a large health care fraud task force, I observed systemic fraud schemes in the delivery of health care that were disproportionately higher than non-health care industries. Further, federal health care programs spawn predatory fraudsters. Internal controls over federal health care programs are weak, and they are demonstrably weaker than their private insurance company counterparts. In some of the lucrative schemes I observed, fraudsters targeted government programs and intentionally avoided private insurance companies for fear of being caught by those insurance company's special investigative units.

In the United States, more losses are incurred from fraud in the health care sector than in any other sector in the economy. To appreciate the magnitude of the problem, the Centers for Medicare and Medicaid Services estimates that 17.9 percent of the U.S. gross domestic product (GDP) pertains to health care related expenditures.[16] The U.S. GDP for 2018 was estimated to be $20.41 trillion.[17] Accordingly, in 2018, the United States is estimated to spend $3.65 trillion on health care. The dollar loss attributable to health care fraud is more difficult to assess. The ACFE estimates that organizations lose an estimated 5 percent of revenues to fraud.[18] By analogy, this percentage can at least be used as a baseline when assessing the percentage of government program funds lost to fraud. Five percent of U.S. health care costs would put the dollar amount attributable to fraud at $182.5 billion. In addition to fraud, the dollar losses associated with waste, abuse, and defensive medicine, could easily add another 5 percent. Assuming that 5 percent or 10 percent of health care expenditures in the United States are attributable to fraud and abuse, the losses would be $182.5 billion and $365 billion, respectively. These are likely conservative estimates, and the actual amounts could be substantially higher.

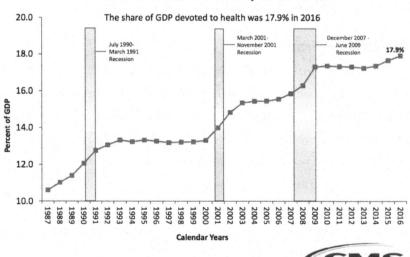

National Health Expenditures as a Share of Gross Domestic Product, 1987-2016

SOURCE: Centers for Medicare & Medicaid Services, Office of the Actuary, National Health Statistics Group; U.S. Department of Commerce, Bureau of Economic Analysis and National Bureau of Economic Research, Inc.

With this backdrop, it should be no surprise that the most pervasive U.S. program frauds involve the Medicare and Medicaid programs. The underlying cause of losses associated with health care is that the cost of a service or product is not borne by the consumer but by the insurance company. In fact, both the providers and the consumers of health care have incentives to overutilize products or services, and neither have real incentives to report red flags of fraud when observed.

In some schemes, the health care provider and the consumer actually collude. Common examples include waiver of copayments and mischaracterization of a medical procedure code to one that is reimbursable by insurance. A description of the manifold health care fraud schemes is outside the scope of this book because the schemes involve private physicians, hospitals, nursing homes, skilled nursing facilities, durable medical equipment, and so forth, and the schemes can vary depending on the type of medical service or product involved, as well as the fraudsters' latest innovations resulting in a never-ending kaleidoscope of possibilities.

According to the National Health Care Anti-Fraud Association, a national leader in the prevention of health care fraud, the following are common health care fraud schemes:

- Billing for services never rendered, either by using genuine patient information, sometimes obtained through identity theft, to fabricate entire claims or by padding claims with charges for procedures or services that did not take place.

- Billing for more expensive services or procedures than were actually provided or performed, commonly known as "upcoding," that is, falsely billing for a higher-priced treatment than was actually provided (which often requires the accompanying "inflation" of the patient's diagnosis code to a more serious condition consistent with the false procedure code).

- Performing medically unnecessary services solely for the purpose of generating insurance payments, seen very often in nerve conduction and other diagnostic-testing schemes.

- Misrepresenting noncovered treatments as medically necessary for purposes of obtaining insurance payments, widely seen in cosmetic-surgery schemes, in which noncovered cosmetic procedures such as "nose jobs" are billed to patients' insurers as deviated-septum repairs.

- Falsifying a patient's diagnosis to justify tests, surgeries, or other procedures that are not medically necessary.

- Unbundling, that is, billing each step of a procedure as if it were a separate procedure.

- Billing a patient more than the co-pay amount for prepaid services or those paid in full by the benefit plan under the terms of a managed care contract.

- Accepting kickbacks for patient referrals.

- Waiving patient co-pays or deductibles for medical or dental care and over-billing the insurance carrier or benefit plan (insurers often set the policy with regard to the waiver of co-pays through its provider contracting process, although, under Medicare, routinely waiving co-pays is prohibited and may only be waived due to "financial hardship").[19]

Qui Tam Litigation

Frauds are most often discovered by someone close to the fraudster. Whether an individual who is suspicious of fraudulent conduct is willing to report it to an appropriate authority will depend on a variety of factors, the most significant of which is the entity's culture. In the health care industry, participants are very hesitant to report wrongdoing, especially when a medical doctor is involved. There is truly a white-coat effect. As an aside, this is not the case in the legal profession.

When managing the Houston Area Health Care Fraud Task Force, I sought to discover the most egregious criminal violations and then prioritize investigations both in an effort to bring fraudsters to justice and to discourage future fraud. As part of this effort, I spoke to a variety of professional groups in the health care industry and encouraged them to report fraud to my office, but this effort was met with limited success. After a particular speaking engagement, however, the attendees wanted to meet with me after my presentation, and others started calling my office. During that particular presentation, I had explained the provisions of the federal False Claims Act, known as a "*qui tam* lawsuit," things changed dramatically.

A *qui tam* lawsuit allows a private individual to collect a substantial reward for reporting government fraud. When I began telling health care professionals that they could personally benefit by reporting fraud, I witnessed a dramatic change in their behavior. This became a major "Aha!" moment for me! Whatever influence the white-coat effect had on discouraging individuals from reporting fraud was clearly overcome when they learned that they stood to gain a financial reward. Whistleblower awards work by incentivizing those with knowledge to take action.

The *qui tam* provisions are found in the federal False Claims Act. Rewards resulting from a successful *qui tam* actions can be substantial because the False Claims Act provides for a civil penalty of not less than $10,957 and not more than $21,916[20] plus three times the amount of damages that the government sustained because of the fraud.[21] The chart below shows the magnitude of recoveries for both the government and the whistleblower, also known as a "relator," since the government began keeping statistics in 1987.

Qui Tam Recoveries (1987-2017)

Year	#Qui Tams	Total Recovery	Relators' Recovery
1987	30	0	0
1988	43	2,343,104	97,188
1989	87	15,113,400	1,446,970
1990	72	40,558,367	6,611,606
1991	84	70,453,931	10,686,287
1992	114	134,943,903	24,381,432
1993	138	190,246,787	29,343,137
1994	216	381,840,528	70,292,246
1995	269	240,659,292	45,628,096
1996	340	137,883,636	25,851,597
1997	547	627,940,474	67,515,904
1998	468	469,082,921	78,751,017
1999	493	497,992,288	64,392,552
2000	363	1,210,059,645	184,054,520
2001	311	1,344,113,067	218,252,350
2002	319	1,103,960,162	165,960,141
2003	334	1,540,048,263	338,690,598
2004	432	570,979,382	112,600,348
2005	406	1,156,529,117	170,612,237
2006	385	1,513,816,862	225,623,908
2007	365	1,411,973,849	197,505,111
2008	379	1,058,261,165	204,679,759
2009	433	1,997,132,735	259,251,282
2010	576	2,390,156,737	401,772,542
2011	634	2,822,441,117	559,917,069
2012	652	3,389,726,844	448,837,485
2013	756	2,995,867,418	558,761,955
2014	715	4,467,703,859	711,636,578
2015	639	2,408,840,181	482,039,295
2016	706	2,921,939,136	526,799,613
2017	674	3,437,037,099	392,959,388
Total	11,890	$40,549,645,269	$6,584,952,211

Source: Department of Justice[22]

Case Example

The size of the reward that a *qui tam* relator (plaintiff) may recover is staggering. Consider a scenario occurring in the ambulance service industry. A Medicare recipient needs dialysis three times a week. The patient is otherwise healthy and is completely ambulatory. Despite being completely ambulatory, the patient likes the convenience of using an ambulance service to transport her for recurring dialysis treatments. The ambulance provider knows the patient does not qualify for the rides under the Medicare regulations but finds the allure of recurring high-dollar payments irresistible. Through marketing efforts in the area around the dialysis treatment center, the ambulance provider can easily recruit 20 dialysis patients.[23]

Now let's do the math under the False Claims Act. The 20 patients receive three two-way trips a week. The ambulance service provider bills Medicare $400 for each one-way trip, resulting in revenue of $2.49 million annually (3 x 2 x 20 x 52 x $400). This also results in 6,240 (3 x 2 x 20 x 52) false claims being submitted to Medicare per year by the ambulance service provider. The False Claims Act allows the whistleblower to recover three times the actual loss amount (3 x $2.49), or $7.47 million, plus up to $21,916 for each false claim associated with the medically unnecessary ambulance ride. In this case, the damages could be in excess of $144 million ($7.47 + (6,240 x $21,916)) per year streaming from a patient base of only 20 individuals. The whistleblower is entitled to up to 30 percent[24] of this amount, or about $43 million.

As this example demonstrates, the potential damages under the False Claims Act can easily be in excess of the net worth of the corporate fraudster. The solvency of the enterprise is easily put at risk. Accordingly, defendants often settle these claims, and the whistleblower walks away with a substantial reward. Once the whistleblower is educated about these realities, the whistleblower has a strong incentive to report fraud outside the company.

Insurance Fraud

According to the FBI, the insurance industry includes over 7,000 companies that collect over $1 trillion in premiums annually, and the cost of insurance fraud (nonhealthcare) is estimated to be more than $40 billion.[25] As with any industry, insurance companies can be both the victim of fraud and the perpetrator.

The most common type of insurance fraud involves exaggerated submission of claims associated with an actual loss by the insured. More aggressive schemes include staged thefts, staged car accidents, and even arson. All of these frauds will include insurance claims for property or injuries that do not exist. Arson has been committed by owners of troubled businesses that experience cash flow or debt service issues. After torching their business, these owners will cause false claims to be filed for the property they damaged, other property not damaged, inflated inventory values, the repayment of a mortgagee, and the lost profits.

Although we generally think of worker compensation fraud as being committed by employees feigning injury, it is also committed by employers. In the United States, each state requires that employers provide workers' compensation to their employees for injuries suffered on the job. Employers will engage in a variety of schemes to lower their premiums, including misrepresentation of data concerning their employees. An employer may misclassify the job classification to an occupation with a lower risk profile. Other schemes include understatement of payroll expenses or falsely claiming employees work in a lower-risk jurisdiction. An employer with a high claims history may form a new company to obtain lower premiums.

The insured can also be the victim of fraud by predatory insurance companies. An unscrupulous insurance agent can collect a premium but never remit it to the insurance company in hopes that the insured will never make a claim. In a more aggressive version, fraudsters sell insurance policies that purportedly are based in an offshore territory, like Bermuda. In reality, the premiums are deposited into a shell company and then laundered. Once substantial claims are made, the company goes belly up and the fraudsters vanish.

Another type of fraud associated with insurance policies involves a viatical settlement. An owner of a life insurance policy who is terminally ill can sell the policy to a third-party investor for an amount that is less than the death benefit. The insured gets the benefit of having disposable funds before death, and investors make a profit. Admittedly, it's morbid to contemplate the risk involved, but the insured is betting on a prolonged life, and the investor is betting on a shortened life. Although the insureds dealing with end-of-life issues may not make sound decisions when dealing with sophisticated settlement providers, most frauds involving viatical settlements are against insurance companies, viatical settlement providers, and investors.

A fraud known as "clean sheeting" involves the insureds misrepresenting their poor health as good in order to obtain a life insurance policy. A fraud known as "dirty sheeting" involves the insured claiming poor health to entice viatical settlement providers to purchase their insurance policy. Fraudulent viatical settlement providers may encourage investors to invest even though they may not have the necessary licenses and/or fail to conduct due diligence involving the viatical settlements. In a DOJ and SEC investigation involving Mutual Benefits Corporation, a Fort Lauderdale-based company that purportedly specialized in viatical settlements, the operators were charged with running a $1 billion Ponzi scheme, victimizing more than 29,000 investors.[26]

Financial Institution Fraud

More is known about financial institution fraud (commonly known as bank fraud) than any other type of fraud because these institutions are required to file suspicious activity reports (SAR) with the Financial Crimes Enforcement Network (FinCEN), an agency of the United States Department of the Treasury, when violations of law are suspected and/or when a transaction has no apparent business purpose. In 2016, almost one million SARs were filed with the FinCEN, capturing suspicious activities in 79 categories, including money laundering, mortgage fraud, check fraud, and identity theft.[27]

Financial institutions are at a high risk for fraud because their greatest asset is capital. Financial institutions can be victimized by outsiders, insiders, or a combination of both. Insiders commit two distinct categories of fraud. One category involves loan frauds and bribery schemes from which the insider personally benefits. A second category involves accounting fraud to inflate regulatory capital in an attempt to prevent the financial institution's regulator from taking control of the institution. The discussion below pertains primarily to outsiders that attempt to victimize a financial institution.

I supervised the investigation of a very bizarre case of fraud involving a bank. In actuality, the matter was likely an insurance fraud, as the bank had gained from what had happened. The case involved the famed racehorse Alydar. Alydar finished second to Affirmed in all three races of the Triple Crown. The owner of both Alydar and Kentucky's storied Calumet Farm was accused of intentionally causing the death of Alydar. At the time, the owner began defaulting on $50 million in loans at a Houston bank. Alydar had been insured for $36.5 million.[28] The insurance proceeds were used to pay down the loan. The prized racehorse may have been worth more dead than alive. While the owner was ultimately convicted on other bank fraud and bribery charges, the cause of Alydar's death was never conclusively proven.

Mortgage Frauds

The 2007–2008 financial crisis is believed by most economists to have been triggered by the U.S. housing bubble. Although the causes of this bubble are multifaceted, fraud certainly played a significant role. When financial institutions learn of a potential mortgage-related fraud, they are required to file a SAR. Financial institutions generally do not learn of a mortgage fraud until the mortgagor stops making a mortgage payment. Accordingly, a lag time will occur between the date of the actual fraud and the filing of a SAR. These two dates are tracked in the chart below depicting all mortgage-fraud related SARs filed from 2001 to 2013.

Number of Mortgage Fraud SARs by Activity Start Date and Year Received

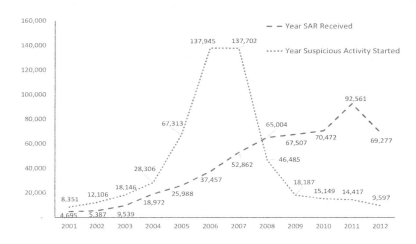

Source: Financial Crimes Enforcement Network Press Release August 20, 2013[29]

This chart is significant because the data was available to federal law enforcement, federal regulators, and, most importantly, the U.S. Congress. What this chart reflects is that U.S. government officials in positions of authority were clearly on notice that a spike in mortgage fraud activity was under way in 2003 and proceeded for another five years before peaking in 2008. In my estimation, policy makers were more interested in rising real estate markets than in sound fiscal policy.

Mortgage frauds generally victimize a financial institution, and in some schemes, a home owner. According to the FBI, the following are common mortgage fraud schemes.[30]

Foreclosure Rescue Schemes: The perpetrators identify home owners who are in foreclosure or at risk of defaulting on their mortgage loan and then mislead them into believing they can save their homes by transferring the deed or putting the property in the name of an investor. The perpetrators profit by selling the property to an investor or straw borrower, creating equity using a fraudulent appraisal and stealing the seller's proceeds or fees paid by the home owners. The home owners are sometimes told that they can pay rent for at least a year and repurchase the property once their credit has been reestablished. However, the perpetrators fail to make the mortgage payments, and usually the property goes into foreclosure.

Loan Modification Schemes: Similar to foreclosure rescue schemes, these schemes involve perpetrators purporting to assist home owners who are delinquent on their mortgage payments and are on the verge of losing their home by offering to renegotiate the terms of the home owners' loan with the lender. The scammers, however, demand large fees up front and often negotiate unfavorable terms for the clients or do not negotiate at all. Usually, the home owners ultimately lose their homes.

Illegal Property Flipping: Property is purchased, falsely appraised at a higher value, and then quickly sold. What makes property flipping illegal is the fraudulent appraisal information or false information provided during the transactions. The scheme typically involves one or more of the following: fraudulent appraisals; falsified loan documentation; inflated buyer income; or kickbacks to buyers, investors, property/loan brokers, appraisers, and title company employees.

Builder Bailout/Condo Conversion: Builders facing rising inventory and declining demand for newly constructed homes employ bailout schemes to offset losses. Builders find buyers who obtain loans for the properties but who then allow the properties to go into foreclosure. In a condo conversion scheme, apartment complexes purchased by developers during a housing boom are converted into condos, and in a declining real estate market, developers often have an excess inventory of units. Developers recruit straw buyers with cash-back incentives and inflate the value of the condos to obtain a larger sales price at closing. In addition to failing to disclose the cash-back incentives to the lender, the straw buyers' income and asset information are often inflated in order for them to qualify for properties that they otherwise would be ineligible or unqualified to purchase.

Silent Second: The buyer of a property borrows the down payment from the seller through the issuance of a nondisclosed second mortgage. The primary lender believes that the borrower has invested his or her own money in the down payment when in fact, it has been borrowed. The second mortgage may not be recorded to further conceal its status from the primary lender.

Home Equity Conversion Mortgage (HECM): A HECM is a reverse mortgage loan product, insured by the Federal Housing Administration, for borrowers who are 62 years or older, own their own property (or have a small mortgage balance), occupy the property as their primary residence, and participate in HECM counseling. It provides home owners access to equity in their homes, usually in a lump sum payment. Perpetrators taking advantage of the HECM program recruit seniors through local churches, investment seminars, and television, radio, billboard, and mailer advertisements. They then obtain a HECM in the name of the recruited homeowner to convert equity in the homes into cash. The scammers keep the cash and pay a fee to the senior citizen or take the full amount unbeknownst to the senior citizen. No loan payment or repayment is required until the borrower no longer uses the house as a primary residence. In the scheme, the appraisals on the home are vastly inflated and the lender does not detect the fraud until the home owner dies and the true value of the property is discovered.

Commercial Real Estate Loans: Owners of distressed commercial real estate (or those acting on their behalf) obtain financing by manipulating the property's appraised value. Bogus leases may be created to exaggerate the building's profitability, thus inflating the value as determined using the "income method" for property valuation. Fraudulent appraisals trick lenders into extending loans to the owner. As cash flows are lower than stated, the borrower struggles to maintain the property and repairs are neglected. By the time the commercial loans are in default, the lender is often left with dilapidated or difficult-to-rent commercial property. Many of the methods of committing mortgage fraud that are found in residential real estate are also present in commercial loan fraud.

Air Loans: This is a nonexistent property loan for which there is usually no collateral. Air loans involve brokers who invent borrowers and properties, establish accounts for payments, and maintain custodial accounts for escrow. They may establish an office with a bank of telephones, each one used for the fake employer, appraiser, credit agency, and so forth to fraudulently deceive creditors who attempt to verify the information on the loan applications.

Kiting

Check kiting involves floating checks among multiple accounts, resulting in an illegal, unsecured, non-interest-bearing loan to the kiter. More specifically, the scheme involves the kiter drafting a check on an account that has insufficient funds to cover the check. Before the check clears the account on which it is written, the kiter deposits funds in that account with funds from another account that also has insufficient funds. The scheme, which requires two or more checking accounts, continues in a vicious cycle until the check kiter either deposits sufficient legitimate funds to end the scheme or it collapses upon discovery by a bank. The scheme works because of the "float time," or the time it takes a check to clear.

In modern times, these schemes are harder to execute due to shorter float times and check-clearing policies at banks. Now, a successful scheme usually involves a bank insider who overrides a bank procedure to allow this to happen.

Bankruptcy, Matrimonial, and Business Divorce Fraud

What do creditors, spouses, and business partners have in common? Their assets may be taken, misappropriated, or otherwise hidden from them. Each of these relationships started out with mutually beneficial interests. When circumstances change, the parties in control of the assets begin hiding them for their personal benefit. Each of these scenarios can also involve legal proceedings in which individuals must declare assets, provide depositions, and testify at trial. Throughout all of these processes, individuals will hide assets, sign false statements, and give perjurious testimony. The propensity for fraud under these circumstances is quite common. In my experience, the fraud is so common that law enforcement will rarely get involved.

Bankruptcy Fraud

Bankruptcy is a legal process in which a debtor can seek relief from a creditor. In the United States, bankruptcy is controlled by federal law and is adjudicated in the federal courts. The current bankruptcy code resulted from the passage of the Bankruptcy Reform Act of 1978, 11 U.S.C. §§101 *et seq.* (Code). For our purposes, the Code contains six Chapters that merit discussion.

Chapter 7: Also known as a "Chapter 7 Liquidation." The purpose is to entirely liquidate the debtor's assets and discharge all liabilities allowed by the Code. Chapter 7 is available to both individuals and businesses and can be filed both voluntarily or involuntarily.

Chapter 9: Applies to municipalities defined as a political subdivision or public agency or instrumentality of a state. However, federal bankruptcy law does not apply to the states themselves.

Chapter 11: Also known as a "Chapter 11 Reorganization." The purpose is the rehabilitation of the debtor and allows the debtor to emerge from bankruptcy as a viable going concern. It applies to businesses and individuals whose debt exceeds Chapter 13 limitations or who have complex financial affairs and can be filed both voluntarily or involuntarily.

Chapter 12: Applies to the family farmer and family fishermen.

Chapter 13: Applies to individuals and allows them to keep most of their assets as they execute a plan to repay creditors. Requires individual debtors to use this chapter when their means-tested income is too great for a Chapter 7. Chapter 13 petitions can only be filed voluntarily.

Chapter 15: Deals with international or cross-border insolvency cases that involve assets, claimants, debtors, and parties of interest in multiple countries.

By far the most common type of bankruptcy fraud involves filing false declarations and property concealments. The debtor simply does not want to make assets available to a creditor to apply to a debt owed. A debtor may fraudulently convey assets to family, friends, or other nominees in an attempt to keep the assets out of the bankruptcy estate. One type of bankruptcy fraud known as a "bust-out scheme" occurs when a fraudster orders large inventories of merchandise on credit with no intention of repaying the debt.

Unfortunately, fraud runs rampant in the bankruptcy system. The U.S. Bankruptcy Trustees, who are charged with managing bankruptcy cases, are required by law to report all potentially fraudulent conduct to the appropriate United States Attorney. As a matter of practice, these referrals are provided to the FBI, which has responsibility for investigating bankruptcy fraud. As an FBI manager, I routinely reviewed these criminal referrals and was continually frustrated to see the number and magnitude of the allegations. The reality is that the FBI does not have the resources to investigate all of these frauds, and therefore, the courts and the creditors have to pursue civil remedies available under the Code. However, just to show the bankruptcy fraudsters that the FBI cares, I always tried to ensure that my squad was at least investigating one large Chapter 11 corporate bankruptcy fraud and a handful of Chapter 7 and 13 frauds. Another common practice that I adopted was to have the FBI work with the United States Attorney and the United States Trustee to indict several of these cases all at the same time to publicize the frauds occurring in our nation's bankruptcy courts. The purpose was to deter those availing themselves of our bankruptcy system from committing fraud.

Case Example

Lenders are frequently subjected to fraudulent credit applications that can be difficult to detect during the underwriting process. Indeed, the more sophisticated fraudsters can dupe a lender into approving and funding a loan, and the lender may not uncover the fraud until months or years later after the loan is in default.

Attorney Kevin Stine of Baker Donelson assisted one such bank client who had loaned in excess of $400,000 to an individual, ostensibly for the purpose of a real estate investment. The borrower's credit application included a personal financial statement and income tax returns reflecting substantial net worth and annual earnings as a physician.

Following default, the bank retained Baker Donelson to enforce the loan, and Baker Donelson secured a money judgment in state court. The borrower sought refuge in bankruptcy court, after which the bank successfully fought efforts to discharge the judgment with evidence that the borrower materially misrepresented her net worth and earnings in her credit application. Indeed, the borrower was not even a college graduate—let alone a physician—and the income tax returns she included in her application were bogus. The bankruptcy court ended up issuing an order that the bank's judgment was excepted from discharge, preserving the bank's right to pursue collection of the judgment from the debtor post-bankruptcy.

THE HONEST TRUTH ABOUT FRAUD

Matrimonial and Business Divorces

Like bankruptcy fraud in which a debtor is trying to defraud a creditor, spouses and business partners may hide assets from each other. When assets are hidden before the unsuspecting victim is aware of it, it can be difficult to discover later where the assets are located. This can be particularly effective when assets are sold for cash and records are destroyed. Money laundering can be effective and is discussed in more detail in Chapter 9.

Fraud committed by partners in a small business occurs frequently, and following is a common scenario. A company may have 3 to 5 members, and the company is very successful. The business could be a bar, restaurant, printing business, or construction company. In each of these businesses, a trusted CFO handles all of the finances and accounting. As the business becomes successful, money flows into the company. Due to a lack of internal controls and the trust among the members, the CFO begins embezzling funds.

Fraud Detection

When I receive calls from individuals who have just discovered that their spouse or business partner is hiding assets, it is never pleasant. They are naturally very panicky and do not know what to do. In the case of divorcing spouses, the calls seem invariably to come from the wife. In the case of business partners, the calls come from the hard-working or creative member of the business who has just learned that the CFO is likely embezzling company funds.

If the party hiding the assets is not aware that the victim knows of the wrongful conduct, then collecting information can be done without obstruction. Regardless of the scenario, I want to obtain all of the available records. Finding hidden bank accounts will usually be very important. Although this can be difficult, there are techniques that I have learned to discover them. Important information to obtain quickly will include:

- Accounting Records
- Accounting Data (QuickBooks Files)

- Tax Returns (Personal and Company)

    ○ W-2 Forms

    ○ Schedule K1

    ○ Depreciation Schedules (helps with concealed assets)

    ○ Interest and Dividend Income

    ○ Investment Interest Expense Deductions

    ○ Real Estate Tax Deductions

    ○ Interest Expense Deductions

    ○ Miscellaneous Deductions

    ○ Foreign Income

- Bank Accounts

- Brokerage Accounts

- 401(k) and other Retirement Accounts

- Credit Card Statements

- Loan Applications

- Insurance Policies

- Credit Reports

- Public Databases

- Fee-for-service Databases

Bust-out Scheme

One of the purposes of forming a legal entity (e.g., corporation or a limited liability company) is to limit liability. A fraudster may attempt to hide behind a legal entity when committing fraud. Examples include a bust-out scheme in which a company borrows money to purchase inventory with no intent to repay. In fact, this can occur in any contractual relationship where the buyer accepts a good or service, refuses to pay, and argues that only the company can be held liable. To defeat this argument, courts have adopted an equity doctrine known as "piercing the corporate veil." The legal theory is that a dominant shareholder or member is acting as an *alter ego* ("second self" in Latin) for the legal entity.

Some of the legal elements for finding an *alter ego* are:[31]

- The company must be influenced and governed by the person asserted to be the *alter ego*.

- The unity of interest and ownership is inseparable from the other.

- The facts must be such that adherence to the corporate fiction of a separate entity would sanction a fraud or would promote injustice.

Further, the following factors, though not conclusive, may indicate the existence of an *alter ego* relationship allowing for a plaintiff to "pierce the corporate veil" and go after a member of a company personally for the debts and/or liability of that company:[32]

- A general commingling of corporate activity and/or funds and those of the person or persons who control the company.

- Undercapitalization (i.e., members removing unreasonable amounts of funds from the company, endangering its financial stability).

- Unauthorized diversion of funds.

- Treatment of corporate assets as the individual's own.

- Failure to observe corporate formalities.

- Corporate debt is knowingly incurred when the company is already insolvent.

- Required annual meetings are not held.

- Corporate records, especially minutes of member meetings, are not properly or adequately maintained.

- There is a pattern of consistent nonpayment of dividends or payment of excessive dividends.

- A failure to maintain separate offices, the company has little or no other business and is only a facade for the activities of the dominant shareholder, who is, in fact, the corporate *alter ego*.

Theft of Intellectual Property and Information

Theft of intellectual property (IP) and information is an enormous problem that continues on an upward trajectory. Although it is not technically fraud because it is really theft, there are many deceptive techniques that are used to gain access to IP. As I will discuss in Chapter 8, Cyber Fraud, a common method of stealing IP is through hacking techniques, including social engineering.

IP can be placed into two categories. One category is tangible IP that can be protected by copyrights, patents, and trademarks. Because this type of IP has to be disclosed to be utilized, various laws have been created to protect it. The other category of IP is trade secrets. Trade secrets by their very nature must be kept secret to be protected and include financial, business, scientific, technical, economic, or engineering information whether tangible or intangible (e.g., the formula for Coca-Cola).[33] Trade secrets can be stolen by anyone, including competitors, company insiders, and foreign governments. When trade secrets are stolen by a foreign government, it is known as economic espionage.[34]

The 2018 Annual Intellectual Property Report to Congress[35] highlights some astonishing numbers. The Department of Commerce has designated 81 out of 313 U.S. industries as IP-intensive, collectively accounting for $6.6 trillion in value added in 2014, or 38.2 percent of the U.S. GDP.[36] The United States estimates that counterfeit goods, pirated software, and theft of trade secrets, which includes cyber-enabled trade secrets, directly cost the U.S. economy $225 to $600 billion annually, or 1 to 3 percent of GDP in 2016.[37] Furthermore, China accounts for 87 percent of counterfeited goods seized that are coming to the United States.[38] China has a thriving counterfeit industry that is made possible by its technology to produce the fake goods, websites to market products, acceptance of credits cards for purchases, and commercial carriers to deliver counterfeited goods to the United States and abroad. Between 2013 and 2017, total inbound international packages mailed to the United States tripled.[39]

Throughout history, sovereign nations have actively engaged in espionage. Citizens of any nation probably believe this conduct is appropriate when the information is gathered—albeit through theft, deception, or hacking—in the defense of the country. However, a country actively engaging in theft of trade secrets to enrich the country is quite another matter. This is exactly what China is doing! Since it is a communist country, the distinction between the military and commerce are blurred because the state is running both, and its citizen's may find China's prolific espionage industry more palatable, as it increases its military and economic competitiveness around the world.

Thefts of IP are also perpetrated by company insiders. Employees with a need to access this data can easily misappropriate it by connecting an electronic storage device to a company computer. The data can be sold, or the employee can leave the company and use the data to compete with the victim's competitors. Unfortunately, IP thefts have become all too common. The challenge for attorneys and forensic accountants is to prove that the IP was stolen, demonstrate that the victim (company) was harmed, and calculate the damages incurred.

The prevention of IP theft must include a multifaceted approach. Efforts need to be made to clearly communicate that this conduct will not be tolerated. Employees without a "need to know" must be restricted from accessing sensitive data. The company's information technology function must be designed to create digital footprints in order to document employees downloading company information. To the extent that it is consistent with the company's e-mail retention policy, e-mail traffic should be preserved for investigative purposes and to create an evidence trail should any IP be stolen via e-mail. When detected, a company should quickly assist in a "noisy" prosecution by making all employees aware that theft of IP will not be tolerated. A potentially more pernicious act is electronic sabotage, which can be done, often by a disgruntled or fired employee, to harm the company.

CHAPTER 8
Cyber Fraud

*"A company can spend hundreds of thousands of dollars
on firewalls, intrusion detection systems and encryption
and other security technologies, but if an attacker can
call one trusted person within the company, and that
person complies, and if the attacker gets in, then all
the money spent on technology is essentially wasted."*

—KEVIN MITNICK
TWO-TIME FELON AND AUTHOR OF *THE ART OF DECEPTION:
CONTROLLING THE HUMAN ELEMENT OF SECURITY*

In this chapter, we will cover frauds and other crimes that use or target a computer or a computer network. This conduct is known as "cybercrime," "computer crime," or "network crime." This does not include those acts in which a computer is simply used as a modality for committing a crime (e.g., a Nigerian 419 e-mail scam), since those frauds are covered in other chapters. The focus of this chapter is on computer attacks done for a variety of purposes, including fraud, theft of property, trespassing, computer damage, or a combination of any of these. Although the purpose of the attack may be something other than fraud, I will discuss a variety of these cybercrimes because the prevention, detection, and investigation of them is similar regardless of the motivation of the offender.

Of all of the criminal activities that the FBI is responsible for investigating, none have changed more than cybercrime. The technology used by cybercriminals to commit crimes and the technology used by the FBI to investigate crimes changed dramatically during my 25 years with the FBI. The FBI's protocol for executing search warrants in the early 1990s was to send a team of FBI agents to the file room with dollies, where they would roll out all of the file cabinets onto a large truck until the file room was empty. Back at the FBI field office, the poor case agent could easily spend the next year poring over all of the documents that the FBI had taken from the files.

In January of 2002, the FBI began actively investigating Enron. Three teams were assembled: an interview team, a document search team, and a digital search team. Over nine days, I led the document search team, which grew to over 125 FBI agents. Another FBI agent led the digital search team. Looking back, the year 2002 was probably the transition time in corporate history when half of the evidence resided in a document format and half resided in a digital format. Currently, digital media could easily account for 80 percent or more of the evidence in a typical federal case.

Before I get into the details of cybercrime, a brief discussion of two legal terms drawn from the implementing regulations of the Health Insurance Portability and Accountability Act (HIPAA) of 1996 will be very helpful, since variations of these terms are used in several federal and state statutes.

- **Security Incident:** A security incident means the attempted or successful unauthorized access, use, disclosure, modification, or destruction of information or interference with system operations in an information system.[1]
- **Breach:** A breach is the acquisition, access, use, or disclosure of information that compromises the security or privacy of the information.[2]

A security incident is a broad term that means a cyber-related matter has occurred. Once a security incident has been identified, a regulated entity may be required to respond to the threat, mitigate its effects to the extent possible, and document the incident. A breach (or data breach) is a more serious event because it indicates that the malicious actor may have control over the victim's data. Depending on the federal or state law triggered, the victim (company) may also be required to notify other victims whose records have been compromised, a regulatory authority, or the media about the circumstances surrounding the breach.

When an organization experiences an event that may be a cyberattack, management should be careful in describing the event. Whether an event is a security incident or a breach is a fact-specific determination. If a breach has occurred, certain legal obligations may be triggered. A company encountering any cyber-related event should not conclude that it is a security incident or a breach until an attorney who is competent in this area of law says it is.

Cast of Characters

As you might expect, cybercrime encompasses a variety of bad actors. Here is the cast of characters (they can be individuals or organizations):

Cyberterrorist: A terrorist motivated by a political, religious, or ideological cause who targets a victim's computer or network with the intention of causing serious harm to the network or the underlying infrastructure that the network controls.

Financial Hacker: An insider or an outsider who hacks a computer or a network for financial gain.

Hacktivist: A politically or socially motivated individual who targets a computer or a network of an organization that has an opposing view.

Nation State Actor: A foreign government that attacks a computer or a network for political, economic espionage, or warfare reasons.

Script Kiddie: An unskilled individual, often a juvenile, who follows the scripts of other attackers to attack a computer or a network.

Former Employee: A disgruntled current or soon-to-be-former employee who is seeking revenge, company data, or a cover-up of illegal activity.

Social Engineering

Social engineering is the psychological manipulation of a person for the purpose of obtaining information or causing a specific action. In the cyber-crime context, the information wanted can include online credentials (user name and password), bank account information, or insider information. The fraudster's goal is to create a scenario in which the victim will disclose information by any means, including by mail, phone, or computer, or through direct personal contact. Because many victims are too savvy to disclose this information, fraudster have developed another technique. The fraudster, who is generally thought of as a hacker, will manipulate the victim into taking a specific action, like clicking a mouse or touching a key. The victim may download a weaponized document containing malware or be directed to a malicious website where malware is downloaded. Either of these scenarios can lead to a whole host of bad things, which can include theft of intellectual property, business e-mail compromise (BEC) fraud, or a ransomware attack. Even when a company follows all of the current protocols to detect and defeat malware, if the attacker is introducing malware that has never been seen before, the company may still become vulnerable to what is known as a "zero-day attack."

Social media has radically changed the way people communicate around the world. Most of us will recognize popular social media platforms that include Facebook, YouTube, Instagram, Twitter, LinkedIn, and Pinterest. A critical piece of business intelligence includes social media data mining. I am constantly amazed at what analysts can piece together from social media alone. Combine this information with fee-for-service databases, and a person's complete background can be obtained, including all previous addresses, jobs held, education, relatives, and neighbors. Socially oriented information can include favorite sports teams, vacations, and hobbies. Also obtainable are assets that include real estate, automobiles, and, most importantly, bank accounts and brokerage accounts. After mining a person's personal and social history, just think what a sophisticated hacker can then do with that information!

Social Engineering Schemes

There are a variety of schemes that fraudsters will use to gain access to information to include the following:

Phishing: A social engineering technique in which a bad actor sends many e-mails enticing multiple victim-recipients to disclose information or to take a specific action.

Spear Phishing: A tailored e-mail that targets a specific victim or class of victims with a phishing e-mail.

Whaling: A phishing attack that is directed at a specific individual in authority, which could include a company executive.

SMSishing: A phishing attack that uses text messages (short message service).

USB Thumb Drop Attack: A thumb drive containing malware is positioned near a target company—for example, a parking lot, storefront entrance, or company cafeteria—to entice an employee to place it into a company computer's USB port. The thumb drive may have a company logo or label on it, suggesting important information.

Pretexting: Using false pretenses to obtain information from another person. Pretexting may be illegal under state or federal law, especially if it involves obtaining bank, phone, or tax records.

Dumpster Diving: The process of searching discarded trash for the purpose of finding sensitive information.

Case Example

A hacker wants to cause a high-level employee to either download a weaponized file or to click on a link to a malicious website. The attack may occur on the company's computer or on the employee's home computer. The employee is security savvy, having attended social-engineering awareness training that the company requires of all of its employees. What can a hacker do?

The hacker learns through online searches that the employee is an alumnus of the local university. The football team played the previous Saturday and won. The hacker then visits the employee's LinkedIn page and learns of the employee's associates. The hacker notices an associate's name, which in this case is Ralph Hodges. With that name, the hacker creates a Gmail account with a very similar spelling, ralphodges@gmail.com. This bogus e-mail address is spelled with only one "h," and this deceptive change is highly unlikely to arouse suspicion. On Monday morning at around midday, the employee gets an e-mail from the close associate that says, "Hi Buddy—I saw you at the game Saturday but did not have a chance to say hi. I can't believe what the local reporter said about our team. Check out this link to read more." The scam may also encourage the employee to download a document.

This is an example of whaling, in which the hacker has taken the time to tailor an attack to a specific high-level individual. In reality, a hacker has an unlimited number of ways to commit this attack, and the victim only has to fall for it once.

Social engineering is usually the first step of various types of predatory frauds. As discussed in the Chapter 1, "the Fraud Triangle" provides limited insight into the motivation of a predator. To understand how social engineering works, consider it from the perspective of both the fraudster and the victim. Consider how social engineering works in frauds like ransomware or business e-mail compromise. The fraudster may never have met the victim and may reside in a foreign country. Let's explore social engineering from a psychological perspective.

The predators who engage in social-engineering-related frauds do it for a variety of reasons, but financial gain may not be their primary motivation. In my experience, they are likely to be males in their twenties or thirties. One can imagine that they have not gotten electronic gaming out of their system, and now they want to prey on real people.[3] Many of these schemes require a variety of fraudsters and hackers with various skill sets to be successful. However, from a psychological perspective, the chart below is more telling of what happens in this type of fraud. Think about a phishing campaign to install ransomware on as many computers as possible. The damage done to all of the victims will be enormous. The actual payout to the predators will be a small fraction of the actual damage done. The predators likely feel a sense of excitement. However, their true feelings are masked in the bogus e-mails sent to victims. Victims are deceived by the fraud when acting out of a sense of compliance or other motivations. See the chart below for the emotions of the predator and the victim.

Emotions in a Social Engineering Attack

Predator's Motivation	Predator's Demeanor	Victim's Emotions
Greed	Nice	Cooperativeness
Excitement	Authoritative	Friendly
Challenge	Knowledgeable	Compliant
Desiring	Helpful	Trusting
Fun	Confident, Persuasive	Fearful
Enjoyment	Successful, Connected	Curious

For predatory frauds, there may not be a way to control the fraudster's actions. Accordingly, the focus should be on the victim's reactions. Through social engineering awareness training, these psychological concepts will hopefully cause intended victims to pause before disclosing sensitive information or infecting a computer with malware.

Verizon Report

Verizon is one of the leading telecommunication companies that tracks data breaches and related incidents, and it produces an annual report that covers security incidents and data breaches. Verizon's *2018 Data Breach Investigations Report* captured 53,000 security incidents and 2,216 confirmed data breaches. Some of the more significant findings in the Verizon 2018 report are shown in the charts below.[4]

Who's behind the breaches?

73%
perpetrated by outsiders

28%
involved internal actors

2%
involved partners

2%
featured multiple parties

50%
of breaches were carried out by organized criminal groups

12%
of breaches involved actors identified as nation-state or state-affiliated

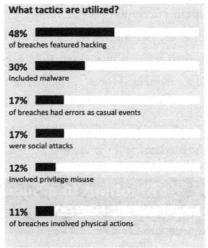

What tactics are utilized?

48%
of breaches featured hacking

30%
included malware

17%
of breaches had errors as casual events

17%
were social attacks

12%
involved privilege misuse

11%
of breaches involved physical actions

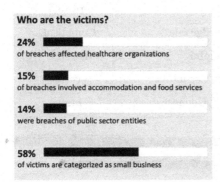

Who are the victims?

24%
of breaches affected healthcare organizations

15%
of breaches involved accommodation and food services

14%
were breaches of public sector entities

58%
of victims are categorized as small business

What are other commonalities?

49%
of non-POS malware was installed via malicious email

76%
of breaches were financially motivated

13%
of breaches were motivated by the gain of strategic advantage (espionage)

68%
of breaches took months or longer to discover

Source: *Verizon 2018 Data Breach Investigations Report*

As previously noted, a single cyberattack can include fraud, theft of property, trespassing, computer damage, or a combination of any of these. The challenge for most cyberattackers is to first gain access to a computer or a network. Attackers can deploy a variety of technical hacking techniques, most of which are outside the scope of this book. However, the most powerful and cost-effective technique will likely be social engineering. Cyberattacks may be perpetrated by a diverse array of actors pursuing various goals, the Verizon 2018 Report shows that 76 percent of breaches were financially motivated.

DoS and DDoS Attacks

Although it may not be associated with a financially motivated cyberattack, one type of cyberattack should be addressed due to its prevalence. The Verizon 2018 Report found by a very wide margin that a denial-of-service attack (DoS) is the most frequent type of cybersecurity incident.[5] A DoS attack occurs when an attacker floods a network with traffic until the targeted victim can no longer respond, thereby shutting down services to legitimate customers. A more virulent form of the attack is known as a "distributed denial-of-service attack" (DDoS). In this type of attack, the attacker conducts a large-scale DoS attack through the use of multiple Internet protocol addresses. The attacker uses a botnet, a portmanteau term derived from *robot* and *network*. The botnet controls a group of computers, potentially thousands of computers previously infected with malware. On command, this malicious actor can cause the botnet to flood the victim's network with traffic. Since the attack is coming from multiple IP addresses, the victim's use of ingress filtering to validate an attack is more difficult.

Identify Theft

Identify theft is the use of someone else's personally identifiable information (PII) for some type of benefit, usually financial. PII can be stolen and used to commit financial crimes that require the victim's name, social security number, date of birth, Medicare number, address, passport number, bank account, credit card number, password, telephone number, and biometric data. With this type of information, bank accounts and credit card accounts can be established, loans can be obtained, fraudulent tax refunds can be requested, and purchases can be made.

The Federal Trade Commission (FTC) is a great resource for anyone who has been the victim of identity theft. The FTC also produces an annual report that tracks identity theft. The FTC's *Consumer Sentinel Network Data Book 2017* found that credit card frauds resulting from identify theft continue to be the number one reported complaint.[6] The report also found that 133,000 victims complained of their information being misused on an existing account or being used to open a new credit card account.[7]

Prior to organizations aggregating large quantities of PII, identify theft was more difficult. Previously, identify theft was more likely the result of a stolen wallet or a burglary, in which thieves stole information. Identity thieves can still rummage through discarded trash to find information in a technique known as "dumpster diving."

Case Example

As an FBI agent, seniority on a squad has its benefits. This is especially the case when it comes to "dumpster diving" at a business or doing a "trash run" at someone's residence. Both of these techniques involve going through material that someone has discarded in hopes of finding something that advances the investigation. This can be very helpful for discovering assets listed in insurance policies, obtaining bank account and credit card statements, or obtaining information when looking for a fugitive.

A downside exists to going through someone's garbage. The pivotal piece of information someone is looking for may also be right next to last week's coffee grinds, spaghetti, or even worse, the dreaded dirty diaper. As a case agent needing to make a trash run, I always looked for the rookie agent who had just arrived from Quantico for assistance.

In this digital age, identity theft is a multistep process that requires the skill set of many bad actors. The first step is to harvest data from a company that aggregates data. Some of the more recent hacks receiving notoriety include Target Stores, Home Depot, and Equifax. The Equifax hack is very significant due to the volume and type of data stolen. In September of 2017, Equifax announced that an incident had occurred involving 143 million U.S. consumers in which names, social security numbers, birth dates, addresses, and driver's license numbers had been compromised. Additionally, 209,000 credit card numbers had been accessed.[8]

Once in possession of this bevy of data, the hacker then sells the PII to a broker on the dark web. The dark web is part of the Internet that is not indexed and is usually accessed by an Internet search engine called Tor (The Onion Router) to protect anonymity. Purchases are made with cryptocurrencies like Bitcoin, which also help protect anonymity. The sales price is like any other commodity and is determined by quantity and quality. The recency of the hack is also very important. Highly valued data includes online credentials like user name and password, social security number, birth date, and, of course, credit card numbers. The brokers can sell the data to fraudsters who can exploit it in a variety of ways. In the case of credit card numbers, the data is sold to "carders" who may purchase gift cards or high dollar items that can be easily resold. More complicated frauds can involve using the data to hack bank accounts and then transfer funds to other accounts opened in the victim's name.

Due to the multiple parties and the time involved, the time between exploitation to victimization can take six months. This six-month time delay should be appreciated. When possible, hackers will naturally steal credentials including user name and password. Because many of us are creatures of habit, we often use the same password for multiple accounts. However, if individual computer users change their passwords every 90 days, this would minimize account takeovers associated with stolen passwords. This concept should be incorporated into company policy so that system administrators require all users to change their password every 90 days.

Business E-mail Compromise

Business e-mail compromise (BEC) is a sophisticated fraud often targeting businesses that work with foreign suppliers or that frequently perform wire transfers. The fraudsters, who are often part of foreign organized crime groups, compromise their victims through a social engineering technique, causing an employee to conduct a transfer of funds, or the company's e-mail system is compromised through intrusion techniques.[9]

BEC fraud is wreaking havoc on businesses worldwide. The FBI estimates that between October of 2013 and December of 2016 there were actual or attempted losses of $5.3 billion. I can assure you that once a company has suffered from this type of fraud, the impact will have management's full attention. I encourage you to devote your attention to this fraud now, so that you can prevent it. When working with organizations on fraud prevention, I devote a considerable amount of time to BEC fraud. The real focus is on the social engineering threat due to the potentially catastrophic consequences involved.

The FBI has spent considerable efforts to educate businesses, financial institutions, and the public. In one of its public service announcements, the FBI described the following five scenarios involving BEC fraud:[10]

Scenario 1: Business Working with a Foreign Supplier

A business that typically has a long-standing relationship with a supplier is requested to wire funds for an invoice payment to an alternate, fraudulent account. The request may be made via telephone, facsimile, or e-mail. If an e-mail is received, the subject will spoof the e-mail request so that it appears to be a legitimate request. Likewise, requests made via facsimile or a telephone call will closely mimic a legitimate request. This scenario has been referred to as the "Bogus Invoice Scheme," "Supplier Swindle," and "Invoice Modification Scheme."

Scenario 2: Business Executive Receiving or Initiating a Request for a Wire Transfer

The e-mail accounts of high-level business executives (Chief Financial Officer, Chief Technology Officer, etc.) are compromised. The account may be spoofed or hacked. A request for a wire transfer from the compromised account is made to a second employee within the company who is typically responsible for processing these requests. In some instances, a request for a wire transfer from the compromised account is sent directly to the financial institution with instructions to urgently send funds to bank "X" for reason "Y." This particular scenario has been referred to as "CEO Fraud," "Business Executive Scam," "Masquerading," and "Financial Industry Wire Fraud."

Scenario 3: Business Contacts Receiving Fraudulent Correspondence through Compromised E-mail

In this example, an employee of a business has his or her personal e-mail hacked. This personal e-mail may be used for both personal and business communications. Requests for invoice payments to fraudster-controlled bank accounts are sent from this employee's personal e-mail to multiple vendors who have been identified from the employee's contact list. The business may not become aware of the fraudulent requests until that business is contacted by a vendor to follow up on the status of an invoice payment.

Scenario 4: Business Executive and Attorney Impersonation

Victims report being contacted by fraudsters who typically identify themselves as lawyers or representatives of law firms and claim to be handling confidential or time-sensitive matters. This contact may be made via either phone or e-mail. Victims may be pressured by the fraudster to act quickly or secretly in handling the transfer of funds. This type of BEC scam may occur at the end of the business day or work week and may be timed to coincide with the close of business of international financial institutions.

Scenario 5: Data Theft

Fraudulent requests are sent utilizing a business executive's compromised e-mail. The entities in the business organization who are responsible for W-2s or maintaining PII, such as the human resources department, bookkeeping, or the auditing section, have frequently been identified as the targeted recipients of the fraudulent request for W-2 and/or PII. Some of these incidents are isolated, and some occur prior to a fraudulent wire transfer request. Victims report that they have fallen for this new BEC scenario even if they were able to successfully identify and avoid the traditional BEC scam. This data theft scenario of the BEC scam first appeared just prior to the 2016 tax season.

The best way to prevent BEC fraud is to educate all employees who are involved in any process that an organization uses to make payments, especially wire transfers. Since these frequently occur through social engineering schemes involving phishing e-mails, a heightened state of awareness in the employees must be prevalent. This must be done through routine training of employees throughout the organization. The FBI recommends the following methods to avoid becoming a victim:[11]

- Internally verify the approving official by talking face-to-face or over the phone.

- Create intrusion detection system rules, flagging e-mails with extensions that are similar to those of the company's e-mail. For example, legitimate e-mail of abc_company.com would flag fraudulent e-mails of abc-company.com. Note the minor difference.

- Create an e-mail rule to flag e-mail communications in which the "reply" e-mail address is different from the "from" e-mail address shown.

- Color code virtual correspondence so that e-mails from employees' internal accounts are one color and e-mails from nonemployees' external accounts are another color.

- Verify changes in a vendor's payment location by adding an additional two-factor authentication such as having secondary sign-off by company personnel.

- Confirm requests for transfers of funds by using phone verification as part of a two-factor authentication; use previously known numbers, not the numbers provided in the e-mail request.

- Carefully scrutinize all e-mail requests for transfer of funds to determine if the requests are out of the ordinary.

Never assume prevention will stop all frauds. So, what should you do if you are a victim of a BEC? First, understand how the fraud works. With this type of fraud, there is a fair chance the fraudster resides in an Eastern European country. The e-mail that the fraudster used will commonly provide wire instructions to a bank in Hong Kong or China. From there, the funds may travel through another bank before being withdrawn by the fraudster. What is most frustrating is that due to bank privacy laws, foreign banks will not readily cooperate with U.S. law enforcement. In practice, a victim has about 24–72 hours to notify his or her bank and law enforcement that a BEC fraud is in progress. This fraud is so prevalent that banks, the FBI, and FinCEN have protocols to assist victims. The key is for a victim to contact the right officials if the fraud is discovered in the early hours after a fraudulent wire transfer has occurred.

A fraud akin to BEC involves keylogger malware. A user's computer can become infected with a keylogger as a result of social engineering. As the name suggests, the software can track each one of your keystrokes, giving a hacker access to your username and password when you are logging onto key websites like financial institutions. Armed with the victim's identifiers, the hacker turned fraudster can establish other accounts in the victim's name and drain the accounts.

Ransomware

In March of 2018, my hometown of Atlanta, Georgia, became the victim of a ransomware attack that was estimated to cost the city $17 million.[12] This estimate included neither the city's secondary costs associated with a shutdown of 424 software programs, 30 percent of which were deemed mission-critical, nor any of the costs associated with inconvenienced citizens who interact with the city on a daily basis.[13] The city's attorney said that her office lost 71 of 77 computers as well as a decade's worth of legal documents.[14] The City of

Atlanta was hit with the pernicious SamSam[15] malware, in which the attackers asked for a ransom of approximately $52,000 worth of Bitcoin, and the city said it did not pay the ransom.[16]

Ransomware works by an attacker introducing malware into a victim's computer, encrypting data, and then extorting money, usually in the form of a cryptocurrency like Bitcoin, to obtain the digital key to decrypt the data. The most common introduction of the malware to a victim's computer or network is by attackers tricking users to disclose a password, download a virus-laden attachment, or click on a link to a malicious website.[17] In other words, attackers are using social engineering techniques. The problem is so well recognized that a federal interagency working group, including the FBI and 13 other agencies, have produced guidelines for dealing with ransomware, *How to Protect Your Network from Ransomware.*[18] The guidelines also state that 4,000 ransomware attacks were occurring daily in 2016. Be mindful that these are just attacks, and only a small portion of them were successful.

As demonstrated from the city of Atlanta case, the losses associated with ransomware can be difficult to calculate precisely. The costs associated with consultants, security experts, and attorneys can be quite high, and the costs related to the reputation of organization can eclipse all of those. In fact, in the larger scheme of things, the amount of the ransom demanded can actually be quite small compared to the actual amount of damage done. The larger losses are associated with the erosion of trust and impact on the organization's reputation.

This brings us to the next question: Should ransomware attackers be paid? Law enforcement officials do not encourage paying a ransom to these criminal actors.[19] The rationale for not paying is that it only encourages more attacks. Of course, this admonition may be easier to understand than follow when an attack actually occurs to your organization. Stakeholders will have to consider a cost-benefit analysis, including the fact that the attackers may not provide the decryption key after the ransom is paid. Aggregating factors may be present in industries like health care where patient care may be a factor.

Hospitals and other health care providers can be particularly vulnerable when they have legacy medical equipment attached to their systems and patches and updates are not available. In fact, Hollywood Presbyterian Medical Center paid a $17,000 ransom to a hacker in an attack that prevented the hospital from sharing communications electronically.[20]

The effects of a ransomware attack on an organization can be debilitating, and all organizations should take steps to mitigate this threat. In this regard, the FBI details best practices for minimizing and mitigating this threat. The biggest takeaway is to continually have a data backup in a safe environment, and redundancy of this process is just as important. If all else fails, the computer or network can be reconfigured, and the organization's data will have been protected throughout the attack. The FBI recommends the following safeguards for dealing with ransomware:[21]

- Make sure employees are aware of ransomware and of their critical role in protecting the organization's data.

- Patch operating system, software, and firmware on digital devices (which may be made easier through a centralized patch management system).

- Ensure that antivirus and antimalware solutions are set to automatically update and conduct regular scans.

- Manage the use of privileged accounts—no users should be assigned administrative access unless absolutely needed, and only use administrator accounts when necessary.

- Configure access controls, including file, directory, and network share permissions appropriately. If users only need read-only information, they do not need write-access to those files or directories.

- Disable macro scripts from office files transmitted via e-mail.

- Implement software restriction policies or other controls to prevent programs from executing from common ransomware locations (e.g., temporary folders supporting popular Internet browsers, compression/decompression programs).

- Back up data regularly and verify the integrity of those backups regularly.
- Secure backups. Make sure backups are not connected to the computers and networks that they are backing up.

Federal Criminal Statutes

The primary federal statute used to prosecute cybercrimes was initially passed by Congress as part of the Comprehensive Crime Control Act of 1984. That Act was significantly enhanced by the Computer Fraud and Abuse Act of 1986 and has been modified several times. The law is codified at 18 U.S.C. 1030. This statute generally prohibits accessing a protected computer without authorization or exceeding authorization to engage in certain prohibited conduct. The statute has both criminal and civil provisions, and it covers any protected computer. The definition of a protected computer is broad and includes any device connected to the Internet, including a cell phone.[22] This statute can be used to prosecute many of the offenses described in this chapter including fraud-related cybercrimes. More specifically, 18 U.S.C. 1030 outlaws the conduct described in the chart below.

Criminal Conduct Under 18 U.S.C. 1030	
Computer Espionage; Obtaining National Security Information	1030(a)(1)
Obtaining Information; Trespass; Hacking	1030(a)(2)
Trespassing in a Government Computer	1030(a)(3)
Accessing a Computer to Commit Fraud	1030(a)(4)
Distribution of Malicious Code	1030(a)(5)
Trafficking in Passwords	1030(a)(6)
Extortion Involving Computers	1030(a)(7)

Congress has also passed statutes that specifically deal with identity theft including 18 U.S.C. 1028 and 18 U.S.C. 1028A. These statutes cover a variety of identity theft scenarios, including network intrusions like the Equifax hack that compromised 143 million U.S. consumer identities. Section 1028A, known as the "Aggravated Identity Theft statute," requires that a federal judge sentence a defendant to a two-year mandatory minimum sentence that runs consecutively with any other count of conviction. Defendants get a bonus time-out for identity theft—good stuff for those of us who don't like their identity to be stolen.

CHAPTER 9

Money Laundering and Tax Fraud

"The Panama Papers expose the internal operations of one of the world's leading firms in incorporation of offshore entities, Panama-headquartered Mossack Fonseca. The 2.6 terabyte trove of data at the core of this investigation contains nearly 40 years of records, and includes information about more than 210,000 companies in 21 offshore jurisdictions."

—INTERNATIONAL CONSORTIUM OF INVESTIGATIVE JOURNALISTS[1]

Money laundering is the process of concealing the origin of assets that one controls. By this definition, money laundering is not inherently illegal. Lawful reasons may exist for disguising the origins and extent of one's wealth. High-net-worth individuals are at risk for their personal safety, loved ones being kidnapped, and being victims of various frauds. Other individuals may want to make their wealth difficult for judgment creditors to pursue. Citizens fleeing corrupt regimes may need to launder their wealth in an attempt to prevent confiscation. Although legitimate reasons for laundering money exist—and you should be highly suspect when you hear them—that is not the subject of this chapter. This chapter is about the process of making dirty money appear clean—hence the term "money laundering." This discussion is also a logical place to address tax frauds, since many money-laundering schemes are orchestrated so that the bad actor will not have to pay tax on the proceeds of illegal activity.

Whether it is covered in a mystery novel or on the big screen, money laundering is often one of those enigmatic, murky, and shadowy concepts that always seems to involve attorneys, accountants, and a Swiss banker but is never really adequately explained. Because money laundering is a process, and therefore inherently intangible and conceptual, it is naturally the subject of some amount of intrigue. Money laundering will be explained from three perspectives: theoretical, regulatory, and criminal.

Money Laundering Theory

Money laundering starts with proceeds from a specific source, which for a variety of reasons the launderer wants to obfuscate (e.g., hide the money trail). While we often think of the proceeds starting from a criminal offense, as we will see, this is not always the case. Money laundering takes place in three distinct stages: placement, layering, and integration. Throughout this discussion, consider the challenges that money launderers, including drug dealers, fraudsters, tax cheats, and terrorists, face when moving money through these three phases.

Placement

The placement of funds into a financial institution is the first stage of money laundering, and for many money launderers, this is the most difficult. The challenge is particularly difficult for drug dealers because they usually deal in currency. The large drug cartels become a victim of their own success when they try to move their billions in drug proceeds back to Latin America. Their problem is the massive amount of cash, which can include one-, five-, ten- and twenty-dollar bills. Placing this cash into a financial institution undetected has proven to be a challenge, particularly since countries like the United States and Canada require the bank to file a report with the government for all cash deposits in excess of $10,000.

To avoid their deposits being reported to the government, launderers will use a technique known as "smurfing." Smurfing is a spoof on the cartoon characters the Smurfs. Smurfs, also known as "mules," are individuals recruited to open bank accounts and deposit cash in amounts less than $10,000. When money launderers are moving millions of dollars, this can be a time-consuming proposition. Also, due to the regulatory framework discussed below, financial institutions are required to detect this type of suspicious financial activity. To avoid the risk of detection, money launderers often purchase businesses that deal in cash, like restaurants, bars, laundromats, or night clubs and comingle their illegal proceeds with the funds of the business. Another placement technique is to bulk smuggle the cash to a country with favorable bank secrecy and privacy laws, where the cash can be deposited into the financial system. For fraudsters, the placement of funds is less of a hurdle because the proceeds of fraud usually originate in the financial system.

Layering

Once the proceeds have been placed in a financial institution, the next stage is layering transactions by moving the proceeds through various banks or financial transactions. The extent of the layering and the sophistication of the process is only limited by the creativity of the launderer. Law firms specializing in creating offshore accounts can be used to set up shell companies or even shell banks. The bank secrecy and privacy laws of some jurisdictions allow the money-laundering industry to flourish. The more layering there is, the more difficult it is for law enforcement to do its job.

When a prosecutor or a civil litigant wants to obtain corporate or financial records in a foreign jurisdiction, various legal procedures must be followed. In the case of a transnational criminal matter, a prosecutor can use a Mutual Legal Assistance Treaty (MLAT) if both the prosecutor's country of origin and the subject's country of origin have entered into an MLAT. In civil matters or criminal matters for which there is no MLAT in place, a more archaic form of legal process, known as "letters rogatory" (letters of request) are used to facilitate communications between the courts of the two countries. Letters rogatory are slower and more cumbersome than MLATs. Due to the time delay pursuing either an MLAT or letters rogatory, an astute money launderer could move funds through a number of foreign jurisdictions, effectively preventing law enforcement from tracing the money within the statute of limitations of the underlying criminal offense. To deal with this issue, Congress provided the DOJ with a tool that allows prosecutors to extend the statute of limitations up to three years while investigating money-laundering offenses.[2]

In conjunction with an effective layering scheme, a launderer may also want to layer corporate entities in the names of various nominees. Here again, law firms can assist with creating legal entities and can use the names of employees on staff at the law firm to serve as officers and directors. In order to be in compliance with the jurisdiction in which they incorporate, the law firm may have to properly identify the client. However, law firms that are either lax or are churning out too many shell entities to conduct due diligence may not be in compliance with local laws or may even be lied to by their client as to the true owners of the corporate entities.

As a manager of the forfeiture team in the Houston Division and later the Atlanta Division of the FBI, I spent a considerable amount of time tracking the proceeds of federal crimes for the purpose of seizing the assets. Despite all of the experience I gained in investigating the tradecraft of professional money launderers, I learned more about money laundering from the Panama Papers leak that was published in May of 2016 and the Paradise Papers leak that was published in November of 2017.

The Panama Papers is the name given to the leak of decades worth of client files from the Panamanian law firm Mossack Fonseca. The leaker, who has only been identified as "John Doe," provided 2.6 terabytes of data to a German newspaper that collaborated with the International Consortium of Investigative Journalists (ICIJ).[3] During a year of secrecy, the ICIJ worked with more than 100 media partners worldwide to mine the data.[4] The ICIJ discovered that the law firm's records contained more than 214,000 offshore companies connected to people in more than 200 countries and territories.[5] The data is available on the Internet at www.icij.org for everyone around the world to continue to investigate. The Panama Papers continue to expose the offshore holdings of world political leaders, provide links to global scandals, and detail the hidden financial dealings of fraudsters, drug traffickers, billionaires, celebrities, and sports stars.

One of the many interesting finds in the Panama Papers is that Russian President Vladimir Putin's very close friend since the 1970s, Sergey Roldugin, controlled offshore accounts.[6] Roldugin had a role in introducing Putin to his future wife, and he is also the godfather of Putin's oldest daughter.[7] Roldugin is a world-class cellist and became the director of the St. Petersburg State Rimsky-Korsakov Conservatoire and Artistic Director of the St. Petersburg House of Music.[8] More significantly, Roldugin is the owner of three offshore companies found in the Panama Papers. These companies controlled significant interests in Russia's largest truck maker and Russia's largest television advertising buyer.[9] One of Roldugin's companies was assigned the rights to a $200 million loan for $1.[10] Do you think that it is possible Roldugin is a nominee for Putin?

In 2017, the files of the Bermudian law firm Appleby were leaked in what has become known as the "Paradise Papers." The ICIJ again took the lead in investigating this matter and collaborated with more than 380 journalists.[11] The Paradise Papers leak contains more than 13.4 million files from a combination of offshore service providers and the company registries from 19 jurisdictions.[12] The Paradise Papers leak contains information about more U.S. citizens than the Panama papers, estimated to be at least 31,000 U.S. citizens.[13] The U.S. authorities, including regulators and law enforcement personnel, mined this treasure trove of information for enforcement actions.[14] All of this information is also publicly available on the ICIJ's website.

As a result of the Panama Papers and Paradise Papers leaks, more is known about hiding wealth, obfuscating corporate ownership, tax evasion, and money laundering than ever before. At a minimum, more is known about the techniques, the makeup of the individuals who engage in this activity, legal structures, and which countries are being used to facilitate the process. The leaks demonstrate how law firms assisted clients in layering transactions and forming legal entities in nominee names in an effort to hide the beneficial ownership of companies that control bank accounts and other assets.

Integration

The last stage of money laundering is moving the proceeds into an account that appears to be for a legitimate purpose. The launderer has now accomplished one of several potential goals, like hiding the source of the wealth or keeping tax authorities and prosecutors at bay. Here again, the integration process is only limited by the creativity of the launderer. Funds can be moved into the "clean" bank account with bogus explanations such as a consulting fee, loan, dividend, or proceeds of the sale of an asset. In more sophisticated schemes involving international financial accounts, the last step is likely a wire transfer to a U.S. bank from an overseas shell company's bank account.

Reverse Money Laundering

Money laundering is generally considered to be the process of taking criminally derived funds and making them clean. However, sometimes bad actors have legally derived funds that they do not want to be associated with their dirty acts. In this scenario, the source of the funds still needs to be hidden. Examples can include a large bribe to a foreign official, terrorism financing, and tax evasion. Under U.S. law, the act of obfuscating the source of the funds to commit an illegal act may not actually be illegal unless the funds move into or out of the United States.[15] Nevertheless, the laundering process is the same since it accomplishes a similar goal of hiding the source of the funds.

Regulatory Aspects of Money Laundering

The world community has been relatively slow to adopt anti-money-laundering laws and regulations. As with most illegal activities plaguing the world, countries do not act until the United States leads. When it comes to anti-money-laundering laws, the United States was slow to enact laws to prevent and prosecute money laundering. The first significant legislation in the United States was the Currency and Foreign Transaction Reporting Act, more commonly known as the Bank Secrecy Act of 1970 (BSA). The name— Bank Secrecy Act—is a serious misnomer because it does nothing to promote secrecy. In fact, the BSA mandates financial institutions to report customer information to the U.S. government. One of the more significant requirements is that financial institutions must file currency transaction reports (CTRs). The BSA was met with resistance by banks due to increased costs of reporting and by individuals on privacy grounds, arguing that the government was searching their private bank records.

The BSA was enacted to prevent and detect money laundering. This was accomplished in large part by requiring financial institutions to keep certain transactional records, thereby creating a paper trail for investigators. However, banks were slow to adopt appropriate procedures, and the regulators and law enforcement were slow to make effective use of the information when they received it. By the 1990s, the banks were likely in compliance and filing CTRs, but law enforcement, especially the FBI, was not making effective use of the information. This was due in part because the BSA required information to be filed with the Department of the Treasury, which had jurisdictional squabbles with the Department of Justice about timely sharing of information. Further, the process had not been fully automated. For example, when I was a bank fraud supervisor in Houston, I might receive a couple of hundred BSA filings each month. The names on those paper documents had to be manually checked against an FBI database to see if there were hits against active cases. A year could easily pass from the time a bank customer engaged in a suspicious activity and I had enough actionable intelligence to use in an active case or to open a new investigation. The keeper of the BSA information is the Financial Crimes Enforcement Network (FinCEN), a bureau of the Department of the Treasury. Things have dramatically changed in the last decade. I am now happy to observe that FinCEN and the FBI share information in a timely manner. A customer can make a suspicious deposit in a bank, and the FBI case agent with an active investigation involving that customer will be automatically notified of the Suspicious Activity Report (SAR).

The next major anti-money-laundering legislation was the Money Laundering Control Act of 1986. Below is a discussion of the creative lengths that Congress went to when it criminalized money laundering. This federal statute criminalized money laundering in the United States for the first time. Since that time, the majority of states have followed suit and have enacted anti-money-laundering laws.

In 1989, an international intergovernmental organization established the Financial Action Task Force (FATF). FATF is a standards-setting organization that promotes measures for combating money laundering and terrorist financing. FATF is a helpful resource for reporting the latest in money-laundering trends and identifying countries that are at high risk. It should come as no surprise that FATF has identified the Democratic People's Republic of Korea and Iran as the highest risk countries for both money laundering and terrorism financing due to their failure to adopt international standards.

In 2001, the USA Patriot Act was signed into law. Title III of this act, International Money Laundering Abatement and Financial Anti-Terrorism Act of 2001, is a broad statute designed to enhance the prevention, detection, and prosecution of money laundering. The Act strengthens rules for banks that are engaged in international business. Banks are required to identify foreigners who gain beneficial ownership of a U.S. account or use a payable-through account to gain access to the U.S. banking system. The Act also prohibits shell banks with no physical presence in any country from using correspondent banking services to gain access to the U.S. banking system. The Act requires financial institutions to implement anti-money-laundering programs, as discussed below. Lastly, the Act enhances law enforcement's access to bank records in money-laundering investigations. Virtually all fraud investigations are money-laundering investigations. Accordingly, the FBI can conduct nationwide queries of financial institutions to search for accounts in most fraud cases.

Criminals often use offshore accounts to hide money because they offer greater privacy, less regulation, and reduced taxation. To address the substantial tax evasion by many of America's wealthy, Congress passed the Foreign Account Tax Compliance Act (FATCA) that became law in March of 2010. FATCA addresses taxpayer noncompliance by focusing on both individuals and foreign financial institutions. FATCA requires certain U.S. taxpayers holding foreign assets to report information on IRS Form 8938. FATCA also requires foreign financial institutions to report directly to the IRS certain financial account information held by U.S. taxpayers. The objective of FATCA is to increase U.S. taxpayer compliance through transparency.

Banking Terms Relating to Money Laundering

The terms below are used in banking and by those professionals who create complex legal structures to move and secure money in various jurisdictions. The terms are also helpful for discussing money laundering.

Bearer Shares: A bearer share is an equity or stock security owned by whoever possesses the stock certificate. The owner is not listed in any official registry, and this enables the owner to hide his or her ownership when dealing with third parties.

Correspondent Bank: A bank that serves as an agent by providing services on behalf of another financial institution (respondent bank). Correspondent banks can provide service transactions that originate from a respondent bank in a foreign country.

Respondent Bank: A bank using the services of another bank (correspondent bank). Respondent banks can be in foreign countries and use U.S. banks to assist in providing services to its customers through the use of a payable-through account.

Nested Services: Nested services are provided to foreign customers having accounts at a third-party foreign bank in order to gain access to the U.S. financial system because their bank has a relationship with a foreign respondent bank that uses a U.S. correspondent bank for services. See the diagram below. Foreign customers using nested services are considered a high risk for money laundering due to the challenges that the U.S. correspondent bank faces in conducting due diligence on the third-party customer.

International Banking Relationships & Nested Services

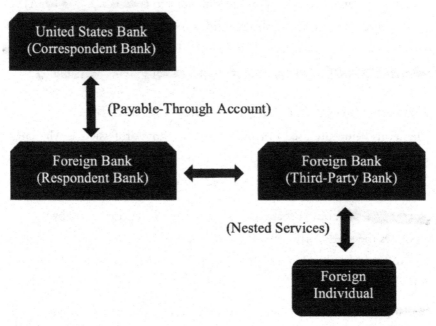

Payable-Through Account: An account in which a U.S. bank grants check-writing privileges to customers of a foreign bank through a correspondent–respondent banking relationship.

Shell Bank: A bank that does not have a physical presence in any country but does hold a license in the country of origin. The USA Patriot Act generally prohibits a U.S. correspondent bank from providing services to a foreign shell bank.

Shell Company: A company legally formed in the country of origin but without a physical presence, employees, or products. The company may be used to conceal the ownership of assets or facilitate tax evasion and/or money laundering but generally does not function for a legitimate purpose. Shell companies are often formed by professional money launderers.

Trust: A three-party contract in which the *trustor* funds the trust with assets for the *trustee* to manage on behalf of a *beneficiary*. The legal owner of the assets is the trust. The existence of a trust does not have to be disclosed to a regulatory authority to be valid.

Offshore Trust: A trust formed in a country other than the country of origin of the true beneficiaries. A few countries, including Cook Islands, Nevis, and Belize, offer very strong asset protection through a trust. In those countries where the law permits, a trustee may refuse an order from a foreign court to turn over funds. Depending on local law, the trust's assets may be subject to favorable tax treatment.

Regulatory Compliance

Since its enactment in 1970, the Bank Secrecy Act has been amended several times, resulting in various regulatory filing requirements to document transactions by those engaging in currency transactions. These requirements, along with certain provisions of the Internal Revenue Code, are a major part of the government's anti-money-laundering and tax compliance efforts. The BSA requires financial institutions to keep certain records of cash purchases of negotiable instruments, file reports of cash transactions exceeding $10,000, and file suspicious activity reports when money laundering, tax evasion, or other criminal activities is suspected. The BSA's definition of "financial institution" applies to 25 different entities that handle financial transactions, including traditional banks as well as pawnbrokers, travel agencies, insurance companies, phone companies, and other organizations.[16] Other reporting requirements are required by the IRS for U.S. persons in conjunction with their annual tax returns.

As part of the U.S. government's anti-money-laundering and tax compliance efforts, the following forms are required to be filed with either the FinCEN or the IRS.

BSA Forms

Currency Transaction Report: A CTR Form 112 must be filed electronically with FinCEN by a financial institution for any deposit or withdrawal of currency greater than $10,000. Multiple currency transactions totaling more than $10,000 during any one business day are treated as a single transaction.

Suspicious Activity Report: A SAR Form 111 must be filed electronically with FinCEN by a financial institution for suspicious activity. Reporting thresholds may vary by the type of financial institution. For banks, suspicious activity must be reported for any insider abuse; criminal violations of $5,000 or more when the suspect is known; criminal violations of $25,000 or more regardless of a potential suspect; and any transaction of $5,000 or more for money laundering, evading the BSA, or any transaction that has no apparent lawful purpose. SARs are commonly filed when a customer makes multiple deposits below $10,000 over a period of days in an apparent attempt to evade a CTR requirement. SARs are also filed when a customer attempts a currency transaction of more than $10,000, learns a CTR will be filed, and then declines to continue with the transaction. The filing threshold for a money service business is $2,000.

Report of Foreign Bank and Financial Accounts: An FBAR (foreign bank account report) Form 114 must be filed by a U.S. person if that person has a financial interest in or signature authority over at least one financial account located outside the United States and the aggregate value of all foreign financial accounts exceeds $10,000 at any time during a calendar year. Form 114 must be filed electronically with FinCEN no later than April 15 of each year.

Report of International Transportation of Currency or Monetary Instruments: A CMIR (currency and monetary instrument report) Form 105 must be filed for each person who physically transports, mails, or ships currency or monetary instruments in an aggregate amount exceeding $10,000 at one time either into or out of the United States. Travelers carrying currency or a monetary instrument must file this form at the time of entry or departure from the United States. Shippers or recipients of currency or monetary instruments have other due dates for filing the form.

Registration of Money Services Business: A money service business must register with the FinCEN by completing Form 107 and is subject to the BSA regulatory framework. The record-keeping provisions of the BSA create a paper trail that regulators and law enforcement can follow.

IRS Forms

IRS Form 8300: IRS Form 8300 must be filed by any person in a trade or business who receives more than $10,000 in cash in a single transaction or related transactions within one year. The report must be filed within 15 days after the receipt of cash. The customer paid in cash must be notified by January 31 of the following year.

Form 1040, Schedule B: Schedule B is part of the annual tax return for individuals and asks a question that each taxpayer must check with a yes or no answer: "In the prior year, did you have a financial interest in or signature authority over a financial account (such as a bank account, securities account or brokerage account) located in a foreign country?"

Foreign Account Tax Compliance Act, Form 8938: Form 8938 must be filed by U.S. residents who have assets in foreign countries if certain thresholds are met. The threshold is $50,000 in foreign assets held at the end of the year or $75,000 held at any time during the year. These thresholds are doubled for married individuals. Taxpayers living abroad have different thresholds.

AML/BSA Compliance Program for Financial Institutions

A financial institution is required by the USA Patriot Act to establish anti-money-laundering programs, which have become known as the "five pillars of an AML/BSA compliance program." These rules require financial institutions to:

1. Develop a system of internal controls to ensure ongoing compliance.

2. Designate a BSA compliance officer or individual who will be responsible for compliance.

3. Independently test the BSA/AML compliance.

4. Train appropriate personnel.

5. Develop risk-based procedures for conducting ongoing customer due diligence.

The customer due diligence (CDD) step is based on "know your customer" (KYC) rules. Effective May of 2018, this rule has been enhanced to require banks to obtain the identities of the beneficial owners behind legal entities. A beneficial ownership is ownership by anyone who directly or indirectly owns 25 percent of the legal entity(ies) that created the account. This requirement had been proposed for a period of years but was finally implemented after the Panama Papers story broke. Prior to this rule, a legal entity could conduct business with a U.S. bank without disclosing the beneficial owners.

Civil Discovery

While the purposes of the BSA and IRS regulations are to curtail money laundering and tax evasion, an understanding of this framework can also be helpful to civil litigants. I am suspect of attorneys and accountants who promote schemes to wealthy clients to transfer their assets to overseas financial accounts for the purpose of making their clients "judgment proof" if they are sued. The taxpayer may also be inclined to falsify tax returns by answering "no" to the foreign bank account question on IRS Form 1040, Schedule B, which is a felony. During litigation, opposing counsel can ask for the tax returns, including Schedule B, Form 8938, and any FBAR that was filed. These forms will yield another round of discovery, and opposing counsel will ask for the documents surrounding any undisclosed assets, financial accounts, or asset protection trusts. Opposing counsel may ultimately be able to obtain post-judgment relief through an order to repatriate the foreign assets back into the United States under threat of imprisonment for contempt. The bottom line is that if the client is truthful during the discovery process and was truthful when filing the tax returns, all of the expense of hiding assets overseas may not make the client judgment proof at all. For those who are determined to keep their funds offshore, the law in some jurisdictions potentially allows the foreign trustee to take control of the assets and not honor a foreign court order.

Criminal Aspects of Money Laundering

The earlier discussions addressed the theoretical underpinnings for money laundering and how U.S. authorities have set up a regulatory framework to assist with the prevention, detection, and investigation of both money laundering and tax evasion. Now, let's review the various money-laundering schemes and how U.S. law enforcement agencies prosecute them. Money launderers are adapting to new technologies like cryptocurrencies and prepaid access cards. The schemes vary depending on whether currency is involved, as is often the case for drug offenses. Certain techniques are used by the money launderer who wants to purchase assets with the proceeds of the dirty funds in a bank account. Other techniques are used by the tax evader who starts with clean funds but wants to hide them from taxing authorities like the IRS.

The Schemes

Money launderers user various schemes to launder their proceeds. Some of the more common schemes are as follows:

Shell Companies and Trusts: An effective way to launder money is to move the funds through a series of countries with strong bank secrecy and customer privacy laws using shell companies with bank accounts. The funds can then be placed in a shell company, a trust or a foundation used to purchase assets internationally. An offshore trust may enable the trustee to refuse an order from a foreign court. All of this can be managed by a foreign attorney, adding another layer of protection through the attorney–client privilege if applicable in the foreign country.

The example in the diagram below demonstrates a complex movement of funds used to purchase assets. The movement of funds accomplishes several objectives, including making it expensive and time-consuming for any investigator to follow. The funds are commonly deposited into a trust or a foundation, likely controlled by a law firm. The structure of the trust may prevent disclosure of the beneficial owners, and the terms of the trust may prevent the transfer of funds to a beneficiary when under court-ordered duress. In this context, court-ordered duress can mean providing the funds to a judgment creditor or a spouse in the United States. Although the court-ordered duress language may not always be upheld, the legal and investigative expenses in getting a defendant to this posture may be cost prohibitive. This process effectively hides both the source of the funds and the ownership of the assets.

Complex Money Laundering Scheme

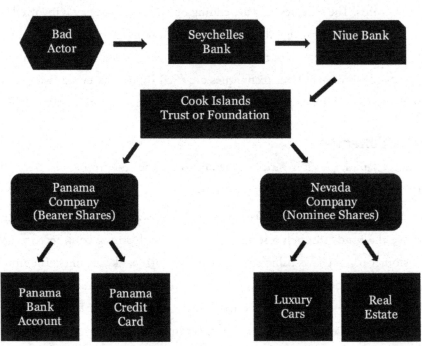

Front Businesses: A front business is a common solution for criminals who are generating a large amount of cash and cannot effectively use structuring or smurfing techniques to get funds into a financial institution. The money launderer purchases a cash-intensive business and commingles the illegally obtained cash with the legitimate funds of the business. As noted earlier, common "facade" businesses are restaurants, bars, laundromats, and nightclubs. The owner may choose to account for the illegal cash as revenue and pay taxes. Alternatively, the owner may keep the revenue off the books and just pass the funds through the business's bank account. The latter choice puts the company at risk with the IRS, and either choice can be revealed with effective forensic accounting techniques.

Cryptocurrency: Cryptocurrency is a decentralized digital currency using cryptography to secure transactions and allows for payments to be made anywhere in the world. The technology used is referred to as blockchain. A popular digital currency is Bitcoin. Although Bitcoin provides a lot of anonymity, the transactions are maintained in a public ledger for anyone to see and can be followed from one digital wallet to the next. However, the owners of the digital wallets themselves are anonymous. Although difficult, methods are available that enable investigators to determine the identity of the holder of a cryptocurrency wallet. A *Wall Street Journal* article published an account of Denver-based Shapeshift AG, which facilitated the movement of proceeds of the WannaCry ransomware attack from Bitcoin into an untraceable cryptocurrency called Monero.[17] Since this was done in the United States, the transaction was governed by the BSA requiring money service businesses to keep records of the transactions. This type of cryptocurrency-to-cryptocurrency movement of funds will become more common and will take place in foreign jurisdictions that do not regulate the practice.

Structuring: Cash under $10,000 is deposited into a financial institution in an attempt to evade the CTR filing requirement and is also known as smurfing. For example, a drug dealer has $100,000 in currency derived from criminal proceeds. The cash is broken into 12 separate deposits over a period of days.

Bulk Cash Smuggling: Transporting large amounts of currency to a foreign country for deposit. This is commonly done by creating a hidden compartment in an automobile, which can be driven through a country's border. More sophisticated schemes may involve private airplanes used to cross international borders.

Banks: Possibly the easiest way to launder money is to work with corrupt insider(s) at a bank who are willing to engage in money laundering as coconspirators. HSBC Holdings Plc is a British bank with a presence in the United States. HSBC paid $1.9 billion to the United States to settle money-laundering-related charges after it failed to file SARs, failed to conduct due diligence with correspondent accounts, and allowed the bank to launder the proceeds of various criminal offenses.[18] The bank's money-laundering operations included $881 million involving drug proceeds, $660 million involving movement of funds to U.S. sanctioned countries as well as a failure to monitor $670 billion in wire transfers, and $9.4 billion in purchases of physical dollars from its Mexico Unit.[19] While the HSBC scandal was unusual due to its size, laundering money through banks is nothing new. United States regulators and criminal authorities scrutinize large banks. Privately owned small banks in rural communities are also at a high risk for money laundering because they are less frequently scrutinized by regulators.

Black Market Peso Exchange (BMPE): The BMPE involves a process in which Latin American drug cartels use U.S. trade-based businesses to launder currency and is commonly known as the "black market peso exchange." I witnessed this practice firsthand when I was supervising the execution of warrants for seizure of assets. In Houston, FBI seizures included cocaine and the conveyances transporting the drugs north. In Atlanta, the seizures involved cash and the conveyances transporting the cash south. A problem that the drug cartels have is getting their cash back to Latin America, usually Columbia. One of the techniques used to solve this problem is the black market peso exchange. Drugs are smuggled into the United States through Mexico and other means. After the drugs are sold on U.S. streets, the cash is deposited into a U.S. business that sells products to Latin America. The business will purchase any commodity that is in demand in Latin American (e.g. textiles). These goods are then shipped south of the U.S. boarder and sold for pesos. The black market peso exchange solves the problem of transporting billions of dollars of cash across the U.S. border.

Hawala: The ancient form of transferring something of value from one person to another across great distances originated in the Middle East and is known as a "hawala." The person who manages the process is known as a "hawaladar." For example, a Pakistani taxi driver in the United States can send earnings home to family members in Pakistan by dropping off cash at a local Pakistani business and then notifying the family members with a text message—less a commission—that the money is ready to be picked up in Pakistan. The benefit of this process is that neither of the two Pakistanis actually needs a bank account to move money internationally. This example involves a hawaladar in the United States and a hawaladar in Pakistan. The two hawaladars work in concert with each other in assisting their customers in sending money between various countries for a fee. The process is not illegal if the hawaladar registers the business as a money service business with both the state government and FinCEN. Once registered, the hawala is governed by the BSA's requirements to maintain records and file CTRs, SARs, and other forms. Of course, this defeats the purpose of using a hawala. Operating an unlicensed hawala is illegal but is nevertheless commonly used in the United States to move funds to the Middle East.

Credit Cards: Once funds are successfully laundered into a foreign bank account, a credit card can be issued and used in any country. Online banking services allow the credit card monthly balance to be paid with funds from a laundered account. Another method of moving funds is to prepay the credit card and then transfer the card to another individual.

Prepaid Access Cards: Technology allows for money to be stored on prepaid cards sold by vendors. These cards are commonly used as gift cards but can be used for any purpose, and most are accepted by vendors that accept traditional credit cards. Using smurfing techniques, large amounts of currency can be converted to prepaid cards.

Federal Criminal Statutes

The world community was late in the game to criminalize money laundering. The United States led the way in 1986 when it first criminalized money laundering. If you were Congress, how would you fashion a statute to criminalize money laundering? Congress enacted two statutes to accomplish this, 18 U.S.C. 1956 and 18 U.S.C. 1957. United States law does not directly attempt to criminalize any of the three underpinnings of the theoretical aspects of money laundering: placement, layering, and integration. Rather, the criminal offense of money laundering is simply whatever the applicable statute says it is.

Sections 1956 and 1957 generally require that the property involved be the proceeds of what the statutes define as a specified unlawful activity (SUA). In actuality, almost every federal criminal offense is an SUA including those relating to drug trafficking and fraud. The general rule requiring property to be the proceeds of an SUA has one exception. As described below, when the matter involves international money laundering, the funds do not have to be the proceeds of any crime at all.

Section 1956 is the more complex of the two statutes, and it criminalizes four kinds of money laundering: promoting, concealing, structuring, and tax evasion. Section 1957 is often known as the "spending statute" and is conceptually easier to understand. This statute is likely violated when the money launderer moves more than $10,000 of the proceeds of an SUA through a financial institution. Since most frauds that come to the attention of a federal prosecutor likely involve the movement of funds greater than $10,000 through a bank, §1957 is the statute that will likely be used to prosecute a fraudster.

Most fraud prosecutions involve mail and wire fraud charges carrying a penalty of five years in prison. Money laundering, however, carries significantly higher criminal penalties, including 10 years (§1957) or 20 years (§1956) in prison. Again, it is very difficult for a fraudster not to commit money laundering because the fraudster invariably moves large sums of money through a financial institution before spending the proceeds. By the time the fraudster purchases a dream home, yacht, or airplane, the fraudster has triggered the money laundering statute. Given the increased penalties and prison time, when a prosecutor discloses that he or she may charge a defendant with money laundering, the astute defense attorney often counsels the client to begin plea bargain negotiations.

18 U.S.C. 1956—In General

Section 1956 criminalizes four types of money laundering: promotion, concealment, structuring, and tax evasion. Furthermore, one of these violations must be committed under any of three circumstances: (1) laundering involving certain financial transactions, (2) laundering involving international transfers, or (3) laundering proceeds from an undercover government agent in a "sting" operation.

Penalties for a violation of any of §1956's provisions include a maximum 20-year prison sentence and a $500,000 fine or twice the amount involved in the transaction, whichever is greater.

18 U.S.C. 1956(a)(1): Financial Transactions

Section 1956(a)(1) relating to financial transactions is relatively technical. The statute is violated by one who knows that property involved in a financial transaction represents the proceeds of some form of unlawful activity, conducts or attempts to conduct such a financial transaction that, in fact, involves the proceeds of a specified unlawful activity:

1. With the intent to promote the carrying on of specified unlawful activity; [1956(a)(1)(A)(i)]

2. With the intent to engage in tax evasion or tax fraud; [1956(a)(1)(A)(ii)]

3. Knowing the transaction was designed to conceal or disguise the nature, location, source, ownership, or control of proceeds of the specified unlawful activity; or [1956(a)(1)(B)(i)]

4. An attempt to avoid a transaction reporting requirement (e.g., CTR, CMIR, or Form 8300). [1956(a)(1)(B)(ii)].

This statute is complicated due to the many elements involved. The figure below can assist in determining if §1956(a)(1) is violated.

Laundering Involving Financial Transactions: 18 U.S.C. 1956(a)(1)

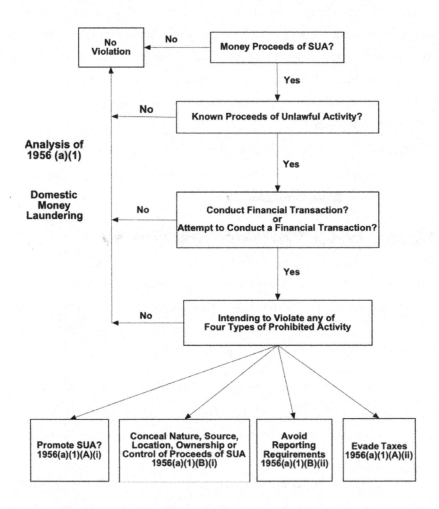

18 U.S.C. 1956(a)(2): International Money Laundering

Prosecutions pursuant to this provision arise when monetary instruments or funds are transported, transmitted, or transferred internationally and the defendant acts with one of three requisite criminal intents: promoting, concealing, or avoiding reporting requirements. In this regard, international money laundering has similar elements as §1956(a)(1) described immediately above. However, the international provision does not pertain to tax fraud or tax evasion.

Another distinction is the international money-laundering provision codified in §1956(a)(2)(A) is unique because it does not require the funds to be the proceeds of any SUA. Rather, the intent to promote any SUA is enough. For example, if a fraudster moved "clean" funds to a foreign bank account with the intent of paying a foreign official a bribe, the wire transfer from a bank within the United States to a bank outside the United States would be enough to violate the statute because the intent was to promote a violation of the Foreign Corrupt Practices Act. This is also an example of "reverse money laundering"—the use of clean funds for an unlawful purpose—which is criminalized under this provision but only when it involves the international movement of funds.

18 U.S.C. 1956(a)(3): "Sting" Provision

The money-laundering statutes are designed to prosecute a defendant who moved the proceeds of a crime for a specific purpose. When law enforcement uses an undercover agent or an informant in a "sting" operation to prosecute professional money launderers, the agent naturally provides government funds to the launderer for the purpose of following the money and documenting the crime. Since the funds are derived from the government and not the proceeds of an SUA, by definition, the movement of these funds cannot be money laundering. Under the sting provision, Congress fixed this technical issue by changing the element of the offense to be property *represented* by law enforcement acting in an undercover capacity to be the proceeds of an unlawful activity.

18 U.S.C. 1957: The Spending Statute

Section 1957 is known as the spending statute because it does not require other elements found in §1956 like promotion, concealment, structuring, or tax evasion. However, Congress replaced those elements with the requirement that the defendant must engage in a transaction that involves more than $10,000.

The elements of this statute are that a defendant must: (1) knowingly engage, or attempt to engage in a monetary transaction, (2) know the funds involved in the transaction are criminally derived, (3) use criminally derived funds in excess of $10,000 in the transaction, and (4) use funds derived from the specified unlawful activity. A monetary transaction is defined as a deposit, withdrawal, or transfer of funds by, through, or to a financial institution. The penalty for a violation of §1957 is a maximum prison sentence of 10 years and a maximum fine of $250,000 or twice the value of the transaction.

For example, in a bogus insurance company scam, the fraudsters may collect insurance premiums and cause them to be deposited into a Bohemian bank account. The fraudster may then want to spend the money on purchasing a home. When the fraudster causes $250,000 in proceeds to be wire transferred to an Atlanta closing attorney for the down payment on a new home, that single act of money laundering violates §1957.

AICPA AU-C Section 250

A CPA who stumbles on a money-laundering scheme can easily be presented with ethical and legal issues to resolve. Take the example of the black market peso exchange. A Colombian financier may purchase a textile business in the United States for the purpose of laundering money. The internal bookkeeper or external auditor may quickly realize that the business has been thrust into an international money-laundering operation. Should the CPA contact law enforcement authorities about what has been discovered? Accountants who are CPAs may be bound by state CPA–client privilege, where applicable, or ethics rules that require confidentiality.

The AICPA rule AU-C, Section 250 (corresponding to ISA 250 (Revised), "Consideration of Laws and Regulations in an Audit of Financial Statements," applies to an external auditor's responsibility to consider laws and regulations in an audit of financial statements. An auditor is required to assess if noncompliance with the laws and regulations has a material effect on the financial statements. If it does, the auditor must report up the management chain but not outside the organization. Of course, AU-C 250 applies to auditors of nonpublic companies. Further, federal securities laws that might require disclosure do not apply to nonpublic companies.

Depending on how the laundered proceeds are accounted for, the money-laundering operation may not make the financial statements misleading. Interestingly, if the proceeds are accounted for as revenue, net income and the tax liability will increase.

Professionals with a duty of confidentiality, such as a CPA, attorney, or doctor, can face ethical dilemmas when they learn of criminal acts. While the FBI will never encourage such a professional to breach this duty, I have dealt with these professionals when they simply came forward and provided information relating to criminal conduct despite confidentiality rules. My impression was that those individuals believed that their moral duty was more important than adhering to a professional code.

Case Example

I supervised the FBI's forfeiture program in Houston and closely worked with drug squads in seizing assets related to conveyances, real estate, and financial accounts. I dealt with one case that was particularly disturbing. The FBI learned from a wiretap that an 18-wheeler was heading north to Houston and was loaded with cocaine. The local police made a stop of the truck, found the drugs, and arrested the Colombian driver. This poor mule, who knew what he was hauling, was beside himself. I soon learned that his

Colombian bosses had kept his child as collateral should the load of cocaine not arrive intact at its destination. Of course, I personally felt very sorry for this man, as he was in some sense another victim caught up in the war on drugs. As requested by the driver, I wrote a letter and provided it to his attorney, detailing the seizure of the truck and drugs. The purpose of the letter was to serve as a receipt, showing that the drugs were seized by law enforcement and were not stolen by the driver. I never learned if the child was returned to the driver's family. The driver was convicted of drug trafficking and was given a lengthy prison sentence.

Tax Fraud

A significant category of fraud pertains to those who engage in tax evasion either through evasion of assessment or evasion of payment. Much of the U.S. collection of taxes is based on voluntary compliance. What is the U.S. compliance rate for paying taxes? An IRS study during the time period 2008–2010 found that the tax compliance rate for U.S. taxpayers was 81.7 percent.[20] In my opinion, this is a troubling statistic, as it reflects a noncompliance rate of 18.3 percent.

The IRS's study also attempted to estimate the tax gap which is defined as the difference between the amount owed and the amount paid. The IRS estimates that the average tax gap for the years 2008–2010 was $458 billion a year.[21] The tax gap was $319 billion for individuals, $44 billion for corporations, $91 billion for employment tax, and $4 billion for estate and excise taxes.[22] This tax gap is composed of three components: $32 billion for *nonfiling*, $387 billion for *underreporting*, and $39 billion for *underpayment*. Although these numbers are difficult to estimate, they do clearly demonstrate that the largest category of tax fraud pertains to individuals and that their method of committing this fraud is through underreporting the taxes owed.

I think I share a minority view on this issue, but I am for aggressive tax enforcement. For those of us who pay our taxes correctly, we are subsidizing those who do not! When put in these terms, I sometimes get some agreement from the taxpaying public. The problem, however, is when law enforcement focuses on an individual personally. When that happens, all bets are off because no one likes aggressive enforcement if they are the ones being scrutinized.

Just like financial statement fraud, tax fraud can also be committed in an almost unlimited number of ways. The schemes used to do this, however, are completely the opposite of financial statement fraud. The goal of someone committing tax fraud is to lower his or her net income by underreporting revenue and overreporting expenses.

Federal Criminal Tax Statutes

In reality, the IRS often works in tandem with its sister agencies like the FBI and the Federal Drug Enforcement Administration. Accordingly, in complex investigations like the Enron case, the criminal charges likely result in mail, wire, securities, and tax charges.

Following are the criminal statutes that the IRS uses to enforce tax evasion:

26 U.S.C. 7201: Willfully attempting to evade or defeat any tax imposed by the Internal Revenue Code (IRC) or failure to pay such tax.

26 U.S.C. 7202: Willfully failing to collect or remit taxes.

26 U.S.C. 7203: Willfully failing to file a return, supply information, maintain records, or pay taxes.

26 U.S.C. 7206(1): Making a false declaration under penalty of perjury.

26 U.S.C. 7206(2): Aiding or assisting a taxpayer in filing a fraudulent or false return.

26 U.S.C. 7215: Failure to remit FICA and income taxes that have been withheld from employees' income and held in trust by the employer.

Case Example

Tax charges may have played a significant role in getting Enron CFO Andy Fastow to cooperate with the federal government. Due to the complexity of the Enron case, investigators needed someone to cooperate with them. In order to go after the kingpins, the government started with lower-level operatives and attempted to move up the chain of command. The strategy was to use the flip-and-roll technique to target Andy Fastow and the former CEOs Ken Lay and Jeff Skilling. Tactically, the government may have made an error in initially focusing on transactions related to several British bankers.[23] After being charged, the British defendants threw a monkey wrench into the process by fighting extradition, thereby slowing the government's investigation.

Inasmuch as Andy Fastow did not seem to be getting the message that the case against him was strengthening and therefore his cooperation would be extremely helpful, the government began focusing on his wife, Lea Fastow. Andy Fastow had formed numerous special-purpose entities (SPEs) to assist in masking the true extent of Enron's debt. Andy Fastow created various SPEs, some of which began with the three letters *LJM*—Lea, Jeffrey, Matthew—the first letters of his wife and two boy's names. Lea Fastow, who was also a Northwestern University Kellogg MBA like Andy Fastow, had also been an Enron employee from 1991 to 1997, holding the position of Director and Assistant Treasurer of Corporate Finance. In various Enron SPEs that Andy Fastow effectively controlled, Andy Fastow and

Lea Fastow caused payments to be made to Lea Fastow and their two sons. The indictment charging Lea Fastow alleged that she had conspired to defraud Enron shareholders, had laundered the proceeds of the fraud with the intent of filing false tax returns, and had filed false tax returns.[24] To conceal the payments from the IRS, the Fastows disguised the payments as gifts.[25] More specifically, the indictment charged Lea Fastow with 26 U.S.C 7206(1), making false declarations on her tax returns.[26] For the tax years 1997–2000, Lea Fastow had signed her tax returns, disclosing the amounts shown below, but she had failed to include in these amounts the fraudulent receipt of proceeds that she had received from Enron SPEs disguised as gifts:[27]

Year	Income Actually Claimed by the Fastows
1997	$1,287,543.00
1998	$2,183,850.00
1999	$9,129,602.00
2000	$48,583,318.00

In the end, both Andy and Lea Fastow pleaded guilty. I suspect prosecutors would have spared Lea Fastow from prosecution if her husband had cooperated in a timely manner. In the best interests of their children, the federal sentencing judge let Lea Fastow serve her one-year prison sentence first, followed by Andy Fastow serving his five-year sentence.

Investigating Tax Fraud

The IRS has the tremendously challenging task of correctly assessing whether taxpayer's returns are accurate, and this task is complicated by the diverse industries filing tax returns across the United States. Consider how diverse the business models and accounting practices are for industries involving farming, automobiles, trucking, insurance, and retail. To assist its personnel with audits and investigations, the IRS has developed the Audit Technique Guides that are available to its personnel and the public.[28] These guides are a rich source of information for any auditor, manager, or forensic accountant who needs to quickly get up to speed about business practices for an industry that includes the players involved, business jargon, internal controls, and accounting practices.

The IRS also provides an extensive manual, the *Internal Revenue Manual* (IRM), for its employees, including examiners, revenue agents, and special agents, and can be found at www.irs.gov/irm. As detailed in the IRM, the IRS uses two basic methods for reconstructing a taxpayer's income: the direct method and the indirect method. Both of these methods are used by the IRS in the enforcement of civil and criminal provisions.

Direct Method

The direct method of reconstructing income, also known as the "specific items method," is used when direct evidence of income exists. The IRS can compare the 1099s that it receives from third parties to a taxpayer's return to determine compliance. The IRS can also subpoena banks account records as direct evidence of tax evasion. Other direct methods include following the proceeds from the sale of real estate, an automobile, stock, or other assets. The direct method is easier to prove and is the preferred method of the IRS.

Indirect Method

The IRS enforces U.S. tax laws by using a variety of civil and criminal tools. The IRS uses its civil authorities to establish deficiencies and to initiate tax collection efforts. The IRS uses its criminal authorities to enforce the criminal statutes referenced earlier. In all of these enforcement proceedings, the IRS may also use what is known as the "indirect method to reconstruct income."

The IRS's authority to use the indirect method is found in 26 U.S.C. 446(b). Section 446 provides that taxable income shall be computed under the method of accounting that the taxpayer regularly uses for bookkeeping, but if no method is used, the IRS can use its own method. All of these methods discussed below have been widely litigated and accepted by the courts, and the IRS uses these methods in civil and criminal enforcement actions.

In the 1990s, the IRS began engaging more aggressively in lifestyle audits, also known as "financial status audit techniques." The IRS would learn of someone exhibiting an extravagant lifestyle that is not congruent with the income reported on the individual's tax return. The IRS would then audit this individual. The American public became frustrated and angry, and Congress responded with the Internal Revenue Service Restructuring Reform Act of 1998. That Act amended the tax code by adding 26 U.S.C. 7602(e), which prohibits the IRS from using financial status audit techniques to detect unreported income unless the IRS has a reasonable indication that there is a likelihood of such unreported income. For our purposes, the financial status audit techniques will be referred to as the "indirect method of computing income." The IRS is required to conduct some initial analysis before using the indirect method of computing income on either nonbusiness returns (individuals) or business returns. This requirement can also be interpreted to mean that the IRS cannot use a lifestyle audit unless it has adequate "predication." I will explore this term more fully in Chapter 11, but the idea is that investigations of any individual should not be initiated unless there are specific facts for doing so, and in this case, Congress statutorily placed this requirement on the IRS. While the threshold for using an indirect method is low, the IRS is still required to obtain a factual basis and to document it in its file.

When the IRS is exercising its civil authority to audit individuals, the IRM requires that the IRS review the tax return, conduct some basic analysis, and interview the taxpayer. An individual is considered a nonbusiness if the tax return does not include a schedule C (sole proprietorship) or schedule F (farming). In connection with this practice, IRS examiners use Form 4822, Statement of Annual Estimated Personal and Family Expenses, to estimate a taxpayer's personal expenses. For taxpayers engaged in a business, the IRS uses other factors to assess if an indirect method is warranted. The IRS will perform an analysis, interview the taxpayer, tour the business, evaluate internal controls, and conduct other procedures.

After these procedures are conducted for either individual or business tax-payers, if there are still indications of unreported income after these inquiries have been made, then an indirect method for computing income is authorized under §7602(e).[29] The IRS will consider the following factors in making a determination if using an indirect method is appropriate:[30]

1. A financial status analysis that cannot be balanced; that is, the tax-payer's known business and personal expenses exceed the reported income per the return, and nontaxable sources of funds have not been identified to explain the difference.

2. Irregularities in the taxpayer's books and weak internal controls.

3. Gross profit percentages change significantly from one year to another or are unusually high or low for that market segment or industry.

4. The taxpayer's bank accounts have unexplained items of deposit.

5. The taxpayer does not make regular deposits of income but uses cash instead.

6. A review of the taxpayer's prior and subsequent year returns show a significant increase in net worth that is not supported by the taxpayer's reported income.

7. There are no books and records. Examiners should determine whether books and/or records ever existed and whether books and records exist for the prior or subsequent years. If books and records have been destroyed, examiners should determine who destroyed them, why, and when.

8. No method of accounting has been regularly used by the taxpayer, or the method used does not clearly reflect income. See IRC 446(b).

At the initiation of any of the indirect methods, the taxpayer should be asked if the taxpayer is a "cash hoarder" or has accumulated cash-on-hand that is not otherwise accounted for in the taxpayer's books and records, tax returns, or bank statements. The purpose of asking the taxpayer this question is that the taxpayer may later claim that he or she kept cash in a safe or other location. In fact, immigrants of some countries do not trust financial institutions and may literally store cash in their mattresses. By asking this question at the beginning of the inquiry, the IRS will lock in the taxpayer's position and prevent the taxpayer from subsequently claiming that he or she is a cash hoarder.

Indirect methods of computing income used by the IRS include the source and application of funds method, the bank deposit method, and the net worth method. Any of these indirect methods can be used by the civil or criminal divisions of the IRS. Although these methods are used by the IRS, they can also be just as helpful to a forensic accountant working with legal counsel in marital or business divorce cases as well as various fraud cases.

Cash T Method

The Cash T method, also referred to as the "T-Account method," is an analysis of a taxpayer's source of income and expenses and is not actually an indirect method of reconstructing income. This method is really the first step in any tax examination and is used for the purpose of gaining an understanding of the taxpayer and whether any red flags immediately appear. At this stage of the IRS's inquiry, the provisions of §7602(e) relating to predication do not apply because the information obtained comes from the taxpayer's return, information in the file, and other information internal to the IRS. As the matter progresses, more information can be added to the Cash T analysis to gain a better picture of the taxpayer. Should the examination turn into a criminal matter, an IRS agent can take the basic Cash T method and fill in the blanks with information from bank accounts, informants, trash runs, and other sources of information.

Basic Cash T			
Gross Receipts		**Business Expenses**	
Schedule C	$200,000	Schedule C	$100,000
		Personal Living Expenses $150,000	
Total	$200,000	Total	$250,000
Potential Understatement of Taxable Income: $50,000			

Source and Application of Funds Method

The source and application of funds method (also known as the "expenditure method") is an indirect method of reconstructing income. This technique is appropriate when the taxpayer's cash does not appear to come from a bank account or when the taxpayer uses cash to pay business expenses. The source and application of funds method is an analysis of a taxpayer's cash flows. The technique compares all known applications of funds with all known sources of funds for the period. The sources of funds should only include the known and legal sources. Conversely, illegal sources (e.g., proceeds from drug trafficking) and unknown cash deposits should not be included as a source of funds. If the application of funds is greater than the sources of the funds, a taxpayer may be understating income on the tax return.

Source and Application of Fund

Sources of Funds		Funds Applied	
Decrease in cash on hand	$10,000	Increase in cash on hand	$20,000
Decrease in cash in bank	$10,000	Increase in cash in bank	$20,000
Decrease in securities	$10,000	Increase in note receivable	$20,000
Increase in note payable	$10,000	Increase in A/R	$20,000
Increase in depreciation	$10,000	Increase in inventory	$20,000
Tax exempt interest	$10,000	Increase in equipment	$20,000
Inheritance	$10,000	Increase in real estate	$20,000
		Increase in automobiles	$20,000
		Decrease in A/P	$20,000
		Decrease in mortgage liability	$20,000
		Personal living expenses	$100,000
Total Sources of Funds	**$70,000**	**Total Funds Applied**	**$300,000**

Total Application of Fund	**$300,000**
Total Sources of Funds	**-$70,000**
Adjusted gross income as corrected	**$230,000**
Less: Itemized deductions	**-$24,000**
Taxable income as corrected	**$206,000**
Taxable income on return	**- $50,000**
Potential understatement of taxable income	**$156,000**

Bank Deposit Method

The bank deposit method is an indirect method of reconstructing income that focuses on the taxpayer's gross receipts. This method is appropriate when most of the taxpayer's income is deposited into a bank account. Prime examples would include professionals who receive payments from customers through checks, credit cards, electronic transfers, or insurance payments.

Conceptually, this method compares the total deposits made into the bank account and the appropriate line on the tax return to assess if the taxpayer has declared all of the income. For this analysis to be accurate, several adjustments have to be made. The process is more complicated when the taxpayer has multiple accounts or has commingled personal and business expenses. Further, inter-account transfers or nontaxable items like a loan have to be factored into the analysis. Let us consider a dental practice as an example. If the dentist decides that she does not want to include the funds received from her credit card merchant account on her dental practice's tax return, this would quickly stand out in this type of analysis.

Net Worth Method

The net worth method is an indirect way of reconstructing income by focusing on the change of a taxpayer's net worth from one year to the next. While the source and application of the funds method focuses on expenditures, the net worth approach focuses on a taxpayer's balance sheet. This technique is appropriate if the taxpayer's net worth continues to increase each year but the reason for the increase cannot be readily explained by the income declared on the taxpayer's return. This method can only be deployed if there are adequate records to reconstruct the taxpayer's net worth. To use the net worth technique, the IRS must first calculate the net worth (assets minus liabilities) of the taxpayer at the beginning of year one. The IRS will then add nondeductible living expenses to the net worth calculation. This total amount is then compared to the net worth of the taxpayer at the end of year one. If the increase in net worth exceeds the income declared on the tax return, the taxpayer has potentially understated his or her income.

PART III:
The Fraud Life Cycle

CHAPTER 10

Fraud Prevention

*"Respect, Integrity, Communication, Excellence—Mr.
Hartman, I don't think we live up to those values"*

—COMMENTS OF FORMER EXECUTIVE ASSISTANT TO ENRON CEO
KEN LAY TO THE AUTHOR WHEN LEADING A SEARCH INTO LAY'S
OFFICE.

The FBI has historically done well at investigating all crimes, including the gangster era's Bonnie and Clyde, foreign spies of the 1950s, civil rights, organized crime, drugs, domestic and international terrorism, and white-collar crime. I am confident that the FBI is the best investigative agency in the world. A criminal act occurs, special agents investigate, and the suspect goes to jail—at least that is how it is supposed to be.

The events of September 11, 2001 ushered in a new challenge for law enforcement. Those orchestrated terrorist attacks demonstrated a failure by the intelligence community, including the FBI. The National Commission on Terrorist Attacks Upon the United States (9/11 Commission) clearly laid out that waiting for an incident to occur, investigating it, and then putting the bad guys in jail is unacceptable when it comes to counterterrorism. Further, the 9/11 Commission noted that clues of the terrorist plots were located within various components of the intelligence community, but the intelligence community had failed to effectively comprehend the overall threat picture. The 9/11 Commission also traced the antecedents of the intelligence community's communication failures: the left hand did not seem to know what the right hand was doing. For a variety of historical reasons, the intelligence community had failed to share vital information with each other, and these same shortcomings also occurred within the branches of the FBI. Because the intelligence was located in various silos, FBI executive management paradoxically observed, "We don't know what we know."

The FBI took the 9/11 Commission's findings to heart and started emphasizing prevention as a key goal in its mission. No longer was being good investigators enough; the FBI had to prevent the next terrorist attack. The bad guys only have to get it right one time; the FBI needs to get it right every time. One of the solutions for the FBI's failure to communicate internally was the creation of the Intelligence Branch. The Intelligence Branch serves as a conduit for the flow of all information through the various FBI components. In other words, the intelligence branch's mission is to connect the dots so that "we can know what we know."

The prevention mission was supposed to transcend all of the FBI's programs, from counterterrorism to white-collar crime and corruption. I don't think this last part of the strategy has been implemented effectively. I don't think the FBI allocates enough of its resources to take lessons learned from its investigations and share them outside the FBI with small and large businesses, not-for-profits, and especially governmental entities that are vulnerable to corruption.

Fraud Life Cycle

Since this chapter focuses on prevention, it is a logical place to introduce the fraud life cycle. The components of the fraud life cycle are prevention, detection, investigation, mitigation, and remediation.[1] These five components form an integrated approach to dealing with fraud. In fact, prevention and detection are closely correlated, and some of the same principles will help to address both of them. Prevention, however, is really a misnomer. In reality, we can never prevent all fraud from occurring in an organization. To attempt to do this would likely result in low employee morale as well as prohibitive costs. Although the correct term is really "deterrence," I will use "prevention" for the purposes of this chapter.

Control Environment

Establishing and managing the control environment is the responsibility of those in charge of governance. This includes establishing the tone from the top, creating policies to address fraud, and providing the resources and attention needed to execute the policies. Without the support of those in charge of governance, a fraud prevention strategy will not be effective. We generally think of those in charge of governance as making up the boards of public, private, and not-for-profit organizations. This, of course, leaves out government. Elected and appointed officials play a very important role in both preventing governmental entities from being defrauded as well as deterring employees from engaging in fraud and corruption.

The internal controls over financial reporting are clearly the responsibility of management. For publicly traded companies, SOX mandates this requirement through the PCAOB's implementing standards.[2] The AICPA has adopted similar standards for private companies.[3]

In this chapter, I will discuss best practices, policies, and procedures for preventing fraud. The effectiveness of these efforts will depend on the control environment. The control environment can be defined as a set of hard controls and soft controls that enable those in charge of governance to efficiently and effectively execute its objectives without the presence of fraud. If both controls are present and functioning, the control environment is strong. If there are deficiencies in either of these two controls, the control environment may be weak and therefore susceptible to waste, fraud, abuse, and corruption. If an organization suffers from systemic fraud or corruption, the root cause is likely to be that the *soft controls* are not present and functioning.

Definitions

An effective fraud prevention strategy will include the application of "hard controls" and "soft controls" defined as follows:

Hard Controls: Hard controls are the policies and procedures that guide employees through financial management, procurement, the handling of assets, and other functions for the purpose of providing management reasonable assurance that it is achieving its stated objectives. Examples include segregation of duties, reconciliations, and management authorizations and approvals. Hard controls can be measured by traditional audit procedures.

Soft Controls: Soft controls are intangible factors derived from an organization's culture or a department's subculture that guide employees through their decision-making processes. Key factors involve the strength of the organization's trust, competency, integrity, training, shared values, and culture. Soft controls can be measured by assessing the difference between the stated organizational values and the values actually practiced.

All organizations incur some fraud, as it is almost inevitable. However, properly implemented controls will minimize the opportunity for fraud to occur. Luckily, very few organizations endure systemic fraud, and more importantly, this type of fraud is preventable. In my experience, systemic fraud is the result of a toxic culture. In this context, culture equates to pressure and rationalization. Now consider how hard controls and soft controls can deter fraud.

Hard controls will minimize the opportunity for fraud to occur. For example, financial statement fraud can be minimized with strong controls around revenue recognition. Corruption can be impacted by awareness and mandatory conflict disclosures. Misappropriation of assets can be minimized through safeguarding assets, especially the checkbook and the P-Card. As previously discussed, there are a variety of ways to stop the opportunity for nonoccupational frauds like the business e-mail compromise and ransomware to occur. Hard controls go a long way in minimizing these frauds by simply stopping the opportunity for them to occur.

Soft controls minimize the pressures and rationalizations that confront employees. These controls work in reverse by creating a culture in which the employees simply do not want to commit fraud. They are extremely important in preventing systemic fraud or fraud that is pervasive throughout the organization. They are also very important for stopping corruption and conflicts of interest because hard controls are often not effective. Due to the importance of soft controls, I think it is best to elevate their prominence in the organization.

The key to minimizing the fraud risk in an organization is to negate at least one of the vertices of the Fraud Triangle: the "low-hanging fruit" here might be to curtail "opportunity," which is what most laws and regulations, such as SOX, seek to do. The control environment must also be evaluated at each level of management to include the board, executive management, middle-level management, and line employees. Effective hard controls mean that these controls are so strong that the *opportunity* for employees to commit a fraud is minimized. Effective soft controls mean that the culture of the organization is so robust that employees are unlikely to succumb to internal or external *pressures* or feel comfortable using *rationalization* as an alibi. Without the presence of *opportunity, pressure,* and/or *rationalization,* we have drastically lowered the risks for occupational fraud occurring in the organization.

Consider the Control Environment Assessment diagram below. On a scale of 1 to 10, with 10 being the best score, how would you rate your organization's soft controls? How would you rate your organization's hard controls? The challenge, of course, is to ensure that you have enough information to accurately answer these two questions, but the results will give you a calibration as to how vulnerable your organization is to fraud. Just as important, this information should be used as a baseline for future improvement.

Control Environment Assessment

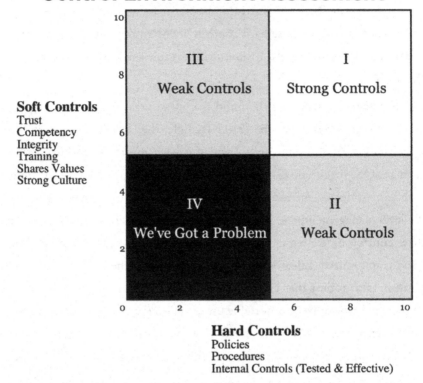

Soft Controls
Trust
Competency
Integrity
Training
Shares Values
Strong Culture

Hard Controls
Policies
Procedures
Internal Controls (Tested & Effective)

Fraud Risk Ownership

When an organization is undergoing an investigation because of a major fraud event, it often engages in a "circle the wagons" approach to crisis management. No one takes responsibility—not the board, not executive management, not internal audit, and not compliance. The list of those not taking responsibility is long. What I see is finger pointing, sometimes at the investigators. Uncovering fraud and assessing blame can be an occupational hazard. The motivations for this behavior are the fear of being blamed, fired, or more significantly, being named as a defendant in a civil or criminal matter. Of course, the fraudster(s) bears the ultimate blame, but those in charge of governance and others may have acted as enablers, only sometimes unwittingly, and thus may also be at fault. In fact, directors can be held personally liable for losses relating to fraud in their company when they have failed to establish a system of internal controls.[4]

For organizations that are serious about fraud prevention, the fraud risk must be owned. This is conceptually easy to do— just delegate it to someone. In actuality, it is much more difficult. When Walmart discovered a serious FCPA violation in its Mexico unit in 2011–2012 and its internal probe showed signs of such violations expanding to other parts of their global operations, such as Brazil, India, and China, Walmart promptly named an "FCPA Czar," someone who would be primarily responsible for looking into FCPA non-compliance matters.[5]

For the fraud risk to be owned, it must first be understood. The frauds described throughout this book can be placed into the following categories:

- Frauds Involving Privity of Trust
- Predatory Frauds
- Occupational Frauds: Financial Statement Fraud, Corruption, and Asset Misappropriation
- Nonoccupational Frauds

The distinctions among these frauds is important for fraud ownership. The three occupational frauds—Financial Statement Fraud, Corruption, and Asset Misappropriation—occur in different ways and often by employees working in different functions in the organization. The nonoccupational fraud list is lengthy, and each must be separately understood. When considering all of these frauds, the Fraud Triangle—opportunity, pressure, and rationalization—really only applies to those in privity of trust. Conversely, predatory fraudsters can only be prevented by stopping the opportunity for fraud to occur. Efforts to enhance the organization's culture by addressing pressure and rationalization will have little impact on predators because they may not even be employees in the organization.

Fraud Risk Categories

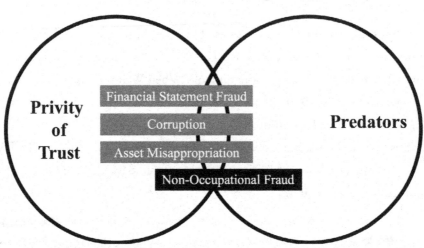

Consideration of the organization's fraud risk and trying to determine the likely type of fraudster who might commit fraud that would impact the organization is a lot to digest. Each fraud risk should be independently identified, and the corresponding hard and soft controls should be developed to minimize the specific risk. Who is going to own the fraud risk? I think it is best to place one person or department in charge of the fraud risk. For organizations in which it would make sense, that individual might be the chief risk officer (CRO). This individual would be responsible for understanding the fraud threat picture and developing controls to mitigate each potential risk to the organization. The organization might consider appointing a fraud risk committee made up of key stakeholders from various departments, which would be overseen by the CRO.

The diagram below illustrates the "Fraud Risk Ownership Model." The model assigns the *opportunity* risk to the CRO or to other management personnel, like legal, compliance, or security personnel. The model assigns executive management (C-suite) as a key stakeholder in ensuring that the soft controls around *pressure* and *rationalization* risks are robust.

Fraud Risk Ownership Model

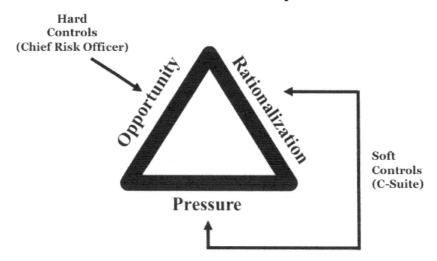

The hard controls are generally evaluated by the internal audit function. The soft controls can also be assessed by internal audit or other stakeholders, like human resources. The takeaway is that hard and soft controls are assigned to accountable professionals within the organization, and these controls are periodically evaluated, monitored, and tested for continued operational effectiveness.

Soft Controls

In January of 2001, I led a team of agents in a search for documentary evidence in the 50-story Enron building. During the search of Enron Chairman and CEO Ken Lay's office, I wanted to personally oversee the agents conducting the search. I was dealing with Lay extensively on the logistics of obtaining documents from his office, but he was also careful enough not to substantively discuss Enron with me. While I was standing in front of Lay's desk, I encountered his long-time executive assistant. Amazingly, she reached over and picked up a beautiful 4 x 4-inch beautiful glass cube that was sitting on Lay's desk. On four sides of the cube were Enron's core values, each of which was separately etched: Respect, Integrity, Communication, and Excellence. Slowly turning the cube to expose the words, she very deliberately read to me each of the four values. She then placed the cube down on Lay's desk, looked me in the eyes, and said with a sigh, "Mr. Hartman, I don't think we lived up to these values."

I found the entire conversation astonishing. Lay was walking in and out of the office during this period and could easily have heard his trusted assistant make those comments. At that time, Lay was the chairman of the board and CEO of Enron. Lay had just returned as CEO when then CEO Jeff Skilling unexpectedly resigned for "personal reasons." More significant, this was very early on in the investigation, and I was not aware of any substantial evidence that had been developed against Lay at that time. Lay was subsequently convicted on fraud charges but died while his criminal charges were under appeal. The irony of having Enron's core values displayed on the desk of the CEO of world's seventh-largest company while in excess of 125 FBI agents were swarming the building was not lost on me. I also knew that a long-time trusted assistant to an executive always knows "where the bodies are buried." I instinctively thought that she was telling me much more than that Enron was not living up to its stated values.

The tone for an organization starts at the top. Although much as been written about Enron's governance failures, a July 8, 2002 report by the U.S. Senate, which was issued after a lengthy investigation, succinctly describes the governance failure in one of its findings:

Finding (1): The Enron Board of Directors failed to safeguard Enron shareholders and contributed to the collapse of the seventh largest public company in the United States, by allowing Enron to engage in high-risk accounting, inappropriate conflict of interest transactions, extensive undisclosed off-the-books activities, and excessive executive compensation. The Board witnessed numerous indications of questionable practices by Enron management over several years, but chose to ignore them to the detriment of Enron shareholders, employees and business associates.[6]

Enron's governance failure is certainly one of the more prominent ones due to its size and economic impact, but unfortunately it is only one of countless such governance failures.

Seven Signs of Ethical Collapse

Professor, attorney, author, and thought leader Marianne Jennings has researched and written exhaustively on the topic of businesses that have suffered ethical collapses. In her book, *The Seven Signs of Ethical Collapse: How to Spot Moral Meltdowns in Companies Before . . . It's Too Late,*[7] she provides details and examples of the following seven signs:

1. Pressure to maintain the numbers

2. Fear and silence

3. Young 'uns and a bigger-than-life CEO

4. Weak board of directors

5. Conflicts of interest overlooked or unaddressed

6. Innovation like no other company

7. Goodness in some areas atones for evil in others

While these seven categories leap from the page as being problematic, I would encourage anyone interested in this subject matter to read Marianne Jennings's book for a comprehensive understanding. Her motivation in conducting this research was to share her findings with those in control of governance for the purpose of actually preventing future ethical failures.

Perception of Detection/Culture of Compliance

I think a carrot-and-stick approach is appropriate for developing a strong control environment. The stick represents the would-be-fraudster who will be caught and prosecuted; the carrot represents employees, who are encouraged to behave ethically and report any potential wrongdoing.

If the *perceived* control environment is strong, a potential fraudster will fear getting caught, and will not even attempt committing the fraud. In essence, we have the perception of detection.[8] Management can strengthen the control environment in a variety of ways. Routine audits serve a dual purpose of testing internal controls and discouraging fraudulent conduct. Appropriately communicating the disciplinary action that will be taken against employees who commit fraud creates a perception of detection. Walking an employee out the front door in handcuffs—the so-called "perp walk"—certainly sends a message. Having cameras in warehouses, even if they do not work, may discourage employee theft. The goal is for management to create an environment in which employees perceive that any inappropriate behavior will be detected and punished. The fraud equation shown below provides an explanation of how fraud can occur by those employees who do not have a healthy appreciation of being detected.

Desire > Fear = Fraud

Management's goal is to decrease desire and increase fear. The fear component is addressed through a perception of detection. How does an organization decrease the desire to commit fraud? Consider the fraud motivators discussed in Chapter 1: the internal and external pressures that employees face.

For internal pressures, we may have to go no further than the human resources department to find the solution. The employee may have been incentivized to make the numbers through a commission or a bonus compensation arrangement. Is the culture of the organization a win-at-all-costs environment? The external pressures including illness, divorce, bankruptcy, drugs, alcohol, gambling, and other life events. Here, an organization may have an employee assistance program to address the issue. Managers should be trained to be attuned to employees' personal issues and offer assistance to the extent that is practicable. Employees under pressure are less likely to defraud the organization that is trying to help them.

The carrot approach encourages ethical behavior through a culture of compliance. This approach is facilitated by executive management, which articulates and mirrors good ethical behavior. The intent is to create an environment where everyone is pulling for the same team and no one wants to see the organization harmed. All employees also understand it is their ethical duty to say something if they see something. Employees should feel comfortable approaching appropriate officials if they witness a red flag that fraud might be occurring. These officials should include their boss, legal counsel, compliance official, or internal auditor. An anonymous reporting system should exist, its presence should be well communicated, and management should appropriately follow through on any complaints received.

Training

Strong ethical cultures are not developed by chance. The values are deliberately created, modeled, communicated, and expected. The requirement for all employees to ethically conform is found in the code of ethics, is communicated during employee onboarding, and is repeated during routine training. When management conducts compliance, ethics, and antifraud training, the message is best provided in person by the managers who are responsible for their respective programs. The presenters should encourage all participants to report any violation of company policy. Presentation of this information in person by the managers who are responsible for their program will bear fruit later. When an employee does witness a potential red flag of fraud, the employee will feel much more comfortable reporting it to a manager whom the employee knows.

During training, senior management should be present to kick off the session, actively participate, and learn the details of the organization's compliance, ethics, and antifraud programs. Senior managers who are too busy to attend the mandatory training sessions unwittingly set a poor tone from the top of the organization. Although computer-based training is widely used in corporate America because it dramatically saves money, it is significantly less effective than a live presentation.

Measuring Soft Controls

To know if the control environment is functioning, management must measure it; that which is measured can be managed. The question is how does the organization's management reliably measure culture or know if it is effectively serving as a soft control? An effective way to quantify an organization's soft controls is to compare its stated values against the values found in practice.

The endeavor to measure culture must have a heartfelt acceptance by executive management for several reasons. Executive management controls the resources to conduct this effort and will be instrumental in instructing everyone in the organization to cooperate. For a large organization, the process must be adapted to account for differing subcultures across various divisions in the organization. When the results of a culture or climate survey are returned, executive management should be the most important consumer of the information. Regardless of the results, high-level findings should be shared with the organization as a whole for the purpose of improving the culture. The results should also be used as a baseline and repeated annually or biannually. Measuring soft controls can be done in a variety of ways:

- Hire a professionally qualified industrial psychologist to assist.
- Use the internal audit function to assess.
- Develop structured interviews.
- Conduct organization-wide surveys.
- Perform focus group interviews.
- Have a 360 review for each manager.

The final results should be aimed at giving executive management some key indicators of performance. How does the way things should be done vary from the way things are done? Are the tone at top, the mood in the middle, and the buzz at the bottom in cultural harmony?

Hard Controls

When hard controls are effectively designed and implemented, they lower the occurrence of fraud. These controls should be developed around known risks. To understand these risks, a risk assessment must be undertaken. Once risks are known, internal controls can be developed. These controls should include preventive controls, detective controls, and corrective controls. One type of preventive control is to ensure that all employees undergo an appropriate background check.

Fraud Risk Assessment

A fraud risk assessment is a study that is done to understand the unique and overall fraud risks that an organization faces. In a sense, it is an investigation in its own right. A good place to start is the last fraud risk assessment that was conducted in the organization. Also, what risks have similarly situated organizations identified? What risks have employees identified? Professional organizations like COSO (Committee of Sponsoring Organizations), IIA, AICPA, AGA (Association of Government Auditors), ISACA (Information Systems Audit and Control Association), and the ACFE are great resources. The assessment should also consider the likelihood of an event and the potential loss to the organization, including loss of reputation.

A key component to conducting a fraud risk assessment is brainstorming. What are the fraud risks the organization may encounter? A review of Part II of this book, "Fraud Threat Picture," is a great place to start. What is the fraud threat picture for the organization? In a nutshell, these include the occupational frauds: asset misappropriation, corruption, and financial statement fraud. The assessment should also address the risks from nonoccupational frauds and cybercrimes. The brainstorming can include a roundtable discussion with key stakeholders, the preferred method, or a fraud risk manager who visits each stakeholder for an in-depth discussion.

I enjoy doing fraud risk assessments for a variety of reasons. When a client asks me to assist in a fraud risk assessment, the organization is demonstrating that it is taking proactive measures to prevent fraud. What I do next is akin to an investigation. I simply ask as many employees as possible several key questions surrounding fraud risks, such as the following:

- What vulnerabilities do you see in the organization?
- If someone wanted to commit fraud, how would the person do it?
- What controls do you think should be put in place?
- If somebody saw something inappropriate, would the person report it?

Not all employees will engage in this type of game theory. I am always suspicious of those who refuse to engage. More often than not, the exercise can actually be fun, since the employees get to put on a sinister hat and think like a fraudster. I will get answers like, "Dick did that 10 years ago and was fired." "Jane did something similar, but management swept it under the rug." "We have recently implemented a new process, and now a vulnerability exists that management isn't aware of." "People are afraid to speak up because they know nothing will be done about it." A skilled interviewer can glean a lot of information by talking to employees. The line employees know where the internal control weaknesses are because they are functioning as the experts in the environment every day. More importantly, they will tell a skilled interviewer if the interviewer asks them.

On various occasions, I was engaged by general counsels for work that included what amounted to a risk assessment. I went through the interview exercise with company employees. I later reported my findings of all potential weaknesses in internal controls. The clients were truly shocked by what I told them. In reality, this process just involved asking the right people the right questions. I have spent an entire career working fraud matters. I am still nowhere near knowing all of the risks a specific organization might face, but the employees know!

The most challenging fraud risk to assess is the risk of management overriding controls. This can be a real dicey endeavor when the assessor has

250

identified this as a risk and begins asking sensitive questions of executive management. This type of a risk assessment is best done by an outside consultant. However, executive management is also just as likely to not allow a consultant to be used for fear of losing control of the assessment and its findings.

One of the benefits of leading numerous investigations over decades is that I have been at the center and have seen the facts. From this vantage point, I have seen the root causes of fraud. A common theme I have observed is the failure of an organization's internal departments to share information. Does this sound familiar? When sizable fraud or corruption happens in an organization, I eventually find the pieces of the puzzle. This is, of course, with the benefit of hindsight, after the fraud has been discovered, but I think a great deal can be learned from these experiences.

Consider this multifaceted example. An accounting technician may have seen signs that an executive manager has padded expense vouchers and has abused the company's P-Card. The IT (information technology) department may have signs that the executive has exceeded network privileges. The security department may have noticed that the executive has entered and exited the building entries at unusual times. The CFO sees a spike in revenue that is out of the ordinary. The HR department may have allegations of sexual harassment. The internal auditor receives an anonymous report on the company's hotline. The executive's personal life may have demonstrably changed through an enhanced lifestyle, and the executive could be going through a divorce. The executive's boss may also have noticed performance issues. All of these issues are noticed, but by different people. No one is connecting the dots. The company does not know what it knows.

The diagram below shows a high-level way of thinking about fraud across an organization. An organization's management can use it as a tool to assess where frauds might reside in the organization. The box is divided into four quadrants, each of which is discussed.

Thinking Outside the Box

We Know What We Know	We Know What We Don't Know
We Don't Know What What We Do Know	We Don't Know What We Don't Know

We Know What We Know: This quadrant represents known risks. The risks can be readily identified from institutional knowledge. Giving employees a P-Card with no controls is like employees having a petty cash fund in their wallet. We know this.

We Know What We Don't Know: This quadrant represents the risks that an organization is willing to take. Such an assessment also invites a discussion as to what the appropriate risk tolerance is for the organization. In essence, we know the risks but assess whether an internal control would be too expensive or cumbersome after considering the downside: the likelihood of a fraud occurrence and associated losses.

We Don't Know What We Do Know: This represents an organization that is so complex that information has been stovepiped into various divisions. The solution is to mandate continued communication among the various divisions. The creation of a fraud risk council can help connect the dots. Assigning the fraud risk to a specific person or division for tracking relevant data is a solution that is known as the "dashboard approach," in which one person or a committee looks at all of the relevant data.

We Don't Know What We Don't Know: The primary purpose of a fraud risk assessment is to discover unknown risks. Here, management knows that it does not know the risks but is willing to go through a process to discover them.

Internal Controls: A Life Cycle Approach

Soft controls and hard controls need to be interwoven into the control environment's fabric. Management should openly discuss the "f-word" with employees—fraud. Obtaining employee buy-in about ethical behavior enables an open discussion to take place on what is expected and why the organization needs to place internal controls around its processes. An organization can develop three types of controls that roughly mirror the fraud life cycle: preventive, detective, and corrective.

Preventive/Deterrent Controls: The goal is to prevent fraud from occurring. The mere presence of internal controls serves as a deterrence to someone attempting to commit fraud. Examples of preventive controls include:

- Background Checks
- Password Protection
- Segregation of Duties
- Approval Requirements
- Job Rotation
- Physical Security
- Network Access Controls
- Securing Assets
- Mandatory Vacations
- Positive Pay System
- Lockbox System
- Document Control Numbers
- Internal Controls Over Financial Reporting
- Drug Testing

Detective Controls: An organization cannot prevent all frauds. Accordingly, they need controls to assist in identifying frauds as or once they occur. The presence and awareness of these controls also doubles as a preventive measure, since a person generally will not attempt to commit fraud if the fear of getting caught exists. Examples of detective controls include

- Hotlines
- Cameras (Closed-circuit TVs)
- Counting Inventory
- Bank Reconciliation
- IT Log analysis
- Data Analysis

- Ratio Analysis
- Management Review
- Continuous Monitoring
- Written Confirmations
- Surprise Checks (e.g., Cash Counts)

Corrective Controls: After fraud has occurred, the organization must take steps to understand and correct the failure of the internal controls. Examples of corrective controls include:

- Training Personnel
- Data Backup
- Insurance
- Disciplinary Action

- Redesign Internal Controls
- Budget Variance Reporting
- Criminal or Civil Action

Background Checks

The best way to avoid having a fraudster in an organization is to not hire him or her in the first place. A background check can screen out known problem candidates. Also, management should be mindful that performing background checks will not prevent fraudsters from being hired. In fact, ACFE data shows that most fraudsters have no prior criminal history. However, background checks will screen known felons and candidates with red flags. Conducting appropriate due diligence before hiring a candidate for a job can save the employer from countless costs associated with hiring a candidate with malevolent intent. Legal counsel should be consulted before background checks are conducted, as federal and state laws govern background checks when organizations are hiring employees. The law may also require certain notifications to the employee, and it may limit the use of the information. If derogatory information is developed and used in the hiring decision, additional disclosures to the candidate may be required.[9]

A "background check" can be defined in many ways. A background check can encompass a quick check of some basic databases, or it can include a comprehensive makeup of the candidate. Background checks should be considered for existing suppliers, customers, and business partners. For candidates being considered for leadership positions or those involving access to financial information, a more comprehensive background checks need to be conducted, and they should also be done for personnel who have subsequently been promoted to those positions. A basic background check should include the following:

- Criminal Background Check
- Credit Check
- Prior Employment Verification
- Driving Record
- Educational Verification
- Licenses and Credential Verification
- Internet and Social Media Checks

For important hires, including those involving financial positions, using a skilled interviewer to check references is helpful. Many fraudsters move from job to job. When the employer learns that an employee has committed fraud, the employer may simply discharge the employee without bringing criminal charges. Gaining confidence, the fraudster then finds another employer to victimize. Diligent calls to prior employers may uncover this type of fraudster. When a previous employer is called, the company policy may be not to provide information on past employees. A call to the employee's prior boss and not the HR department may get around this issue. If the prior boss also says that the company policy is not to comment on past employees, here is an artful question that can be asked: "Would you rehire that employee?" The person asking the question may get an honest "no" answer or may get a very long, awkward pause, followed by, "I cannot answer that question." Either way, the answer is a red flag that the former employee is not welcome at the former employer's business. This answer is certainly grounds for further questioning of the candidate regarding the factors surrounding that employee's departure from the prior company. Should derogatory information be developed in a hiring decision, it may have to be disclosed to the candidate. Here again, the employer needs to seek the advice of counsel.

Fraud Control Policies, Guidance and Models

The good news for those of us who work in creating fraud-resistant organizations is that several professional organizations as well as the federal government have developed policies, guidance, and models that can be adapted and utilized by almost any organization.

Policies

An organization's policies should address a variety of issues. Policies may be found in the employee handbook, a code of conduct, ethics policy, conflicts of interest policy, and antifraud policy. The policies can stand alone, or they can be located in one comprehensive document. Where appropriate, the same policies should also apply to vendors, customers, and partners, and they should be posted on a company's website. An antifraud policy may be less known to some organizations. The ACFE's model "Anti-Fraud Policy" can be found in the Appendix of this book.

Guidance

Several key organizations continue to contribute to the fraud prevention literature, including ACFE, AICPA, IIA, CAQ (Center for Audit Quality), AGA, NACD (National Association of Corporate Directors), and COSO. Following are several helpful guides for managing fraud risks:

- *Managing the Business Risk of Fraud: A Practical Guide*, produced by The IIA, AICPA, and ACFE.[10]

- *The FRAUD Resistant Organization, Tools, Traits, and Techniques to Deter and Detect Financial Reporting Fraud*, produced by the CAQ, FEI (Financial Executives International), IIA, and NACD.[11]

COSO

The Committee of Sponsoring Organizations of the Treadway Commission (COSO) was formed in 1985 with the original purpose of better understanding the causal factors leading to financial statement fraud. In the intervening years, COSO has expanded its focus and now provides guidance on enterprise risk management, internal controls, and fraud deterrence. COSO is composed of the following sponsoring organizations:

1. American Accounting Association
2. American Institute of Certified Public Accountants
3. Financial Executives International
4. Institute of Management Accountants
5. The Institute of Internal Auditors

COSO is the world's leader in establishing an internal controls framework, having first adopted the original framework in 1992 and later revising it in 2013 (2013 COSO Framework). The iconic "COSO Cube" in the diagram below details the 2013 COSO Framework's three objectives on its top, the five components of internal control on its face, and the hierarchy of the organization on its side. A detailed explanation of the 2013 COSO Framework can be found on the coso.org website.

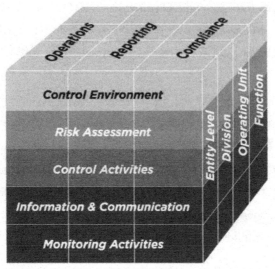

©2013, Committee of Sponsoring Organizations of the
Treadway Commission (COSO). Used by permission.

In 2016, COSO developed the *Fraud Risk Management Guide* (COSO Fraud Guide). This guide uses the five COSO control components and the 17 COSO principles found in the 2013 COSO Framework as a baseline for developing the COSO Fraud Guide. The COSO Fraud Guide details five fraud risk management principles:

1. The organization establishes and communicates a fraud risk management program that demonstrates the expectations of the board of directors and senior management and their commitment to high integrity control and ethical values regarding managing fraud risk.

2. The organization performs comprehensive fraud risk assessments to identify specific fraud schemes and risks, assess their likelihood and significance, evaluate existing fraud control activities, and implement actions to mitigate residual fraud risks.

3. The organization selects, develops, and deploys preventive and detective fraud control activities to mitigate the risk of fraud events occurring or not being detected in a timely manner.

4. The organization establishes a communication process to obtain information about potential fraud and deploys a coordinated

approach to investigation and corrective action in order to address fraud appropriately and in a timely manner.

5. The organization selects, develops, and performs ongoing evaluations to ascertain whether each of the five principles of fraud risk management is present and functioning, and communicates any deficiencies in its fraud risk management program in a timely manner to parties who are responsible for taking corrective action, including senior management and the board of directors.

Federal Sentencing Guidelines

Similarly situated criminal defendants should be sentenced for their crimes similarly—or so one would think. This is not the case in state courts, and it has not always been the case in federal courts. Congress passed the Sentencing Reform Act of 1984 for the purpose of establishing the United States Sentencing Commission (Commission) to set uniform guidelines for sentencing defendants to prison, payment of fines, and setting probation.

Like individuals, organizations can also be found guilty of crimes. An organization can be held criminally liable for the acts of an employee who was acting in the scope of his or her employment even if the employee acted contrary to company policy or instructions. Although organizations cannot be sentenced to prison, they can be punished by fines or ordered to make restitution.

As part of the sentencing guidelines framework, the Commission developed the *Federal Sentencing Guidelines for Organizations* (Guidelines), which became effective November 1, 1991. Due to the harshness of monetary fines that can accrue to an organization, the Guidelines allow for a mitigation of the fines *if* the organization has an effective compliance and ethics program. Accordingly, during sentencing the federal judge hears evidence of whether the defendant (organization) has a qualifying compliance and ethics program, and if the court finds that it does have one, the court's application of the Guidelines may substantially lower the fines that the organization has to pay.

Since these Guidelines were enacted in 1991, compliance and ethics programs have become more robust in corporate America. The Guidelines now provide a standard for an effective compliance and ethics program. In fact, they state that an organization must exercise due diligence to prevent and detect criminal conduct and otherwise promote an organizational culture that encourages ethical conduct and a commitment to compliance with the law.[12] The Guidelines describe how an organization can exercise due diligence and promote an ethical culture through a seven-component framework. This framework was designed to be general for the purpose of enabling implementation to diverse organizations throughout the United States.

Although the Guidelines are not mandatory, by adopting the Guidelines, an organization may significantly reduce a fine should it be found guilty of a criminal offense. Realistically, a prosecutor may also exercise discretion and not even charge an organization if the prosecutor is convinced that there was an effective program in place. A summary of the Guidelines' seven-component framework is as follows:[13]

1. The organization shall establish standards and procedures to prevent and detect criminal conduct.

2. The governing authority shall be knowledgeable about the compliance and ethics program and exercise reasonable oversight. Executive management shall oversee the program. A compliance official shall exercise the day-to-day operation and be given adequate resources and appropriate authority.

3. The organization shall use reasonable efforts to keep bad actors out of the management ranks through the exercise of due diligence.

4. Executive management shall take reasonable steps to communicate the compliance and ethics program's standards and procedures to its officers, employees, and as appropriate, its agents.

5. Executive management shall take reasonable steps to: (a) monitor and audit the program, (b) periodically evaluate its effectiveness, and

(c) provide an anonymous reporting mechanism whereby employees or agents will not fear retaliation.

6. Executive management shall promote and enforce the program through incentives as well as appropriate disciplinary measures for those who engage in criminal conduct or fail to take reasonable steps to prevent or detect criminal conduct.

7. Executive management shall take reasonable steps to respond to criminal conduct, which may include providing restitution, self-reporting, and cooperation with authorities, and prevent similar criminal conduct, including making any necessary modifications to the compliance and ethics program.

The Guidelines and the COSO Framework contain many similarities. An organization desiring to develop either an internal controls framework or a compliance program should consider integrating both of these models into their organization.

Risk Model

The Institute of Internal Auditors has written a position paper that provides a "Three Lines of Defense Model" to assist organizations in deploying risk and control procedures. The model can assist in managing many different risks, including fraud. Details pertaining to the Three Lines of Defense Model can be found on the IIA's website.[14] A graphic of the model is shown below. This is an important model for those who are responsible for the internal audit function.

The Three Lines of Defense Model

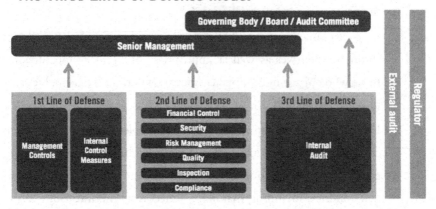

Adapted from ECIIA/FERMA *Guidance on the 8th EU Company Law Directive, article 41*

Prevention and detection are related concepts in the fight against fraud. Since all frauds cannot be prevented, the next chapter will apply some of these same concepts to fraud detection.

CHAPTER 11
Fraud Detection

"The Whistleblowers: Persons of the Year,
Cynthia Cooper of WorldCom, Coleen Rowley
of the FBI, and Sherron Watkins of Enron."

—COVER OF *TIME* MAGAZINE, JANUARY 2003

I n January of 2003, I was waiting in a grocery store checkout line when I noticed that *Time* magazine's "Person of the Year" edition had three women pictured on its cover. Upon closer inspection, I was shocked to realize that I had met each of those women. One woman was an FBI agent whom I had met at the FBI's annual legal conference at FBI Headquarters, and the other two women I had met at their corporate headquarters, Enron and WorldCom, respectively.

Less than two years had passed since Americans had been the victim of some of the worst calamities in modern times. We were attacked externally by foreign terrorists and internally by corporate chieftains. *Time* magazine was highlighting three women who spoke truth to power. WorldCom's internal auditor, Cynthia Cooper, reported to her board that the company's financial statements were bogus. FBI special-agent attorney for the Minneapolis Field Division, Coleen Rowley, wrote a letter to then FBI Director Robert Mueller detailing how antiterrorism agents' efforts in her field division had been stifled by FBI Headquarters' management such that it might have prevented critical information about the 9/11 attackers from being discovered before the attack. Enron's Vice President of Corporate Development, Sherron Watkins, prophetically wrote a letter to Enron's CEO Ken Lay detailing how she was "incredibly nervous that we will implode in a wave of accounting scandals."[1]

Those closest to the facts know the most about the facts. Although this statement is self-evident, it is the linchpin for detecting fraud. If employees are trained to spot the red flags of fraud and are empowered to report it, fraud will be greatly reduced.

I have always found the motivation of whistleblowers fascinating. This fascination has continued into my private practice, in which I now have whistleblowers as clients. In my experience, a whistleblower will initially attempt to report negative information to responsible parties inside the organization. From there, a variety of things can happen. The complaint may be lodged with the wrong official or never taken seriously. The whistleblower may report to a manager, who is either complicit or knowledgeable about the fraud, and the complaint is never elevated. When a complaint does make its way to an appropriate executive or the general counsel, feedback about the status of any internal investigation may not be provided to the whistleblower due to the sensitivity of the issue. When a whistleblower's complaint is mishandled, the whistleblower becomes increasingly disillusioned and fears no one will listen.

Another type of whistleblower can prove to be very frustrating for management. An employee may be under disciplinary action and fears being discharged. The employee may also be knowledgeable about a significant fraud and now fortuitously decides to complain. This a challenge for management because, although the company may have been able to rightfully terminate the employee, to do so at that point could result in the appearance of retaliation against the employee with the newfound grievance.

Regardless of their initial paths, whistleblowers have other options. Whistleblowers may give their complaint directly to a law enforcement agency or a regulator. Others will educate themselves by retaining legal counsel. Whistleblowers may learn that they qualify for a substantial reward under various government programs, including the *qui tam* provisions of the False

Claims Act. These whistleblowers are generally employees who follow the rules but become angered if they see management or others breaking the rules. An important lesson is that a whistleblower will likely report internally before reporting outside the organization. Generally speaking, whistleblowers will not reach out to an attorney or law enforcement agencies unless they have exhausted remedies inside their organization. Management that appreciates this proclivity will foster an environment of compliance in which employees feel comfortable bringing any red flag of fraud to an appropriate official's attention.

Even if employees do not report outside the organization, they may be recruited by law enforcement to provide information. In these cases, the FBI gives the cooperator the name "informant." Complicated white-collar crimes like financial statement fraud can take the government a long time to unravel. The FBI case agent may decide to utilize the historical investigative approach and reconstruct the fraud through a document review and by following the money. I have investigated many cases using this method, and I equate it to an archaeological dig. Sometimes there is a better way for investigators obtain the information they need. The key is to find someone in the organization who is close to the fraud and will cooperate. The crown jewel of investigative techniques is to develop an informant who will wear a wire and engage a potential defendant in an incriminating conversation. When done effectively, this technique can cut months or even years off the length of an investigation and greatly increase the chances of a guilty plea.

If a whistleblower or an informant is present, the organization's control environment has likely failed. First, a fraud is occurring. Second, an employee is seeking redress outside the organization.

All frauds cannot be prevented, and attempting to do so can be counter-productive due to the cost of implementation and diminished morale associated with a restricted work environment. Accordingly, we need organizations to enhance their detection mechanisms in order to catch frauds when they are in progress. The Association of Certified Fraud Examiners' 2018 *Report to the Nations* demonstrates the significance of tips when building a detection framework. Key facts from that report regarding fraud detection are shown below:

- Of all frauds, 40 percent were detected as a result of a tip.

- Employees accounted for 53 percent of all tips.

- For frauds detected as a result of a tip, the median duration was 18 months, with a media loss of $126,000.

- Corruption was detected as a result of a tip 50 percent of the time.

- The loss associated with frauds was 50 percent less at organizations with hotlines.

Below are two charts from the ACFE's 2018 *Report to the Nations* depicting who detects fraud and how it is done.

Who Detects Fraud?

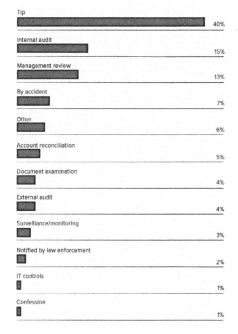

Tip
40%

Internal audit
15%

Management review
13%

By accident
7%

Other
6%

Account reconciliation
5%

Document examination
4%

External audit
4%

Surveillance/monitoring
3%

Notified by law enforcement
2%

IT controls
1%

Confession
1%

How is Fraud Detected?

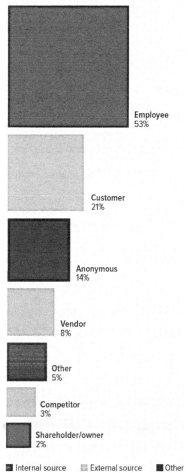

Employee
53%

Customer
21%

Anonymous
14%

Vendor
8%

Other
5%

Competitor
3%

Shareholder/owner
2%

■ Internal source　▨ External source　■ Other

Source: ACFE 2018 *Report to Nations*

Detection Framework

Management must first understand the red flags for fraud. This information should be incorporated into employee training for the purpose of expanding fraud awareness throughout the organization. Every employee needs to feel comfortable detecting and reporting fraud. So how does an organization detect fraud? There are two basic questions that will lead us to the answer:

- ▶ What can go wrong?
- ▶ What does it look like?

"What can go wrong?" was answered in Part II, "Fraud Threat Picture." Following is a short overview of that material:

- Asset Misappropriation
- Corruption and Conflicts of Interest
- Financial Statement Fraud
- Small Organization Fraud
- Nonoccupational Fraud
- Cyber Fraud
- Money Laundering and Tax Fraud

A fraud risk assessment will assist in identifying, "What can go wrong?" However, the "What does it look like?" question is more difficult. Other chapters have provided ideas for detecting specific frauds. Here, the focus is on common, broad-based, and cost-effective ways of detecting fraud. The most important of these is increasing the number of employee notifications (tips) by creating a culture of compliance. The ACFE's 2018 *Report to the Nations* shows that on average, 40 percent of frauds are detected as the result of a tip. For those organizations that are willing to focus on detection, the percentage of frauds detected as the result of tips could be increased substantially.

Behavioral Forensics

Behavioral forensics involves looking for both patterns of suspect behavior and changes in behavior, telltale signs that fraud could be at play. After assuming that an *opportunity* to commit fraud exists, the organization shifts its focus to *pressures* that its employees may face and the *rationalizations* they may use to justify inappropriate conduct. What does that look like?

Those who are likely to defraud their employer are likely under some type of pressure. In this context, "pressure" includes employer-based incentives. The fraudster may have also engaged in some form of rationalization. Now the organization is looking for those employees who may be under pressure and susceptible to rationalization. To do this, the organization needs to juxtapose the three branches of the Fraud Tree with the seven motivators of fraud discussed in Chapter 1.

Three Branches of the Fraud Tree	Seven Motivators of Fraud
• Asset Misappropriation	○ Business Need
• Corruption (Conflicts of Interest)	○ Ego (Pride and Shame)
• Financial Statement Fraud	○ Excitement
	○ Parity
	○ Social Compact of Reciprocity
	○ Slippery Slope
	○ Fear and Greed

Although any of these motivators can be the driving force behind any fraud, in my experience, each of the motivators will have a particular correlation with a branch of the Fraud Tree as shown below:

- **Asset Misappropriation**
  - ○ Parity
  - ○ Fear and Greed
- **Corruption (Conflicts of Interest)**
  - ○ Parity
  - ○ Social Compact of Reciprocity
- **Financial Statement Fraud**
  - ○ Business Need
  - ○ Ego (Pride and Shame)
  - ○ Excitement
  - ○ Slippery Slope

Understanding these relationships can help with both fraud prevention and detection. More specifically, the goal is to develop a fraud-resistant culture by addressing each of these fraud motivators.

Asset misappropriation is the most common form of fraud. The motivators for this type of fraud are also the most recognizable: fear and greed. Fear includes fear of getting fired, fear of missing a mortgage payment, or fear of not having the funds to feed an alcohol or gambling vice. Greed can cause common behavior like an excessive desire to enhance one's wardrobes, drive expensive cars, or take expensive vacations. The lack of Parity—the feeling of not being treated fairly—can also be used as an alibi for committing fraud. Detection includes an organization knowing its employees, periodically running background checks, including credit checks and bankruptcy filings.

Corruption and conflicts of interest are the most difficult to detect. This is an area in which coworkers are the most likely people to detect a problem. Does an employee make references to being affiliated with another business? Does an employee engage in unexpected secrecy when dealing with vendor contracts? Does an employee have too close a relationship with counterparties? Are the employees' conflicts of interest disclosure forms filed in a timely manner, and are they complete? Are these disclosures audited?

Financial statement fraud occurs with the least degree of frequency but can cause the most damage to an organization. What is the tone from the C-suite? WorldCom's CEO Bernie Ebbers had leveraged himself with debt collateralized by WorldCom stock in order to purchase numerous businesses. A declining value in WorldCom's stock was not an option for Ebbers. Has an executive's behavior or personality changed? Is there a general decline in the company's industry? Are there new and unrealistic sales goals for the company?

Frauds get more complicated when more than one bad actor is at play. Are there coconspirators in a business unit? Has the entire organization fallen prey to a corrupt business leader? For a detailed explanation of behavioral forensics and a discussion of organizational frauds, the *A.B.C.'s of Behavioral Forensics* is a must read.[2]

Dashboard Approach

Fraud prevention and detection share a lot in common. In Chapter 10, I discussed the fraud risk assessment as a key tool in preventing fraud. After an organization knows the fraud risks, it then needs to begin accumulating data that can detect a fraud in progress. I call this process the "dashboard approach." Under this approach, a corporate official such as the chief risk officer is assigned the fraud risk for the organization. This official is now responsible for obtaining the necessary data to be able to assess the fraud threat picture and look for red flags of fraud across the organization. For some organizations, the creation of a fraud risk council can be helpful.

Data can be aggregated. This information is then analyzed for the purpose of identifying the fraud and the fraudster. Software products can be used to gather and track this type of data. The techniques used to collect data may be produced by different stakeholders across the organization, but all of the information can be put into the dashboard system for earlier fraud detection.

Analytical Procedures

A robust internal audit function is important for both preventing and detecting fraud. The mere fact that financial processes are audited is a significant deterrent. The ACFE's *2018 Report to the Nations* shows that 15 percent of all frauds are caught by the internal audit function.

Continuous monitoring is a process that tests all or substantially all transactions at or near the time of occurrence. If the transaction meets a predetermined criterion, an event notification is logged. There are risks with false positives and false negatives. Continuous monitoring can also be expensive to establish on the front end. Consider P-Card fraud as an example, since most organizations face this risk. Continuous P-Card monitoring analyzes all the relevant data at or near the time any P-Card is used to make a purchase. This data includes dollar amounts, vendor names, merchant category codes, products or services purchased, dates of purchase, and other criteria. For example, a P-Card monitoring system can catch a machine operator who is authorized only to purchase diesel fuel but has purchased gasoline or has made the purchase on a holiday or a weekend. Continuous monitoring of a P-Card will flag a supply clerk that makes a jewelry purchase. The system can also be designed to catch split purchases if two or more department employees used P-Cards to get around a purchasing threshold.

If bank account funds are suspected of being misapplied, the long-lost art of the proof-of-cash technique can be applied for any period in question. This technique validates whether the company's records accurately reflect the bank deposits, withdrawals, and transfers made. For a detailed explanation of the technique, four forensic experts have written an article on the subject, *The Proof of Cash Should be King Among Forensic Auditing Techniques*.[3]

Benford's Law

Benford's Law of expected frequencies, or "Benford's Law," was named for physicist Frank Benford. This law posits that in any naturally occurring data sets, the first digit of any number is most likely a 1, and then a 2, and then a 3, and so on through 9. The exact percentages are shown in the table below. The rule also holds true for the second digit of a number in question, but then becomes of little use with the third digit.

Benford's Law of Expected Frequencies			
Digit	1st Place	2nd Place	3rd Place
0	N/A	12%	10.2%
1	30.1%	11.4%	10.1%
2	17.6%	10.9%	10.1%
3	12.5%	10.4%	10.1%
4	9.7%	10%	10%
5	7.9%	9.7%	10%
6	6.7%	9.3%	9.9%
7	5.8%	9%	9.9%
8	5.1%	8.8%	9.9%
9	4.6%	8.5%	9.8%

Source: *Benford's Law: Applications for forensic accounting auditing, and fraud detection.*[4]

The law only applies to naturally occurring numbers like the ones you would find in a general ledger account. Benford's Law does not apply to sequential numbers, such as those found on invoices, or to social security numbers. So why is Benford's Law important? For those attempting to detect fraud, the data can be sorted to look for anomalies. Just because some of the data is not consistent with Benford's Law does not necessarily mean that fraud is present; it just means that the reason for the anomalies needs to be investigated. All of the accounts that one would generally find on a ledger can be sorted in this fashion, including the check register, accounts receivable, asset accounts, as well as other data like wire transfers. For example, an embezzlement scheme may be uncovered if the dollar amount of checks starting with a 9 (e.g., $9,900) appear in 12 percent of the data instead of 4.6 percent.

Unstructured Data

To understand unstructured data, let's first define "structured data." Structured data includes clearly defined data sets that are easily searchable, such as spreadsheets, transaction registers, or journal entries. The data sets qualifying for a Benford's Law search are structured data. Comparing all vendor bank account numbers with employee bank account numbers for the purpose of detecting a conflict of interest is an example of structured data analysis.

Unstructured data is everything else in the universe of data. This data cannot be easily sorted by its underlying content. For our purposes, the most important example of unstructured data is e-mails. Other examples include social media, websites, text messages, calendars, and video content. To further clarify the distinction, the metadata associated with voicemails is structured data and could be sorted by date, but the audio file itself could not be sorted.

As an investigator, I am more interested in reviewing e-mails as opposed to structured data. If e-mails are available for the subject I am investigating, I will always review them. Invariably, the e-mails will be used as lead information, and more likely than not, will contain the smoking gun to be used at trial. In this regard, I am referring to investigations in which adequate predication exists (discussed in Chapter 12) to investigate a specific person.

Using unstructured data in an audit function or as a fraud detection technique raises legal and organizational culture issues. Always seek advice of legal counsel before reviewing unstructured data as a fraud detection technique. Even when legally permissible, management must consider whether the technique violates cultural norms as an invasion of privacy or a violation of trust.

Whether used to detect or investigate fraud, the e-mail review technique is invaluable. Industry-specific key words can be used to assist in discovering the incriminating e-mail. For example, corruption is always hard to uncover, especially a violation of the Foreign Corruption Practices Act in a foreign country. E-mail searches can be conducted of all sales employees who interact with foreign officials using the following search criteria: gratuity, entertainment, and gifts. A search yielding an e-mail that says, "We need to double the gift amount to our friend in China," may just be the thread that unravels a FCPA case.

Hotline

Shortly after the 1962 Cuban Missile Crisis, President John F. Kennedy realized that there was a need to have a "hotline" between the United States and Russia to communicate urgent messages. Since then, companies have coined the term for a system that enables employees to report inappropriate activity in the workplace anonymously. The Sarbanes-Oxley Act of 2002 mandated hotlines for all publicly traded companies, and the presence of hotlines is a standard part of most companies' compliance programs.

Just because a company has a hotline does not mean it will ring. To be effective, the hotline should be integrated into the code of conduct and employee training, and it should be appropriately advertised. The hotline is for all company stakeholders, including vendors, customers, and the general public. The tone from the top should include favorable messaging so that all stakeholders feel encouraged to report misconduct. The hotline can also be communicated on the company's webpage, on invoices, and on pay stubs.

Hotlines help in gathering more than just fraud information. In fact, many complaints are likely HR related because employees have a venting mechanism to complain about their boss. Sexual harassment and other violations of a code of conduct are also reported through hotlines. Bogus claims may also be made for the purpose of harassment. The hotline results must be forwarded to management in a timely manner so that management can review and triage the results.

Hotlines may fail to be successful for many reasons. Employee buy-in is required so that employees believe that complaints will be heard by management and that action will be taken. Not only must the hotline provide for anonymous reporting, but there must also be a general belief by those making complaints that they will remain anonymous. The hotline can be outsourced to a third party, which enables a company to have a hotline that works twenty-four hours a day, seven days a week. For international companies, a third-party will have professionals who speak multiple languages. Lastly, management should test the hotline to ensure that quality control and critical information will make their way to the appropriate parties.

Whistleblowers

If company management knows that the primary way fraud is detected is from tips from employees, then a culture of compliance can be fostered to encourage all employees to report anything suspicious. As part of the culture survey discussed in Chapter 10, employees should be asked, "How likely would you report a violation of the company's code of conduct?" The answer to this question will enlighten management about the strength of the company's fraud control environment.

As mentioned earlier, *Time* magazine's 2003 "Person of the Year" were three women. I do not think the gender of these three whistleblowers is a coincidence. Of the whistleblowers I have known, a majority (greater than 50 percent) have been women. What makes this number more striking is that the organizations in which they worked and complained about were predominately male, which makes this gender percentage significantly understated. I am not aware of a study backing these observations, but I would be shocked if this phenomenon did not hold true. I attended the book signing for Enron whistleblower Sherron Watkins when she released her book, *Power Failure: The Inside Story of the Collapse of Enron.*[5] During the event, she was asked the question why the *Time* magazine story involved three women. Watkins answered that women's close friends are usually outside the workplace, and men's friends are usually inside the workplace. If her thesis is true, maybe there is a cultural explanation for a potential whistleblower's (un)willingness to report on the top brass. Also, for women who do not want to climb the corporate ladder or believe they cannot, whistleblowing on the "boy's club" may be easier for them than for their male counterparts.

I have seen the success of the government's whistleblower programs while I was an FBI agent, and I am observing the same success now that I am in private practice. Many whistleblowers are committed to shining the light on fraud because they think it is the right thing to do. For others, their hesitancy to report wrongdoing is overcome when they learn that they may qualify for a monetary reward. Popular federal whistleblower programs include the *qui tam* provisions of the federal False Claims Act, the SEC's whistleblower program pursuant to the Dodd-Frank Wall Street Reform and Consumer Protection Act, and the IRS's whistleblower program.

Qui Tam Actions

A *qui tam* action is rooted in English law. The term is short for the Latin phrase *qui tam pro domino rege quam pro se ipso in hac parte sequitur,* meaning "he who sues in this matter for the king as well as for himself." The *qui tam* provisions are found in the federal False Claims Act (FCA).[6] The history of the FCA statute is also discussed in Chapter 2. A *qui tam* lawsuit may be appropriate any time a false claim made to the government results in a loss of federal funds. Rewards from a successful *qui tam* action can be substantial, as the FCA provides for a civil penalty of not less than $11,000 and not more than $22,000[7] plus three times the amount of damages the government sustains because of the fraud and attorney's fees.[8]

In a *qui tam* lawsuit, the plaintiff or whistleblower is known as a "relator." The relator works with an attorney to file an action under seal with the

Department of Justice (DOJ). The DOJ then decides if it wants to intervene in the lawsuit or let the relator continue without the government's assistance. The goal is generally to develop a strong case so that the government is interested in litigating the case. If the government intervenes, the relator may still assist the government, but the cost of litigation is borne by the government.

Qui tam actions generally fall into one of two categories: procurement fraud and program fraud. Procurement fraud cases often involve false claims for payment involving the delivery of nonconforming goods or services. Program fraud involves making false claims that relates to any of the myriad of government programs involving federal funds. A high percentage of these cases involve health care fraud due to the magnitude of federal dollars spent on federal health care programs. A *qui tam* action may also be brought when a mortgage lender originates loans backed by the Federal Housing Authority but falsely certifies that lending regulations or underwriting standards were met.

Unlike other whistleblower programs, only the first to file the lawsuit can recover damages. Further, any prior public disclosure of the facts in the media or to the government will likely prevent the lawsuit from going forward. The law punishes the whistleblower who procrastinates, complains internally, or goes to the media. The whistleblower needs to remain silent and file the lawsuit quickly. If a potential whistleblower is contemplating *a qui tam* action, retaining legal counsel should be done early in the process.

SEC Whistleblowers

In 2010, the Dodd-Frank Wall Street Reform and Consumer Protection Act was signed into law, creating the Office of the Whistleblower within the Securities and Exchange Commission (SEC). The SEC is *required* to make monetary awards to whistleblowers who voluntarily provide original information that leads to a successful SEC enforcement action resulting in monetary sanctions or a settlement over $1 million.[9] Awards must be made in an amount equal to 10 to 30 percent of the monetary sanctions collected.[10] Whistleblowers can remain anonymous throughout the process, and if the whistleblower is represented by counsel, the SEC does not have to know the identity of the whistleblower until a payment is actually made. The SEC whistleblower program also has strong antiretaliation penalties.

The whistleblower must provide original information relating to a violation of the federal securities laws. "Original information" is information derived from the independent knowledge or analysis of a whistleblower, not previously known by the SEC, and not exclusively derived from an allegation in a judicial proceeding, government report, audit, or the news media.[11] Violations of securities laws can include any of the following:

- Foreign Corruption Practices Act Violations
- Ponzi Schemes
- Insider Trading
- Market Manipulations
- Violating Accounting Standards
- False Financial Statements by Public Companies
- State and Municipal Securities
- Broker–Dealer Violations

IRS Whistleblowers

The IRS has two primary provisions under which it can pay an award to a whistleblower for assisting with a successful tax collection. In fact, the IRS has had a whistleblower provision since 1876 when it enacted 26 U.S.C. 7623(a). Unfortunately, the IRS has not traditionally paid out significant awards under this program even though it has discretionary authority to pay a maximum award of 15 percent up to $10 million per award. The program is at the IRS's discretion, and a whistleblower cannot dispute the amount that the IRS decides to pay, if anything.

In 2006, Congress realized that the IRS had not traditionally embraced the use of its statutory authority to pay whistleblowers, and therefore created a mandatory program requiring the IRS to pay whistleblowers when certain criteria were met. Under the Tax Relief and Healthcare Act of 2006, Congress codified these mandatory provisions at 26 U.S.C. 7623(b) and created the IRS Whistleblower Office to manage the awards program. However, Congress apparently only wanted to apply this mandatory program to significant tax cheaters. Before a whistleblower can receive an award under this program, the tax, penalties, interest, additions to tax, and additional amounts in dispute must exceed $2 million and the taxpayer must have an annual gross income of more than $200,000 for any tax year subject to the IRS's action. Lastly, the whistleblower has to substantially contribute to such action. If these thresholds are met, the whistleblower will recover a mandatory minimum of 15 percent and a maximum of 30 percent of the amount that the IRS recovers. If the whistleblower otherwise meets these requirements but has not substantially contributed, the whistleblower may be eligible for an award up to 10 percent of the awards collected. An example of a less than substantial contribution might be a circumstance in which the whistleblower learned of the matter through a judicial hearing, government report, news media, or audit.

Auditors' Standards for Fraud Detection

External auditors are responsible for detecting fraud that is material to the financial statements. See Chapter 5 for a detailed discussion of financial statement fraud. The ACFE's 2018 *Report to the Nations* shows that frauds are only discovered by the external auditors 4 percent of the time. Although external auditors too often do not detect fraud *material* to the financial statements, the 4 percent number is really misleading because most frauds are not material to the financial statements, and therefore their audits are not designed to detect most of these frauds. The standards for auditors of companies that are not publicly traded have evolved over decades and can now be found in the AICPA's *AU-C 240—Consideration of Fraud in a Financial Statement Audit*. For publicly traded companies, the PCAOB has adopted much of the AICPA's standard, which is found in AS 2401, *Consideration of Fraud in a Financial Statement Audit*. The language in these two standards for the detection of fraud is nearly identical. Auditors are naturally concerned with the financial statements being free of misstatement due to fraud. As previously addressed, financial statement fraud is commonly done through various schemes to inflate revenue. Although we generally do not think of asset misapplication being material to financial statements, it certainly can happen. If executives have misapplied large amounts of cash, inventory, or other assets, the resulting inaccurate account balances may be material to the financial statements.

The external auditor's standards have largely incorporated the Fraud Triangle's three vertices in its discussion of risk factors relating to both misstatements arising from fraudulent financial reporting and from misappropriation of assets. Although the standards do not directly address corruption and conflicts of interest, they do provide very well-reasoned ways of detecting financial statement fraud and asset misappropriation fraud. Portions of AU-C 240 are show below.

Risk Factors Relating to Misstatements Arising from Fraudulent Financial Reporting[12]

The following are examples of risk factors relating to misstatements arising from fraudulent financial reporting.

Incentives and Pressures

Financial stability or profitability is threatened by economic, industry, or entity operating conditions, such as (or as indicated by) the following:

- High degree of competition or market saturation, accompanied by declining margins.
- High vulnerability to rapid changes, such as changes in technology, product obsolescence, or interest rates.
- Significant declines in customer demand and increasing business failures in either the industry or overall economy.

- Operating losses making the threat of bankruptcy, foreclosure, or hostile takeover imminent.

- Recurring negative cash flows from operations or an inability to generate cash flows from operations while reporting earnings and earnings growth.

- Rapid growth or unusual profitability especially compared to that of other companies in the same industry.

- New accounting, statutory, or regulatory requirements.

Excessive pressure exists for management to meet the requirements or expectations of third parties due to the following:

- Profitability or trend level expectations of investment analysts, institutional investors, significant creditors, or other external parties (particularly expectations that are unduly aggressive or unrealistic), including expectations created by management in, for example, overly optimistic press releases or annual report messages.

- Need to obtain additional debt or equity financing to stay competitive—including financing of major research and development or capital expenditures.

- Marginal ability to meet exchange listing requirements or debt repayment or other debt covenant requirements.

- Perceived or real adverse effects of reporting poor financial results on significant pending transactions, such as business combinations or contract awards.

- A need to achieve financial targets required in bond covenants.

- Pressure for management to meet the expectations of legislative or oversight bodies or to achieve political outcomes, or both.

Information available indicates the personal financial situation of management or those charged with governance is threatened by the entity's financial performance arising from the following:

- Significant financial interests in the entity.

- Significant portions of their compensation (for example, bonuses, stock options, and earn-out arrangements) being contingent upon achieving aggressive targets for stock price, operating results, financial position, or cash flow.

- Personal guarantees of debts of the entity Management or operating personnel are under excessive pressure to meet financial targets established by those charged with governance, including sales or profitability incentive goals.

Opportunities

The nature of the industry or the entity's operations provides opportunities to engage in fraudulent financial reporting that can arise from the following:

- Significant related party transactions not in the ordinary course of business or with related entities not audited or audited by another firm.

- A strong financial presence or ability to dominate a certain industry sector that allows the entity to dictate terms or conditions to suppliers or customers that may result in inappropriate or non-arm's-length transactions.

- Assets, liabilities, revenues, or expenses based on significant estimates that involve subjective judgments or uncertainties that are difficult to corroborate.

- Significant, unusual, or highly complex transactions, especially those close to period end that pose difficult "substance over form" questions.

- Significant operations located or conducted across jurisdictional borders where differing business environments and regulations exist.

- Use of business intermediaries for which there appears to be no clear business justification.

- Significant bank accounts or subsidiary or branch operations in tax-haven jurisdictions for which there appears to be no clear business justification.

The monitoring of management is not effective as a result of the following:

- Domination of management by a single person or small group (in a nonowner-managed business) without compensating controls.
- Oversight by those charged with governance over the financial reporting process and internal control is not effective.

The organizational structure is complex or unstable, as evidenced by the following:

- Difficulty in determining the organization or individuals that have controlling interest in the entity.
- Overly complex organizational structure involving unusual legal entities or managerial lines of authority.
- High turnover of senior management, legal counsel, or those charged with governance.

Internal control components are deficient as a result of the following:

- Inadequate monitoring of controls, including automated controls and controls over interim financial reporting (when external reporting is required).
- High turnover rates or employment of staff in accounting, IT, or the internal audit function who are not effective.
- Accounting and information systems that are not effective, including situations involving significant deficiencies or material weaknesses in internal control.
- Weak controls over budget preparation and development and compliance with law or regulation.

Attitudes and Rationalizations

- Communication, implementation, support, or enforcement of the entity's values or ethical standards by management, or the communication of inappropriate values or ethical standards that are not effective.

- Nonfinancial management's excessive participation in or preoccupation with the selection of accounting policies or the determination of significant estimates.

- Known history of violations of securities law or other law or regulation, or claims. against the entity, its senior management, or those charged with governance alleging fraud or violations of law or regulation.

- Excessive interest by management in maintaining or increasing the entity's stock price or earnings trend.

- The practice by management of committing to analysts, creditors, and other third parties to achieve aggressive or unrealistic forecasts.

- Management failing to remedy known significant deficiencies or material weaknesses in internal control on a timely basis.

- An interest by management in employing inappropriate means to minimize reported earnings for tax-motivated reasons.

- Low morale among senior management.

- The owner-manager makes no distinction between personal and business transactions.

- Dispute between shareholders in a closely held entity.

- Recurring attempts by management to justify marginal or inappropriate accounting on the basis of materiality.

- A strained relationship between management and the current or predecessor auditor, as exhibited by the following:

    ◦ Frequent disputes with the current or predecessor auditor on accounting, auditing, or reporting matters.

- ○ Unreasonable demands on the auditor, such as unrealistic time constraints regarding the completion of the audit or the issuance of the auditor's report.

- ○ Restrictions on the auditor that inappropriately limit access to people or information or the ability to communicate effectively with those charged with governance.

- ○ Domineering management behavior in dealing with the auditor, especially involving attempts to influence the scope of the auditor's work or the selection or continuance of personnel assigned to or consulted on the audit engagement.

Risk Factors Arising from Misstatements Arising from Misappropriation of Assets[13]

Incentives and Pressures

Personal financial obligations may create pressure on management or employees with access to cash or other assets susceptible to theft to misappropriate those assets. Adverse relationships between the entity and employees with access to cash or other assets susceptible to theft may motivate those employees to misappropriate those assets. For example, adverse relationships may be created by the following:

- Known or anticipated future employee layoffs.
- Recent or anticipated changes to employee compensation or benefit plans.
- Promotions, compensation, or other rewards inconsistent with expectations.

Opportunities

Certain characteristics or circumstances may increase the susceptibility of assets to misappropriation. For example, opportunities to misappropriate assets increase when the following exist:

- Large amounts of cash on hand or processed.

- Inventory items that are small in size, of high value, or in high demand.

- Easily convertible assets, such as bearer bonds, diamonds, or computer chips.

- Fixed assets that are small in size, marketable, or lack observable identification of ownership.

Inadequate internal control over assets may increase the susceptibility of misappropriation of those assets. For example, misappropriation of assets may occur because the following exist:

- Inadequate segregation of duties or independent checks.

- Inadequate oversight of senior management expenditures, such as travel and other reimbursements.

- Inadequate management oversight of employees responsible for assets (for example, inadequate supervision or monitoring of remote locations).

- Inadequate job applicant screening of employees with access to assets.

- Inadequate record keeping with respect to assets.

- Inadequate system of authorization and approval of transactions (for example, in purchasing).

- Inadequate physical safeguards over cash, investments, inventory, or fixed assets.

- Lack of complete and timely reconciliations of assets.

- Lack of timely and appropriate documentation of transactions (for example, credits for merchandise returns).

- Lack of mandatory vacations for employees performing key control functions.

- Inadequate management understanding of IT, which enables IT employees to perpetrate a misappropriation.

- Inadequate access controls over automated records, including controls over and review of computer systems event logs.

Attitudes and Rationalizations

- Disregard for the need for monitoring or reducing risks related to misappropriations of assets.
- Disregard for internal control over misappropriation of assets by overriding existing controls or by failing to take appropriate remedial action on known deficiencies in internal control.
- Behavior indicating displeasure or dissatisfaction with the entity or its treatment of the employee.
- Changes in behavior or lifestyle that may indicate assets have been misappropriated
- The belief by some government or other officials that their level of authority justifies a certain level of compensation and personal privileges.
- Tolerance of petty theft.

CHAPTER 12

Investigations

"What one man can invent another can discover."

—SHERLOCK HOLMES IN *THE ADVENTURE OF THE DANCING MEN*, BY SIR ARTHUR CONAN DOYLE

In January of 2002, I received an unusual call from my boss. She had just flown to FBI Headquarters to attend an emergency meeting about Enron. She was in a conference room full of FBI and DOJ executives when she advised me, "Vic, we may need you to lead a search of the Enron offices tomorrow." That was the first time I realized that the FBI was going to initiate an investigation into Enron. I was not totally surprised about the comment since Enron had restated its financial statements in November of 2001, had filed for bankruptcy in December of 2001, and the storied company had been making the headlines daily. What did surprise me was that I was told to ready a team to search Enron "tomorrow."

I have participated in over 50 searches, usually conducted pursuant to a search warrant. In each of those searches, we planned for days or usually weeks. The search of Enron resulted in the largest single-site search in FBI history, and I was being asked to lead the search the next day! Such an undertaking with next to no preparation would be a monumental task. As it turned out, that is exactly what I did—undertake a monumental task.

The search lasted nine days. It started under many unusual circumstances. The search was done pursuant to receiving a board-authorized consent to search and not a search warrant. The FBI did not have probable cause to obtain a search warrant, and the board was fearful that if a search warrant was obtained, it would trigger certain reporting requirements and bad publicity. The result was a mutually agreed upon search.

The FBI's interest had been piqued only a few days earlier when it became aware that an Enron vice-president had accused Enron's management of obstruction of justice. The SEC had issued subpoenas, and Enron employees were shredding documents, or so the vice-president said. That was the purpose of the investigation on the first day. The second day was entirely a different story. I quickly determined that Enron employees were shredding documents, but every company shreds documents. The allegation of obstruction of justice by shredding documents could not be substantiated. However, once FBI agents started interviewing Enron employees, we quickly developed a long laundry list of potential federal violations. From the roots of those allegations, the FBI began a lengthy investigation across the organization involving numerous individuals, subsidiaries, departments, and transactions that took years to complete.

An investigation is nothing more than the collection of evidence for a specific purpose. Evidence resides in three different categories or "buckets." These three buckets are witness statements (obtained through interviews), digital evidence, and tangible evidence (usually documents). To collect this evidence at Enron, the FBI formed three teams: an interview team, a digital imaging team, and a document search team. As we will see, interviewing is usually the most critical of these three buckets of evidence. At the end of each day of the Enron search, the team leaders of these three teams exchanged information. This continuous collaboration resulted in an ever-increasing amount of fraud theories, leads, and places to search for more evidence.

As in the Enron case, once the red flags of fraud are present, various stakeholders may ask for an investigation to be conducted. When I am called upon to initiate an investigation, I first determine the forensic posture of the matter by asking a number of questions: Who is my client, and what is their objective? Is this a civil or a criminal matter? If it is a civil matter, am I investigating for the plaintiff, defendant, creditor, spouse, business partner, victim, or potential wrongdoer? Is this a board-led investigation or other internal investigation? Does the matter involve a publicly traded company? Is the company a victim, the perpetrator or both? Are there other ongoing investigations? If so, who is leading them, and what is the theory of their case? For criminal matters, am I working for the prosecution or the defense? If I am working for the defense, I might be called upon to conduct a shadow investigation of the prosecution. If I am trying to prosecute or defend a legal position, I have to know the legal issues involved. If the board wants to use the results of the investigation for disciplinary or firing actions, what are the company's policies? As we saw in Chapter 2, "Fraud Defined," the legal elements of fraud will vary greatly depending on the forensic posture of the case.

Next, I start with the end result in mind. How might this investigation end, and what might the stakeholders do with the information? One possibility is that the suspects would be exonerated—maybe not too surprisingly, but many stakeholders might not want to accept this answer. Another possibility is that the investigation might be inconclusive—bad judgments by multiple parties, a lot of smoke but no fire, or just a confusing but justifiable pattern of facts. Although those are very real possibilities, when the allegation of fraud is at issue, a tangible loss to a victim might have been discovered already, and, if so, one or more individuals would be responsible.

Regardless of the type of assignment it is, I always start with the end in mind. How will I deliver the results of my investigation? Will it be an oral presentation or a written report? Who are the end users, and what are their needs? In a federal investigation of a corporation, when does the end occur? The answer to this question is both fascinating and important. The end may be when the corporation's attorney is making arguments before the sentencing judge to mitigate the fine that he or she it will impose on the corporation. That is the end, and it is the first thing I am thinking about when I initiate an investigation. I need to ensure that the prosecutor, judge, and jury have all of the information they need to meet the ends of justice.

The Federal Sentencing Guidelines for Organizations allows for a federal judge to mitigate or lower a fine if the organization has an effective compliance and ethics program in place. When I am leading an investigation into a corporation, the issue of whether or not there is an effective program in place can be determined if the right questions are asked and the appropriate documentation is obtained. However, none of that information can be obtained if I do not start with the end in mind.

In an FBI espionage or foreign counterintelligence investigation, the end results may never be made public. That too is important information. If the FBI does not want the investigation to become public, then it must tailor the investigative techniques to meet this objective. A client may not want the results of a fraud investigation to become public. In this case, I must start with the end in mind to achieve the objective of a "quiet" investigation.

Preliminary Matters

Once an allegation of fraud arises, management should immediately take steps to address the issue. For our purposes, I will assume that occupational fraud has occurred inside the organization. The concepts that follow will generally apply regardless of the particular forensic posture of the case.

If fraud has occurred, this most likely means that prevention efforts have failed. If the detection systems are working, the fraud may have been caught sooner than 18 months, which is how long frauds last on average before being detected. The organization should have a fraud policy. See the Appendix for the ACFE's "Sample Anti-Fraud Policy." Contained in any policy should be an escalation protocol. This will enable the fraud allegation to be communicated by the person who spotted a red flag of fraud to the person or department that is capable of assessing the allegation and ensuring that it is appropriately addressed. Because frauds vary drastically, each investigation must be tailored to address the specific factual pattern. Here are some preliminary questions that should be addressed as soon as it is practicable:

- Is any branch of the Fraud Tree implicated: asset misappropriation, corruption, or financial statement fraud?
- Is this a nonoccupational or predatory fraud?
- Assuming the worst, how bad could this be?
- Do I have an affirmative obligation to notify any internal or external party?
- Does the potential fraudster(s) know that management has been alerted?
- Is the fraud ongoing?
- If the allegation is true, will the company be a participant in the continuation of the fraud?

Legal Counsel

Legal counsel should be engaged as early in the process as possible. Outside counsel should be considered when legal expertise does not reside internally or there is a need for greater independence. A variety of legal issues will arise at the inception of the investigation. Experienced counsel knows to start with the end in mind because they have litigated these cases and know the pitfalls. Legal counsel may also provide some amount of protection to the investigation through the attorney–client privilege and the work product doctrine.

Fraud allegations will likely trigger the obligation to preserve evidence through a process known as a "litigation hold." A litigation hold is a notice in any form that communicates an affirmative legal duty for any potential party to maintain evidence if litigation can reasonably be anticipated. Evidence includes anything that could be relevant to any future litigation. The most common examples are documents, e-mails, and electronically stored information. The process also requires preservation of less obvious evidence like voicemails and electronic calendar entries. If video surveillance exists, the data should be preserved before it is overwritten. The failure to preserve evidence in a timely manner when litigation is anticipated is known as "spoliation." Spoliation is the intentional, reckless, or negligent failure to secure evidence pursuant to legal requirements. The sanction to a party for spoliation can have a draconian impact on the outcome of the ligation. A court may instruct a jury to presume that the lost evidence is both relevant and favorable to the innocent party. The court could also strike a defense that may have otherwise been available to the party that was responsible for the spoliation. These sanctions can change the outcome of litigation even if the lost evidence is actually innocuous or irrelevant.

Insurance Company Notification

If an insured company has a policy that covers against fraud or cyberattacks, the terms of the policy may require timely notification to the insurance carrier. Legal counsel can assist with evaluating whether a fidelity insurance policy or bond covers the matter at issue and when notification to the carrier is appropriate.

Predication

Predication is an articulable, factual basis that would cause a reasonable person to believe that a fraud has occurred, is occurring, or might occur in the future. No fraud investigation should be initiated until adequate predication has been established. This is true for the FBI and for law enforcement, and the rule holds true for those working in the private sector. In the criminal context, initiating investigations without predication can raise issues relating to entrapment, the First Amendment, and abuse of authority. Predication is just as important in the private sector to avoid privacy and discrimination issues. Committing investigative resources without adequate predication is a waste of those resources and can unnecessarily harm innocent people. Once an adequately predicated investigation has begun, a corollary principle is that the least intrusive investigative techniques should be deployed to obtain information, or else the investigative team may needlessly invade someone's privacy or unnecessarily cause reputational harm.

A robust audit function should not be confused with a lack of predication. Auditors often take random samples and assess if the audit evidence conforms to a certain standard. Audits serve as both a preventive and a detective control. However, auditors should not randomly select an employee to conduct a fraud audit. Randomly reviewing e-mails, conducting a desk search, surveilling an employee, or conducting a background investigation should never be part of an audit or even an investigative step when predication is lacking.

Contacting Law Enforcement

The decision to contact law enforcement and, if so, when, should be made with legal counsel. Depending on the circumstances, the involvement of law enforcement may not be in the best interest of the victim. Further, the organization and its officers may also be involved in the fraud. The downside to notifying law enforcement is that law enforcement may begin seizing evidence, issuing subpoenas, and interviewing witnesses, sometimes through a grand jury. Any of these steps may hinder a civil resolution of the matter. In other circumstance, law enforcement's presence can greatly enhance the outcome. When I managed the FBI asset forfeiture program, I worked with many victims to recover their funds through asset seizure. For many frauds, if the victim's funds are not quickly seized, the proceeds are laundered by the fraudsters or paid to their criminal defense attorneys. In many of these cases, the FBI had already been investigating the matter for a lengthy period of time before the victim became aware of the fraud. Here, the victim may be able to collaborate with law enforcement, thereby cutting costs, saving time, and potentially recovering the lost funds.

Organize the Investigation

Once the decision to investigate has been made, an investigative team must be formed. Investigations are not a one-size-fits-all solution. A variety of factors must be considered, including the type of fraud, who may be involved, and its potential impact. Internal resources are usually desirable, as the parties know the organization, and it is usually a less expensive proposition than retaining outside attorneys, forensic accountants, and investigators. In other cases, outside resources are a necessity due to the complexity of the matter, the resources required, or the need for independence. Further, a hybrid approach can be practical where the investigation is led by outside counsel that directs internal components to conduct the investigation.

Management should consider whether or not it is appropriate to use various resources to staff the investigation. Talented individuals should be sought regardless of their job title. Traits to consider are knowledge of the organization, interpersonal skills (very important for interviewing), and the ability to deploy resources. The following resources should be considered when an investigative team is being formed:

- Inside Counsel
- Outside Counsel
- Audit Committee
- Executive Management
- Management
- Human Resources
- Internal Audit

- Security
- Forensic Accountant
- Forensic Technology Expert
- Information Technology Personnel
- Certified Fraud Examiner
- Investigator

A member of the management team should be designated as the team leader. After considering inputs from all of the stakeholders, a plan should be developed. The plan should address high-level goals and should be inherently flexible. The underlying facts will drive decision making, and these facts will only be developed as the investigation progresses. A plan should address the following topics:

- Goals
- Resource limitations, if any
- Team members and responsibilities
- Communication protocols

When I lead investigations on behalf of a client, I like to break the investigation into two phases. During Phase One, I immerse myself in all of the known and readily available facts. I review the complaint and interview any available complainant. When appropriate, I obtain and review bank statements, credit cards statements, and accounting system records. Reviewing the personnel file of any potential suspect may disclose prior disciplinary actions and provide insight into the suspect's background. After I know everything that can be reasonably known at that stage, I then develop a plan that I call Phase Two. With all of the information developed to date, I now have a more practical knowledge of the dollar loss, the individuals who are potentially involved, the cost to investigate, and the time it may take to complete the investigation. While all of these issues will be very preliminary and fluid, I am now in a position to begin managing client expectations.

Initial issues that I need to address are whether the fraud is ongoing and whether any potential suspect knows that the fraud has been discovered. The answers to these questions will tell me if I am working on a historical investigation or a proactive investigation. If the fraud is ongoing, I may be in a more favorable position to catch the fraudster in the act through a variety of techniques, including recorded conversations, surveillance, and a review of e-mails.

With a plan in place, the investigative team can begin collecting evidence. As discussed previously, the evidence will be found in three buckets: witness interviews, digital evidence, and tangible evidence.

Interviews

Interviewing is usually the most important part of an investigation. Other investigative techniques are often more costly, time-consuming, and less efficient. If an FBI agent can approach a suspect and obtain a confession, the time and expense of an investigation will be greatly reduced. Likewise, if an interviewer can talk with witnesses and establish all of the elements of the fraud, the investigation can come to a conclusion much more quickly.

An interview should be distinguished from an interrogation. An interview is a nonaccusatory conversation with questions designed for a specific purpose. An interrogation is a conversation with someone suspected of wrongdoing for the purpose of obtaining an admission of guilt and is usually controlled by the interrogator though accusatory and leading questions.

Because the term "interrogation" conjures up a suspect in a dark room under hot lights with cops demanding a confession, the term may be viewed disapprovingly by the uninformed. Accordingly, some may find the term "admission-seeking interview" more palatable. Regardless, this section is about interviewing. I will leave interrogation to law enforcement and those with sufficient experience and training.

Legal Issues

How an interview is conducted, what the interviewee is told, and how the information is used can raise legal issues. An interviewer should be mindful of the various legal issues associated with interviewing.

Upjohn Warnings

In *Upjohn Co. v. United States*, 449 U.S. 383 (1981), the United States Supreme Court addressed an important issue for attorneys who lead investigations. In fact, the word *Upjohn* is now used to describe certain warnings that attorneys may need to provide to employees being interviewed under certain circumstances. The current stature of this case is a little ironic because the warnings generally attributed to *Upjohn* were not actually a part of the case. Instead, the Supreme Court addressed the parameters of the attorney–client privilege involving company lawyers and nonmanagerial employees.

Upjohn involved a pharmaceutical company that realized it may have been paying foreign officials to secure government business. This conduct could not have violated the Foreign Corrupt Practices Act of 1977 because the conduct in question preceded the enactment of the law. However, the deduction of those payments for federal income tax purposes would have been illegal. The company initiated an internal investigation that included employee interviews and sending questionnaires to employees. When the IRS learned of the company's internal investigation, it sought any report of communication between employees and legal counsel. The Court held that the employee communications with company counsel were protected by the attorney–client privilege, and it overturned a previous test used by some lower courts.

The significance of *Upjohn*, however, was not its particular holding, rather, it was the legal community's use of the case to describe the legal and ethical responsibilities of attorneys leading internal investigations. An "*Upjohn* warning" is now the term used in legal parlance to define the admonishments that attorneys should provide to an employee to clearly establish that the attorney represents the company and not the employee being interviewed. Further, the company holds the privilege, not the employee. The warnings also provide that, while the employee can discuss the facts of the underlying matter, the employee cannot later discuss the conversations that were held with the attorney.

The importance of the *Upjohn* warning is that an employee could mistakenly think the attorney represented the best interest of the employee and, therefore, make incriminating statements to the company's counsel. The attorney's obligation is to act in the best interest of the company. The company could cause this information to be provided to law enforcement, and it could be used to prosecute the employee. For our purposes, we should understand that in attorney-led interviews, the attorney may have an ethical and legal obligation to clearly provide this warning to an employee being interviewed.

Miranda Warnings

The well-known *Miranda* warnings emanated from *Miranda v. Arizona*, 382 U.S. 436 (1966), and they only apply to government personnel, generally law enforcement. The *Miranda* warnings are designed to admonish those who are in custody that, before they provide information, they have the right to remain silent, the information they provide can be used against them, they have the right to an attorney, and if they cannot afford an attorney, one will be provided to them.

Two critical elements must be present before *Miranda* is used. The warnings only apply when someone is in *custody* and is being *interrogated* (questioned). Does law enforcement have to provide *Miranda* warnings before engaging in custodial interrogation? The answer is no, but if an interrogation is done without providing these warnings, any resulting statement can be excluded from evidence.

Garrity *Warnings*

An interviewee should also be provided admonishments in another legal context. Consider a government employee who is under investigation and the employee's boss (a government actor) requires the employee to provide a statement as to what happened. Such a compelled statement may incriminate the employee. This is exactly what happened in *Garrity v. New Jersey*, 385 U.S. 493 (1967). Here, a police officer was being questioned in a ticket-fixing scheme and was told he had to give a statement or be subject to termination. The United States Supreme Court held that such a compelled statement was inadmissible in a criminal proceeding because the officer was faced with losing his job or providing a statement that violated both his right of due process and his right against self-incrimination. *Garrity* applies when a government employee is compelling the interview of one of its other employees.

Larger governments may have inspector generals who conduct internal investigations. These more sophisticated agencies understand *Garrity* and will either provide one of two types of warnings to the government employee. One type of warning is that the governmental entity is conducting an investigation and the employee is not compelled to answer questions, but if the employee does answer questions, the answers can be used against the employee in a criminal proceeding. This warning could be bad news for the employee. It probably means that the employer suspects the employee of wrongdoing and is preserving the right to prosecute the employee. The other type of warning is that the governmental entity is conducting an investigation and the employee must answer all questions truthfully or possibly be terminated. This warning could mean that the investigators have already obtained a prosecutive declination and do not intend to prosecute the employee, but they just need the facts.

The failure to appreciate *Garrity* and its implication can impair a prosecutor's case. Consider a local government that does not have an awareness of these issues or hires an investigator who is uninformed. If a government employee's statement is taken under a scenario in which the employee could later argue that he or she feared being fired, not only would the statement be excluded from evidence in a criminal proceeding, but also anything the prosecution developed that was the fruit of the investigation might also be excluded. When conducting an investigation of a government employee, the company should seek legal counsel regarding any *Garrity* warning that could be appropriate under the circumstances.

Defamation

Defamation is a false statement that is published (a third party learns of it) and causes reputational harm to another. When done in writing, it is known as libel, and when done orally, it is known as slander. Issues of libel or slander can arise in an investigation.

Consider the example of an investigator who is attempting to hold a difficult interrogation of an executive who is actually innocent. If the interrogation is inadvertently held in a public environment because, for instance, the conference room door has been left open, any defamatory language may be deemed to have been published. After hearing the wrongful accusations by the interrogator, employees may begin spreading vicious rumors about the executive. This type of reputational harm could provide the basis for a cause of action for slander.

The end result of most investigations is a written report. A report must be factually accurate. A report that contains incorrect information can result in reputational harm and give rise to a cause of action for libel.

False Imprisonment

During an interview, investigators should never give an interviewee the impression he or she is not free to leave. Unless the interviewer is from law enforcement and has a legal right to detain the individual, the interviewer could be liable for false imprisonment. The better practice is to have a witness present and let the interviewee know that he or she is free to leave, take breaks, or be questioned at another time.

Deception

A 20-year old U.S. Marine is suspected of murder. The police interrogate the suspect and falsely tell him that his friend has already confessed to the murder and has implicated him. After considering the false statements made by police, the suspect confesses. Should the police be allowed to lie to a suspect? This was what occurred in *Frazier v. Cupp*, 394 U.S. 731 (1969), and the U.S. Supreme Court affirmed the government's ability to use deception during an interrogation. Although such tactics are not without limits, the use of deception during an interview may be legally permissible.

Should you consider a ruse or deception when interviewing a witness or suspect? Although it is permissible, I strongly recommend against using this tactic. The downside is that other stakeholders may negatively view the tactic. An organization may not want a culture in which management has approved the use of deception with employees. Juries also do not like investigators using deception. On the other hand, an occasion may exist when the need for the technique outweighs the risks. When the use of deception in an investigation is being considered, the organization always should consult legal counsel.

Polygraphs

A polygraph is really a set of closed-ended interview questions but with a machine that is attached to the subject to monitor biological responses. I have been subjected to a polygraph test, and I have witnessed the effectiveness of polygraphs in many FBI cases. Nevertheless, a polygraph can provide false positives and false negatives, and the error rate is controversial. The polygraph is used in three different contexts. In the first context, it is used as part of a background investigation for the initial hiring and continued employment of law enforcement and U.S. national security personnel. In the second context, it is used to assess the truthfulness of witnesses, informants, and suspects.

Lastly, a polygraph is also used as an interrogation tool to obtain a confession from a suspect.

The best way to prevent fraud from occurring in an organization is not to hire a fraudster. Should a company have a policy that requires all new employees to submit to a polygraph test? No. Not only would such a policy be expensive and demoralizing, but also it would likely violate federal law. The U.S. Department of Labor enforces the provisions of the Employee Polygraph Protection Act of 1988 (Polygraph Act). The Polygraph Act prohibits most private employers from using a polygraph for preemployment screening. A violation subjects the employer to a fine of up to $10,000 and creates a legal basis for a lawsuit by the employee.[1]

The Polygraph Act has a couple of significant exceptions. It does allow an employer to administer a polygraph test if four conditions are met: (1) the purpose relates to an ongoing fraud investigation, (2) the employee had access to the property, (3) the employer has a reasonable suspicion that the employee was involved, and (4) the employee is given notice of the employer's basis for administering the polygraph.[2] The other exception exempts federal, state, and local governments, thereby allowing the administration of the polygraph test to law enforcement and national security personnel.[3]

Attorney Ethical Issues

Interviews are often done by investigators or corporate personnel conducting an investigation at the direction of an attorney. Pursuant to state bar rules, attorneys have an ethical duty not to contact individuals represented by counsel without their counsel's consent. The rule also applies to any investigative team member working at the direction of an attorney. When investigations are led by an attorney, the investigative team should always be in communication with the attorney about ongoing investigative steps, including listing the individuals they intend to interview.

Recorded Interviews

To record or not to record interviews—that's the question. First, the interviewer needs to ensure that recording interviews is legal in the interviewer's jurisdiction. If all of the parties who will be involved in the recording consent, there is not a problem. If during the investigation the investigator wants to make a surreptitious audio or video recording, the investigator needs to obtain a legal opinion. The law can vary depending on the state and whether the recording is audio, video, or telephonic. A violation of the law may constitute a felony. For telephonic recordings, the controlling law is likely the state where the device is located, which could be in the state where either party is present or a third-party state when a remote recording service is used.

The upside to recording interviews is that the statement is electronically preserved should the interviewee later deny making a statement. The recording also provides a record for the investigator to review.

The downsides to recording interviews are significant. An audio recording may not fully reflect the exchange of information. Listening to what sounds like aggressive questioning can cast the interviewer in a misleadingly poor light. The decision to record some interviews and not others can lead to the argument that the interviewer destroyed certain exculpatory recordings. Once a recording is made, it becomes evidence. Appropriately extracting, copying, and storing digital evidence is resource intensive. If the matter goes to trial, the recordings may have to be transcribed, which can also be a resource-intensive endeavor.

I always carefully consider the pros and cons of recording an interview. If I believe that a witness or a subject may later recant his or her statements, I will at least ensure that another interviewer is present. This may also be the circumstance when I consider recording the interview. Also, I will be mindful that the interviewee may be recording the interview even if the interviewee says that he or she is not. Lastly, surreptitious recording by an attorney may violate state bar rules.

Eight Steps to an Effective Interview

The most important skill I learned as an FBI agent is the ability to interview people. It is a skill I have now used for 30 years. As an agent, I could be interviewing a U.S. Senator in the morning and a drug dealer in the evening, and it could even be for the same case! The methodology, however, is exactly the same for either interview.

I learned the eight steps for having an effective interview at the FBI Academy, and these have been reinforced during decades of interviewing. They are now completely ingrained habits that guide me through an interview from start to finish. Interviewing is an art form, and I get better when I am participating with skilled interviewers. I am always willing to borrow a tool from a talented interviewer's toolbox and see if it works for me. Interviewers also have to know themselves. Just because a technique works for one interviewer, does not mean it will work for another interviewer. With time and experience, interviewers can master the art of interviewing. Following are the eight steps to having an effective interview.

1. *Preparation*

I want to know as much as possible about the interviewee. There is an amazing amount of information on the Internet and that is also available from fee-for-service providers. The importance of the interview and the particular interviewee will dictate how to prepare for the interview. If the investigation is at a mature stage, I probably will have learned a lot about all of the witnesses and suspects before I interview them. A look at their personnel file can be helpful. Knowledge of their house, the car they drive, and the clothes they wear will tell a lot about them. Their educational background and work experience are also helpful types of information. Knowing if the individuals are straight shooters, exaggerate, or have a reputation for lying is also helpful.

For complex fraud cases, a solid knowledge of the facts is very important. I also want to know the forensic posture and the legal elements of the fraud at issue. I need to understand all of the documents involved, the money flow, and the role of the interviewee. For complex or lengthy interviews, deception detection can be difficult, as no single answer is necessarily false. Knowing the entire scheme and how it differs from a legitimate business arrangement is important. Understanding this dichotomy enables me to develop key questions.

Because I want to know as much about the key witnesses and suspects as possible, the general rule is to interview these individuals at the end of the investigation. I start with peripheral witnesses first and then move toward the center—the important witnesses and suspects. When should an investigator interview the target of the investigation? Preferably it would be the last step, right? Doing that could be a mistake. The larger or the more sophisticated the fraud is, the greater the chance is that the target will "lawyer up" before he or she can be interviewed. Accordingly, it is a judgment call, but I consider interviewing the target earlier in the investigation if I think that the target may retain counsel. For an investigation that starts in a covert phase, the investigator should consider interviewing the target shortly before the investigation goes to an overt phase (becomes publicly known). Because critical witnesses may retain counsel, the timing of the interview is a balancing act for the interviewer between gathering enough information to have a productive interview and ensuring that the interview occurs before the individual retains counsel. If the interview is attempted too early, important questions will not be asked; if the interview is attempted to late, the interviewee may refuse to be interviewed.

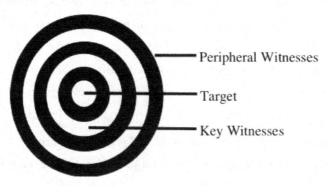

Peripheral Witnesses

Target

Key Witnesses

Before holding any interview, I put a lot of thought into the mind-set of the person I am about to interview. What is the person thinking, and more importantly, what is the person feeling? As an interviewer, I know I have a natural bias to flood my mind with questions that I want to ask and how to deal with my own stress. Interviewing can be very stressful to the interviewer, especially when the interviewee wants no part of the investigation, may want to discredit the ultimate findings, or may be the target of the investigation.

By staying focused on the interviewee's state of mind, I consider what role he or she played in the matter, and how my investigation could have an impact on the interviewee personally. Is the person busy at the time of the interview? How might the interviewee feel about the particular subject matter involved? Might the person view the investigation as being improperly motivated? Understanding the mind-set of the interviewee helps in selecting the place to conduct the interview, developing rapport, and structuring and sequencing questions.

2. *Introduction*

This is a basic step that should smoothly roll into rapport building. I introduce myself, who I am working for in the matter, and the purpose of the interview. This is also a good time to clarify the interviewee's identity, if it is in doubt, and the interviewee's exact role or authority in the matter.

If there is an attorney representing the interviewee, I make sure to identify the attorney's name, firm, and exactly whom the attorney represents. As a practical matter, I usually find it helpful when an attorney is present. The attorney makes the interviewee more comfortable, encourages the interviewee to answer difficult questions, and reduces the chances of the interviewee lying. Furthermore, if the attorney has real concerns about the client talking, the attorney would not allow the client to be interviewed. Investigators should be aware that union employees may have a legal right to have a union representative present during interviews.[4] If the interview is led by an attorney, *Upjohn* warnings may be appropriate at that time.

Ideally, two or more people should not be interviewed at the same time. The interviewer will have difficulty attributing key information to a particular person. This may occur if the two interviewees begin collaborating in order to recall crucial information. Dual interviews can be appropriate when interviewing a child with a parent present. It can also be difficult to avoid when interviewing a spouse, and the other spouse insists on being present. When a dual interview situation arises, the interviewer should attempt to approach the interviewee when he or she is alone.

3. *Rapport Building*

Rapport building is one of the more crucial parts of an interview. Rapport building enables me to develop common ground with the interviewee. Conducting the interview in the interviewee's office enables me to see items like pictures of family members, sports trophies, company awards, and other items that are important to the interviewee. All of these objects are fodder for initiating a lighthearted conversation. When all else fails, a discussion of the weather or the local sports team works just fine.

When building rapport is successful, the interviewee will become more comfortable and possibly build trust with me. However, some individuals do not want to develop rapport, and when I try, the effort actually becomes counterproductive. The interviewee may just not feel comfortable making small talk with a stranger, or it could be a control technique, warning me that the interviewee will attempt to control the interview.

While developing rapport, I am also doing something even more important—calibrating. Calibrating is the process of establishing a baseline of nonverbal behavior when the interviewee is in a nonthreatening environment. We often communicate more through nonverbal expressions than the actual words we speak. Key nonverbal concepts include chronemics, proxemics, kinetics, paralinguistics, and eye contact. These are all concepts that we are familiar with, but giving them names helps us identify and interpret their significance.

Chronemic communication is the use of time to convey meaning whether intentionally or not. This applies to both the interviewer and the interviewee. Is the interviewee is a fast or slow talker? After asking a question, how long does it take the interviewee to respond? Is the interviewee reflective, or does the interviewee just start rattling off information after a question is asked? Chronemics can also be very powerful for the interviewer. When I am asking an important question in which the interviewee might have a motivation to not answer, temper the truth, or lie, I ask the question and stop talking. Then I pause and look at the interviewee. This can actually be quite stressful for both me and the person I am interviewing. I find biting my tongue or discreetly squeezing my leg can help me keep focused on remaining silent. The natural tendency for the interviewer is to fill the awkward silence with chatter so that the stress will dissipate. However, interviewers should not do this; they should just wait for the answer. The interviewee may succumb to the silence by providing information that is key to the entire investigation.

Proxemic communication is the use of interpersonal space to convey meaning. I can often identify the relationship of individuals by how closely they stand next to each other when they are talking. When I am interviewing someone, I can tell the interviewee is comfortable with the subject matter if the interviewee leans slightly forward to make a point. Conversely, if the interviewee leans backwards, this is demonstrating a lack of confidence or discomfort with the answer.

Kinetic communication is the use of body movements, gesturing, talking with the hands, foot-tapping, and so forth. After I observe each interviewee's unique movements (or the lack thereof), I begin learning how the interviewee communicates, especially when the interviewee adds meaning through kinetic emphasis.

Paralinguistic communication is the use of the voice to project volume, pitch, and quality. The way we project our voice can result in the intended meaning being significantly different than the literal meaning of the words spoken.

Eye contact can also be very telling. By observing the interviewee's willingness to make eye contact, I can often detect how confident the interviewee is with the answer. I can also gauge how interested the interviewee is in the conversation in general.

The purpose of observing all of these nonverbal forms of communication is to calibrate the interviewee. In doing so, I am attempting to assess how the interviewee responds to nonthreatening questions. Later in the interview, when I am asking consequential questions, I will observe whether or not there is a change in the interviewee's nonverbal behavior. I am especially looking for changes that occur simultaneously in the form of clusters. Are there changes in voice quality, does the interviewee lean backwards, do hand gestures stop, does the head drop, are arms crossed, does foot-tapping increase, has eye contact decreased, and so forth. I am looking for clusters of behavioral changes.

When there is a substantial change from the interviewee's baseline behavior to what is being observed later, there is a reason for it. The reason is stress. This stress may be the result of several factors or a combination of any of them:

- The interviewee has begun understanding the implications of the investigation.
- The answers are embarrassing.
- The interviewee may fear that he or she will not be believed.
- The answers make the interviewee appear incompetent.
- The answers will implicate someone whom the interviewee knows.
- The answers make it appear that the interviewee is involved with a fraud.
- The answers clearly implicate the interviewee.
- The interviewee is lying.
- The interviewee has committed fraud.

At this point in the interview, all I can really be certain of is that the interviewee is undergoing stress. My job as an investigator is to interpret the cause of that stress after considering all of the possibilities.

Case Example

I once participated in a three-on-one interview—three FBI agents and one witness. We knew going into this interview that three-on-one was generally a bad idea, as it would be intimidating to the interviewee and could be confusing if questions came from multiple interviewers. We each had three separate bank fraud cases, and the interviewee was the number-two executive at a very large and reputable commercial development firm, and he was knowledgeable about the facts of all three of our cases. The interviewee was not a target, but we knew that his boss was implicated in a long list of federal felonies. We estimated that there was only one chance to conduct a surprise interview, and after that, his boss would engage legal counsel for the entire corporation, and we would never be able to talk to anyone.

The interview started out alright. We developed limited rapport, and the interviewee was a talented, smart, charismatic leader who was able to fake his confidence early on. Later in the interview, however, I observed something disturbing that I will never forget. The interviewee had his hands in front of him, just above a wooden desktop, and he was constantly wringing them. Under his palms was a pool of sweat. I could not help but observe that this pool of sweat kept getting larger one drop at a time. Only later in my career—when I investigated a doctor who provided medically unnecessary services for a condition known as excessive sweating or hyperhidrosis—did I reflect on that interview and arrive at an educated guess that the interviewee suffered from this same condition. Regardless, the interviewee was reacting to uncontrollable stress. The reason was obvious. He was providing incriminating information about his boss who was a legend in the community. After an indictment and lengthy federal trial, his boss was convicted of bank bribery, conspiracy, mail fraud, and wire fraud. The interviewee was a key witness.

4. *Questions*

The core of any interview is the actual questions. A question requests the interviewee to recall information, and recollection is tricky. In a perfect world, the interviewee would start at the beginning of an event, sequentially discuss all of the relevant facts, and then describe the impact on the organization. Unfortunately, that is not how recall works. In complicated cases or ones that go back a period of years, the interviewee usually has to randomly jump from fact to fact since recall likely is imperfect.

The goal is to obtain as much of the relevant information as possible. Two types of questions can be asked: open-ended questions and closed-ended questions. I always start with opened-ended questions, the broader the better—for example, "Tell me what you know about the ABC transaction." The question does not suggest the answer. An open-ended question also allows me to observe the depth of the interviewee's knowledge, the ability to recall, and where in the facts the interviewee chooses to start. After various open-ended questions are exhausted, closed-ended questions can be asked to obtain specific information.

Questions to be avoided are leading, compound, unclear, or loophole questions. A leading question may suggest the answer in the question itself. A leading question could mislead the interviewee to providing an inaccurate answer or could give away information that the interviewer does not want to be known. For example, if I am trying to confirm the recipient of a real estate commission on a HUD-1 real estate settlement statement, I will ask the interviewee to start at the beginning of the document and explain each line on the statement. I avoid asking a leading question such as, "Did Mr. Smith receive the real estate commission noted in section 7?"

A loophole question allows an interviewee to provide a truthful but incomplete answer, for example, "Did you ever pay him cash?" This allows for a truthful "no" answer but also allows the interviewee to avoid mentioning the free travel and Rolex watch that he provided to a coconspirator.

Fraud cases likely will require note taking. If two interviewers are present, who should take notes? Several factors should be considered. Note taking creates a barrier to communication because it causes pauses in the communication, and eye contact is dropped. When two people are conducting an interview, the one who is most knowledgeable of the facts should take the lead. Further, the second interviewer may not know the facts as well as the lead interviewer, especially in a complicated fraud matter, and this lack of knowledge can result in poor note taking and possibly have an impact on the quality of the interview report. Unless I am confident that the second note-taker will take good notes, I will likely take the notes myself. This will result in two sets of notes. Both note takers must also agree on every fact in a written report, even if it requires recontacting the interviewee for clarification.

5. *Verification*

Toward the end of the interview, I want to confirm my understanding of the information provided through the verification step. I will go through my notes and reaffirm critical information with the interviewee. For lengthy or complicated interviews, verification may occur at the end of each separate topic. The verification process may also result in additional recollection and start new lines of questioning.

6. *Catch-All Questions*

I was once investigating a bank failure and spoke with a very knowledge-able witness. A couple of years later, when the prosecutor and I were preparing this witness for trial, she provided some key information for the first time.

Feeling blindsided by this critical information, I asked why she was just now telling me this information. Her answer was that I had never asked her for it.

Many interviewees will not volunteer information. They do not want to lie, but if they are not asked a specific question, they will not provide the information. The problem can be aggravated by the fact that I may not know the subject matter well enough to ask the right questions. The solution is the catch-all question. It can be asked in several different ways. Following are some examples: "Is there anything else relevant to this topic?" You are obviously knowledgeable about the facts, so please help me ask the right questions. "What other questions do you think I should be asking?" "Is there anything you are not telling me?

7. *Departure*

Being interviewed about fraud is an unusual event in most people's lives. The interview itself is an attention getter. The implication is that someone did something wrong and that individual may have to face significant consequences. The interview may cause the interviewee to recall information after the interview has concluded. In fact, after the interview, the interviewee may begin checking records, reviewing e-mails, and talking with others. All of these steps may cause the interviewee to recall information or to provide new information. To ensure that the interviewee feels comfortable calling me, I always provide my business card with a request to call me on my cell phone at any time. I also ask if I can follow up on the matter in the future.

8. *Critique*

Interviewing is an art and not a science. I know I can always get better. After an interview, I critique myself as to how it went. This is best done when I have an interview partner and we can discuss the pros and cons of the interview. Was I prepared for the interview? Did I choose the right location? Did I spend enough time on building a rapport with the interviewee? Did I leave any information on the table? I know that taking the time to critique myself will make me a better interviewer.

Digital Evidence

Digital evidence is critical for most investigations. E-mails and texts may show knowledge and state of mind regarding critical facts. Electronic documents and spreadsheets can show planning, transaction details, and movement of funds. All of this information may be found in many diverse platforms. Starting with the end in mind, I assume that any digital evidence will be challenged in a subsequent trial. The first step of my investigation can have a big impact on the last step.

Digital forensic examinations may require involving one or more experts. Digital forensic examinations are very specialized, and the field is constantly changing. Further, the digital evidence may be found on various media including external devices, phones, computers, and the cloud. These computing devices operate on different operating systems and require specialized software to capture and analyze the data. Unfortunately, no single expert may be able to perform all of the necessary tasks. Chapter 14 details a list of questions that investigators should ask when they are engaging a digital forensic expert as well as a list of certifications that an expert may possess.

The exploitation of digital evidence requires two steps: collection and analysis. Software used to identify, extract, collect, and store digital evidence includes commercially available products and open-source software. If open-source software is being used, the forensic expert should be able to provide an explanation as to why it is being used. For example, open-source software may be used because it performs a specific task better than any other software.

There are a variety of software tools and choosing the right one will depend on the digital medium involved. This is a case when having the right tool is in the toolkit is necessary. Commercially available software includes the following:

- EnCase Forensic by Guidance Software
- Forensic ToolKit (FTK) by AccessData
- X-Ways Forensics and WinHex by X-Ways Software Technology AG

- E3 Universal Electronic Evidence Examination by Paraben

Open source software includes the following:

- Penguin Sleuth
- The Sleuth Kit
- Helix

Once the data has been collected in a legally sufficient way, the original data needs to be securely stored. Should an opposing party ever challenge the data, a well-documented report will explain the collection process, and the original data will be available for review. Investigators should only work from copies of the original data.

The second step is analysis. Depending on the type of data or the investigative need, various software packages are available. For analysis of structured data, including financial data to perform forensic accounting or auditing functions, I personally like Microsoft Excel because it can accomplish most tasks, and my learning curve will be short. For robust projects involving complicated data sets, other software products are available, like Interactive Data Extraction and Analysis (IDEA) by Caseware or Audit Command Language (ACL) by ACL Services Ltd. For eDiscovery and review of unstructured data such as e-mails, there are a variety of products, which include RelativityOne or Logikcull.

Documentary and Tangible Evidence

At the heart of any fraud investigation is information. Now more than ever, there is a lot of information at our fingertips. Information is readily available from public sources, proprietary databases, and social media. Documentary evidence is often gathered from witnesses, subjects, and third parties like banks, real estate agents, accountants, and attorneys. Other types of evidence include surveillance photos and videos, items gathered during a trash run, and physical assets. In a counterfeit product case, evidence can include the counterfeit product itself. Although it is technically digital evidence, information from social media can provide investigators with tremendous amounts of information.

When investigators are collecting any physical evidence, they should ensure that it will be admissible in court. Here again, working with legal counsel is important to ensure that the method of collection is legal and that the rules of evidence are followed to ensure admissibility. Chain-of-custody is a legal term used to describe the documentation of the movement of evidence during collection, testing, storage, and its subsequent presentation to a court. For example, the location of a key document may have been found in the CEO's desk. Establishing who found it, its location, and its long journey to the courtroom all needs to be documented on a chain-of-custody form.

Case Example

> While I was in private practice, I worked on a case about a counterfeit matter. I made a purchase of the suspected counterfeit product from a convenience store. I then placed my initials and the date on the original evidence. I kept a receipt of the purchase, took a photo of the product, and created a chain-of-custody form. I then shipped the product and the chain-of-custody form to a laboratory of the manufacturer. Each person that took possession of the product signed the form. When the case went to trial, the evidence was clearly identified, there was a chain of custody, and the expert witness could testify with confidence about the product and its provenance.

The evidentiary value of a document can take many forms. The content of the document itself is generally the most significant. Investigators should always be mindful of fingerprints and handwriting that may be found on a document. If the author of the document or someone who has been in possession of it denies knowledge of the document, sometimes using fingerprints and handwriting analysis is the best way to rebut the denial. When investigators are collecting this type of evidence, they should try to use cloth gloves, limit the number of people who touch it, and place it in a paper envelope for preservation.

Public Records

Although the list of publicly available records is lengthy, fraud investigators should have familiarity with these common sources of information:

- Secretary of State Filings
- Criminal and Civil Court Records
- Real estate Records
- Property Tax Records
- Bankruptcy Records
- Marriage, Divorce, and Birth Records
- Professional Licensing and Disciplinary Records
- Uniform Commercial Code Filings
- Freedom of Information Act to Obtain Federal Government Records
- State Open Records Act to Obtain State Government Records
- Securities and Exchange Commission's EDGAR Database
- Financial Industry Regulatory Authority Database
- Office of Foreign Asset Control Records

Proprietary Databases

More sensitive information about individuals may be found in fee-for-service databases. Sometimes locating a witness, subject, or defendant is the hardest part of the interview process. The databases below also help with locating people of interest, their assets, and other key information that is not available in open-source information.

- Westlaw
- LexisNexis
- Thomson Reuters CLEAR
- TLOxp (TransUnion)
- IRBsearch

- Dun & Bradstreet
- Experian
- Equifax
- TransUnion

Obtaining readily available information about an employee can raise legal issues. As discussed under the topic of background investigations, legal counsel should be consulted when an investigator is gathering information that will be used by an employer when making employment decisions.

Personal and Financial Records

Fraud investigators generally want to obtain sensitive records of an individual under investigation, including bank account statements, credit card statements, tax returns, and phone and medical records. The easiest way to obtain these records is by obtaining the owner's consent. If making such a request fails or is not appropriate, a legal process may be required.

Bank records are usually required in fraud investigations. How does an investigator discover the identity of the suspect's bank? For criminal investigations, the USA Patriot Act enables law enforcement to conduct nationwide canvassing to obtain records relating to money laundering. Private investigators may have contacts who will disclose the location of bank and brokerage accounts. Once the location of the account is known, a legal process will be required to obtain the account statements.

When a fraud investigator is investigating civil cases, uncovering the location of bank and investment accounts can be far more difficult. Investigators may rely on attorneys involved in the matter to issue subpoenas for records from known institutions or from the targets themselves. When tracing funds, investigators may discover previously undisclosed accounts.

Social Media

Social media is a gift to investigators. People will intentionally and unintentionally disclose personal information through social media. I know of a case in which a bank robber used social media to display his loot in a picture with his GPS coordinates located in the picture's metadata. An investigator can glean a lot of information to assist in locating individuals, discovering their assets, and establishing relationships. In a securities fraud case, I determined the identity of a defendant by tying a photograph of a cat in a Twitter moniker (handle) to the person's Facebook account. Common social media platforms include the following:

- Facebook
- LinkedIn
- YouTube
- Pinterest
- Instagram
- Personal & Business Websites
- Twitter

Report Writing

The reporting of investigative results should be closely coordinated with the manager, client, attorney, or other party requesting the report. A report must be accurate; there is no room for factual inaccuracy or sloppiness. On occasion, a report may be requested in an oral format due to the sensitivity of the information or the cost of preparing a written report.

Two different types of reports may be requested in a fraud related matter: an investigative report or an expert report. An investigative report provides the results of an investigation so that stakeholders can make decisions. Such a report may be used for a disciplinary matter, the termination of an employee, a civil lawsuit, or a referral to criminal authorities. An expert report may be required during civil or criminal litigation and will be covered in more detail in Chapter 15.

An investigative report can be organized in various logical formats. A cover letter or a portion of the report should detail who requested the report and for what purpose. The ACFE's *Fraud Examiners Manual* suggests the following flexible format:[5]

1. Background
2. Findings
3. Executive summary
4. Summary
5. Scope
6. Impact
7. Approach
8. Follow-up/recommendation

Missing from the ACFE's recommended format is an appendix. An investigative report should likely cite or refer to exhibits and supporting documentation. I recommend including these documents in an appendix for easy reference by the reader.

The author of a report should never reach an opinion about the guilt or innocence of anyone. This prohibition can be found in federal and state rules of evidence, the AICPA standards, and the ACFE's Code of Ethics.[6] This does not mean that if a fraud has likely been committed that it will not be conveyed in the report. A well-written report will detail the facts and compare them against a company's policy or the legal elements constituting fraud. The reader will then be able to reach a logical conclusion.

Case Example

The following is an excerpt from a fictional investigative report involving an apparent Ponzi scheme.

Facts

The facts show that Bernie Smith told investors he was going to invest their money in an investment scheme known as a split-strike conversion involving publicly traded stocks. Investors were promised annual rates of return in excess of 16 percent and were told that their investment would be risk-free. As of the date of this report, a 52-week U.S. Treasury Bond yield was 2.5 percent. Bank accounts have been reviewed, and all investor deposits have been isolated and traced. The number of investors substantially increased over time. The funds either have been traced to Bernie Smith's personal expenditures, including the purchase of a

$3.1 million home, or were returned to investors. Any investor who redeemed a portion of his or her investment was told that it was a return of both principal and profits. No funds have been found to purchase any type of investment including stocks, bonds or other security. Bernie Smith has appeared in various social columns as an up-and-coming professional in the investment community and a most eligible bachelor.

Definition of a Ponzi Scheme

A Ponzi scheme can be defined as a fraud in which the operator promotes a bogus investment opportunity to lure investors. The operator pays purported profits to earlier investors with proceeds from newer investors. Because the operator is repaying investors with their principal, the scheme is only viable if it can attract new investors. Ponzi scheme operators generally promise higher than market rates of return and tell investors that their investment is safe.

Recommendation

We found the facts surrounding Bernie Smith's receipt and disbursement of investors' funds to be consistent with the operation of a Ponzi scheme. We recommend that this matter be referred the FBI for evaluation.

The executive summary is probably the most important part of the report, especially for lengthy reports. The body of the report really serves as the documentation for the key findings provided in the executive summary.

To make the report user friendly, complicated concepts can be illustrated or described using charts, diagrams, and spreadsheets. Lastly, investigators should always assume that their report will find its way to the front page of a newspaper. This potential reality causes investigators to focus on the accuracy of the facts, whether they are disclosing unnecessary information, and the phraseology of sensitive information.

CHAPTER 13
Fraud Crisis Management

"We cannot solve our problems with the same
thinking we used when we created them."

—ALBERT EINSTEIN

In 2001, Enron ushered in a wave of accounting and governance malfeasance scandals. The FBI was certainly unprepared for the magnitude of the problem—it did not have a plan. From my involvement with these cases, I observed the victimized corporations did not have a plan either—they never thought fraud would ever happen to them. Once an investigation is under way and problematic facts begin mounting, an organization will have to broach the last two components of the fraud life cycle: mitigation and remediation.

Mitigation is a process of minimizing the collateral effects of fraud on the organization as well as ensuring that the particular type of fraud never occurs again. Mitigation efforts are more important if the fraud rises to the level of an organizational crisis. Remediation is the process of attempting to make the victim whole through financial recovery. Conceptually, these two processes should occur simultaneously; however, remediation usually involves legal processes that are likely to continue long after mitigation efforts are completed.

For high-impact frauds, an organization's ability to deal with these issues may depend on whether fraud was appropriately addressed in the organization's crisis management plan. A crisis management plan can be viewed as a continuum. On one end, the leadership team can envision a crisis (any crisis) that would be so significant that it would need time and resources to address its eventuality. On the other end, the leadership team mistakenly convinces itself that such a crisis could never happen to their organization, so they fail to plan. A fraud risk assessment will assist an organization in designing an appropriate plan.

Of course, fraud is only one of many possible organizational crises. These crises can include:

- Technology Crisis
- Data Breach
- Crisis Malevolence
- Natural Disaster
- Workplace Violence
- Financial Crisis
- Systemic Fraud
- Governance Corruption

A crisis can damage corporate infrastructure, impact customer good will, or drive down a company's stock price. The long-term impact on an organization can be significant. In fact, a crisis can be so significant that it can raise the prospect of whether or not the organization will be able to survive the event.

For our purposes, I will focus on fraud-related events and how they impact an organization. Most frauds will not rise to the level of a corporate crisis, but material frauds will. The suspected perpetrators of the fraud may also dictate how the organization responds. A fraud caused by a midlevel manager or an outside predator is easy enough to resolve: pour investigative resources on the issue, and the facts will come flooding out. Change the fraud to a significant financial statement fraud or a C-suite level conflicts-of-interest matter, and it can be a paralyzing event. Key stakeholders may try to circle the wagons, and if successful, the discovery of the facts may slow to a trickle.

Once fraud is discovered, management should consider the mitigation and remediation solutions discussed below to best effect an outcome.

Mitigation

Mitigation involves addressing the collateral effects that fraud imposes on an organization. Outside experts may have to be engaged on short notice. The fraud may have caused reputational harm or may have impaired the trust of employees, vendors, and customers. Timely, accurate, and appropriate communication must be made to all stakeholders. Mitigation will also involve a risk assessment to assess how the problem occurred and the development of internal controls to ensure that this particular type of fraud never happens again. In fact, a board has a legal obligation to safeguard corporate assets from fraud through the development of a system of internal controls.[1] Because crisis management is inherently deployed in real time, its effectiveness will be enhanced if a plan exists and the plan has been rehearsed either notionally or through a formal tabletop exercise.

Consider the example of the now all-too-common ransomware attack. Inside the organization, data is rendered inaccessible, organizational processes are crippled, and personnel are in various stages of panic and stress. Outside the organization, customers, vendors, and other constituents are immediately and negatively impacted. Regulatory and law enforcement authorities will converge on the organization, wanting access to information. Victim notification requirements may be legally required. All the while, the media is having a frenzy reporting on a calamity that could likely have been prevented in the first place. Unfortunately, this series of events occurred in 2018 when the city of Atlanta was hit by the SamSam ransomware attack.

When these events happen in real time, an organization has no time for reflection or pontification. Consequential decisions have to be made rapidly. Accordingly, a crisis management plan should be in place. Executive management should develop a framework around these critical components:

- Understand the potential threats
- Identify team members and responsibilities
- Have resources to stop the ongoing issue
- Establish internal communication protocols
- Communicate externally with a united voice
- Identify and stabilize stakeholders

- Establish preventive measures
- Restore stakeholder trust

This model is flexible enough to accommodate most organizations despite varying industries, business models, and the threats they may face. A fraud crisis management plan could be a stand-alone plan, or it could be incorporated into a larger crisis management plan.

Remediation

Remediation is an attempt to make the victim whole by holding responsible parties accountable. This can also include seeking recovery from a fidelity insurance policy, fidelity bond, or cyber insurance policy. Further, management should not overlook using the criminal justice system to obtain recovery through asset forfeiture or court-ordered restitution. Remediation strategies should be considered in tandem with the ongoing mitigation efforts. Remedial processes are inherently longer-term solutions, as they usually will involve civil and criminal litigation.

Remediation and mitigation efforts can also result in conflict. Management may believe its first duty is to stop the fraud, cyberattack, or other incident. Although immediate efforts to stop such an incident may be appropriate, this focus can also damage efforts to collect evidence. Management may also believe that the honorable thing to do is to accept blame for a portion of the underlying issue. Admission of liability at an early stage in the investigation may be detrimental to subsequent civil or criminal litigation.

Pressure to terminate, sue, or prosecute anyone could be mounting from the media or those impacted by the fraud. Despite this pressure, decision makers should not jump the gun when it comes to remediation. A crisis event will likely be a challenge for any board or leadership team when forced to make consequential decisions with incomplete information. An investigation can unfortunately be a lengthy process. When more facts are known, better decisions can be made. When it becomes increasingly clear that an employee (or employees) is involved in a fraud, those in charge of governance will need to make critical decisions. Complicating the matter, when there are ongoing parallel investigations, multiple investigators are trying to collect from a single body of evidence. Further, these separate investigations may reach varying results.

As an FBI agent, I always appreciated that criminal processes like a federal grand jury subpoena or a search warrant took precedence over civil processes to collect evidence. Unfortunately, other stakeholders—the board, potential plaintiffs, creditors, business partners, or even a spouse— are left struggling to obtain the same evidence in order to make critical decisions and relevant claims.

At the conclusion of the mitigation and remediation efforts, the organization will have moved through the entire fraud life cycle. The organization will have learned of its ability to handle a fraud crisis. This is now an excellent time to start at the beginning of the fraud life cycle and renew prevention efforts by conducting an enterprise-wide fraud risk assessment

PART IV:
Forensic Experts

- The Professionals
- Starting with the End in Mind

CHAPTER 14
The Professionals

"None of us is as smart as all of us"

—KENNETH HARTLEY BLANCHARD

Fraud can occur in every industry, in every company, and within every division or segment of a company. Fraud investigations are challenging, especially at the start of the investigation because the investigators must learn about the industry in which a fraud is alleged to have occurred. For example, investigating a bribe of a foreign official in the pharmaceutical industry is quite different from investigating an early revenue recognition scheme in the software industry. A fraudulent invoicing scheme by a subcontractor is quite different from an elected official having an undisclosed interest in a company that is doing business with the government.

The resolution of fraud-related issues generally requires a team of professionals. The team for a typical "internal investigation" is often led by an attorney or a representative of management. While the investigative methodology remains the same, its application will vary with each engagement. The end goal is to have a final product that resolves the fraud allegation. This chapter focuses on the professionals or specialists who are needed to staff fraud engagements.

Professional Licenses

There are a variety of professionals who may become involved in an investigation: attorneys, CPAs, private investigators, forensic accountants, forensic computer specialists, and other subject matter experts. Of these, three types of professionals are generally required to hold professional licenses: attorneys, CPAs, and private investigators. Private investigators are required to be licensed in all states except Alaska, Idaho, Mississippi, South Dakota, and Wyoming.[1] All of these professionals' licenses can be confirmed by going to the webpage of their particular licensing board. Management may also be able to find out if a professional's license is active and whether there have been any disciplinary actions filed against the license holder. These various professionals sometimes serve in overlapping functions. Depending on the state, a licensed attorney or CPA may be exempt from needing a private investigator's license. The rules vary greatly by state, so each professional should always check state law to see if an exemption applies. For example, an attorney in Georgia is generally exempt from needing a private investigator's license. A CPA in Texas is likewise exempt from needing a private investigator's license.

The need for an attorney in most fraud engagements is readily apparent. Legal issues can arise at almost any stage in the investigation. A fraud investigator will need to know the legal elements of the particular fraud being investigated. Access to subpoena authority through counsel is almost always required in contested matters. The party seeking the investigation will likely benefit from the attorney–client privilege and work product doctrine.

Each of these three unique professionals (attorney, investigator, and CPA) are bound by a code of ethics that can impact a fraud-related matter. An attorney may not be able to surreptitiously record another party. A CPA typically is not able to take a case on a contingency fee basis. Further, a CPA may not report a conclusion on the ultimate issue of fraud or other legal determinations. All of these professionals are ethically bound to protect the confidentiality of their client's information.

Accountants

Accountants can play a crucial role in fraud cases because of their knowledge of financial matters. The term "accountant" includes a diverse field of professionals who possess important knowledge, skills, and abilities as described below.

Forensic Accountant

The definition of "forensic accountant" can vary significantly. The profession does not require a license, and there is no formal standards-setting board. The term is better understood if we define the two words separately. The term "forensic" is defined as, "used in, suitable to, courts of law or public debate."[2] The term "accounting" in this context should more broadly mean "knowledge of financial matters." So, a working definition of "forensic accounting" can be "the presentation of financial matters in a legal forum."

The AICPA's new Statement on Standards for Forensic Services defines "forensic accounting services" as "the application of specialized knowledge and investigative skills to collect, analyze and evaluate certain evidential matter and to interpret and communicate findings."[3] The AICPA further defines "forensic engagements" as either a "Litigation Engagement" or an "Investigation Engagement."

The AICPA has a certification known as Certified in Financial Forensics (CFF), which can be obtained by a CPA who is an AICPA member and passes the rigorous CFF examination. The CFF Core Focus Wheel shown below describes the various skills needed to become a CFF.

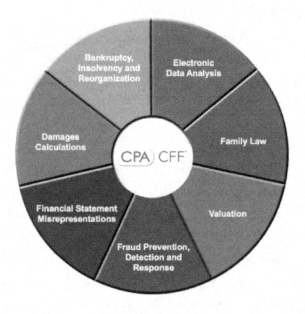

Although relatively new, a highly respected and comprehensive forensic accounting certification is the Master Analyst in Financial Forensics (MAFF) sponsored by the National Association of Certified Valuators and Analysts (NACVA). Most NACVA members are CPAs. Unlike most financial litigation training that tends to be general in scope, MAFF training, continuing education, and related resources provide attendees with an understanding of the professional responsibilities and legal underpinnings necessary to providing credible financial forensics services. The seasoned financial forensics experts who teach in the MAFF program also dive into the methodologies and approaches for calculating damages; financial investigative and forensic accounting techniques; skills development for communicating with judges, attorneys, and juries; and practice building strategies that are being employed by successful and emerging financial forensics analysts.

Forensic accountants specializing in fraud-related issues should have a broad but also fairly deep knowledge base. Accounting and financial knowledge is required to understand complex fraud issues. Investigative knowledge is required to appropriately gather evidence for potential litigation. Legal knowledge is required to ensure that the forensic accountant's services will be legally appropriate and sufficient. Knowledge of psychology is required and quite indispensable in the prevention and detection of fraud and during investigations, which include holding interviews and interrogations. Simply put, fraud is committed by human beings; psychology and psychiatry encompass the study of the principles of human behavior; therefore, in such circumstances, how can organizations not utilize these disciplines whenever fraud is being investigated?[4]

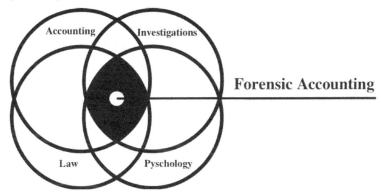

External Auditor

An external auditor is charged with reaching a professional opinion on the financial statements prepared by a company's management. Regarding the financial statements of a publicly traded company, the PCAOB requires the external auditor to reach an opinion "on the fairness which they present, in all material respects, financial position, results of operation, and its cash flows in conformity with generally accepted accounting principles."[5] The standards further require the external auditor to plan the audit to obtain reasonable assurance about whether the financial statements are free from material misstatement whether caused by error or fraud.[6]

External auditors are not necessarily fraud experts. When they are planning their audit procedures or when they encounter suspicious issues, they may consult with accountants possessing greater fraud expertise. Most importantly, external auditors are responsible for finding fraud when it has a material impact on the financial statements.

Internal Auditor

According to the IIA, an internal auditor is charged with providing independent assurance and consulting activities to improve an organization's operations, which can be done by evaluating the effectiveness of risk management, control, and governance processes.[7] Chapter 5 describes the internal audit function in detail. Internal auditors can obtain the certification Certified Internal Auditor (CIA) from the IIA. Internal auditors are not necessarily CPAs.

Although the fields of external auditing, internal auditing, fraud investigation, and forensic accounting are similar, the work is done by different professionals, with different skill sets, and for different purposes, as shown in the chart below.

Auditors, Accountants, and Fraud Specialists				
Issue	External Audit	Internal Audit	Fraud Investigation	Forensic Accounting
Objective	Verify financial statements of a company	Assess activities and operations, provide recommendations	Determine if fraud has occurred, parties involved, and remediation	Financial analysis of a specific issue resolved in a legal forum
Conducted By	External CPA	Employee with auditing knowledge	Attorney, CPA, CFE, private investigator, management	CPA, professional with specialized knowledge
Users	Various stakeholders	Management	Any party	Any party
Scope	Financial statements	Decided by management	Allegation resolution	Issue driven
Methodology	GAAS, GAAP	IIA standards, management's request	Evidence and forensic posture driven	Evidence and standards based
Timing	Annual	Recurring	Issue specific and predication based	Party need and issue driven
Relationship	Nonadversarial; professional skepticism	Professional skepticism	Adversarial	Independent

Other Professionals

There are a variety of professionals who may be needed in a forensic engagement, including certified fraud examiners and computer forensic experts.

Certified Fraud Examiner

A certified fraud examiner (CFE) is a certification by the Association of Certified Fraud Examiners. A CFE has expertise in fraud prevention, detection, and investigation. CFEs have specialized knowledge in fraud, and the CFE credential is often held by internal auditors, forensic accountants, private investigators, and loss prevention specialists.

Digital Forensic Experts

The importance of retaining digital forensic experts was emphasized in Chapter 12. These experts are not all the same, and when retaining them, management should ask several questions:

- What is your expertise?
- What type of devices can you examine?
- What type of software do you use? Commercial or open source?
- Do you have a certification for that software?
- Does your firm use the latest versions of the software?
- Have you ever provided digital forensic support in litigation?
- Have you testified at a deposition or a trial?
- What certifications do you hold?

There are many certifications that a digital forensic expert may possess, and more is generally better. The list below contains some of the more common certifications for digital forensic experts along with the credentialing organization.

- AccessData Certified Examiner (AccessData Corporation)
- Certified Computer Examiner (International Society of Forensic Computer Examiners)
- Certified Forensic Computer Examiner (The International Association of Computer Investigative Specialists)
- Computer Hacking Forensic Investigator (EC-Council)

- Digital Forensics Certified Practitioner (Digital Forensics Certification Board)
- Digital Forensics Certified Associate (Digital Forensics Certification Board)
- EnCase Certified Examiner (Guidance Software Incorporated)
- GIAC Certified Forensic Examiner (SANS Institute Global Information Assurance Certification)
- GIAC Certified Forensic Analyst (SANS Institute Global Information Assurance Certification)
- PCI Forensic Investigator (Payment Card Industry Security Standards Council)

Professional Certifications

Fraud-related engagements often require professionals with a specialty: forensic accountants, internal auditors, and private investigators. The chart below lists some of the certifications that these professionals may hold.

Professional Groups and Certifications

Organization	Certification	Description
American Board of Forensic Accounting	ABGOV—Government Forensic Accountant	Forensic accounting knowledge in the government sector
	CCSA—Certified Cyber Security Accountant	Forensic accounting and analysis pertaining to cyber security and fraud prevention and detection
	CRFAC—Certified Forensic Accountant	For CPAs with knowledge of forensic accounting, fraud, litigation services, cyber security, and valuation
	LHA—Licensed Healthcare Auditor	Forensic accounting and analysis as it pertains to healthcare auditing and fraud prevention and detection
	RFI—Registered Forensic Investigator	Forensic accounting and analysis for non-CPAs
American Institute of Certified Public Accountants	CFF—Certified in Financial Forensics	CPAs who are members of the AICPA with a knowledge of forensic accounting
	ABV—Accredited in Business Valuation	CPAs and other professionals who are a member of the AICPA with knowledge in business valuation
	CITP—Certified Information Technology Professional	CPAs who are a member of the AICPA with a knowledge of information technology
Association of Certified Anti-Money Laundering Specialists	CAMS—Certified Anti-Money Laundering Specialist	Specialized knowledge in money laundering and financial crime risks
Association of Certified Fraud Examiners	CFE—Certified Fraud Examiner	Expertise in fraud examination
Association of Certified Fraud Specialists	CFS—Certified Fraud Specialist	Expertise in the investigation of fraud
Forensic CPA Society	FCPA—Forensic Certified Public Accountant	CPA with a knowledge of forensic accounting
Institute of Internal Auditors	CIA—Certified Internal Auditor	Knowledge of the internal auditing function
National Association of Certified Valuators and Analysts	CVA—Certified Valuation Analysts	Expertise in the valuation of a business
	MAFF—Master Analysts in Financial Forensics	Knowledge of the NACVA's financial forensics body of knowledge

CHAPTER 15

Starting with the End in Mind

"It is not what we know, but what we can prove"

—SHERLOCK HOLMES IN *THE HOUNDS OF THE BASKERVILLES*, BY
SIR ARTHUR CONAN DOYLE

"All rise. Jury foreperson—has the jury reached a verdict?" "We have, your Honor." "What say you?" "We the jury, in the case of the *United States v. Bernie Smith*, find the defendant guilty on all counts."

That is how the case typically ends. The case will likely have begun with a complaint from the victim to law enforcement. Progressing from a complaint to a conviction takes a lot of effort. The case will only be successful if the evidence is gathered in a legally appropriate and sufficient manner and introduced into court under the rules of evidence. If an expert witness testifies, various professional standards and rules will apply. To have a successful case, I always start with the end in mind.

Our legal system is based on a lot of rules. In criminal cases, the U.S. Constitution plays a significant role. For any case, the attorney, investigator, or forensic accountant needs to know how the case will likely end. Is the case a civil or a criminal matter? If it is litigated, will the case be tried in federal or state court or in an administrative hearing? The answer to each of these questions will dictate which rules of procedure and rules of evidence should be followed.

Navigating these rules is the responsibility of the attorney. This reason alone is why an attorney is needed early in an investigation. The federal rules apply in all federal courts. The states rules, however, can vary from state to state. For our purposes, I will discuss the federal rules. Increasingly, the states are adopting the federal rules with or without variations.

Civil Case versus Criminal Case

Both civil and criminal fraud cases begin with an allegation. An investigation ensues to verify the facts. A charging document or civil complaint is filed in court to initiate the court action. The case goes through a discovery process between the parties. The case is resolved at trial. From here, the civil and criminal systems diverge. The differences in these two systems arise from U.S. Constitutional guarantees, the inherent purposes of the two systems, and the development of rules over time.

In a criminal matter, the government is a party and is asserting that an individual has committed a crime. In a civil matter, there is no charge that a defendant has committed a crime. Rather, the plaintiff is seeking monetary damages or equitable relief in the form of an injunction to prevent the defendant from doing something.

The burden of proof for the government in a criminal matter is beyond a reasonable doubt, whereas the burden of proof in a civil matter is a preponderance of the evidence. Another practical distinction for investigators and forensic accountants is that in a criminal matter, most of the investigation occurs before the defendant is criminally charged. In a civil matter, most of the investigation occurs after a complaint is filed through a process called "discovery."

Various sets of rules are followed to navigate a case through the legal system. The chart below tracks the federal rules. For a civil case, the Federal Rules of Civil Procedure control how a case makes its way through the system prior to a trial. For a criminal case, the Federal Rules of Criminal Procedure control how a case makes its way through the system. For both civil and criminal cases, the Federal Rules of Evidence control the admissibility of evidence at trial.

Distinction Between Civil and Criminal Processes		
Time Line	**Civil Matter**	**Criminal Matter**
Pre-Court Involvement	Something Happened Interviews Evidence Collection Internal Investigation	Something Happened Interviews Undercover Operations Any investigative Technique Evidence Collection
Grand Jury	N/A	Subpoena Witnesses Subpoena Documents
Complaint	Civil Complaint – Allegation FRCP 9 – Fraud Answer – Deny or Admit	"Criminal Complaint" Rarely Used in Fraud Cases
Indictment / Information	N/A	Criminal Charging Instrument
Discovery	Broad Discovery FRCP 26 Depositions Interrogatories Expert Witnesses	FRCrP 16 Brady and Giglio Material Prior Statements of Defendant Documents and Objects Expert Witnesses
Burden of Proof	Preponderance of the Evidence	Beyond a Reasonable Doubt
Judgment	Injunction Dollar Judgment	Guilty, Acquittal, Hung Jury
Sentencing		U.S. Sentencing Guidelines Prison Sentence Fines Restitution

Consultant versus Expert Witness

An attorney litigating a fraud-related case may need a forensic accountant to assist in the case. More specifically, the forensic accountant may be engaged in the capacity of a consultant or an expert witness. As a consultant, the forensic accountant assists counsel in collecting, analyzing, and evaluating evidential matter. The opposing party may never learn that a consultant has been retained. In contrast, an attorney may retain a forensic accountant to provide expert testimony at trial. Before the expert is allowed to testify, the expert may be required to produce a written report, may be subject to a deposition, and may be subject to scrutiny by the presiding judge prior to trial in what is known as a "Daubert hearing."

Neither of these two types of witnesses (consultant or expert) should be confused with the CPA who serves as a "fact witness." For example, an auditor who stumbles across fraud during an audit may speak with witnesses, examine documents, and substantiate findings in his or her work papers. Should the auditor later be called to testify about knowledge of what he or she has observed, the auditor will testify as a witness to the facts in the case.

Since most forensic accountants are CPAs and therefore members of the American Institute of Certified Public Accountants, the distinction between a consultant and an expert is important under both the AICPA Code of Professional Conduct and the AICPA's professional standards. In fact, the distinction also has significant legal implications under the Federal Rules of Civil Procedure Rule 26 as well as a state's comparable rules. Let's look at some of the professional and legal requirements when a CPA serves as either a consultant or an expert witness.

AICPA Code and Standards

A summary of the applicable AICPA's Code of Professional Conduct (Code) are discussed below:

- The Code distinguishes between a consultant and an expert witness. Because the services of an expert witness create the appearance that the expert witness is advocating or promoting a client's position, the expert witness is deemed to not be independent.[1] In this context, this lack of independence means that the Code will not permit the expert witness to also engage in attestation services (audit work) for the same client. This lack of independence may also impair the attestation services of the expert witness's firm can ethically provide.[2] Conversely, this prohibition will generally not apply to a CPA who is also serving as a factual witness, providing an investigative service or other service as a nonexpert witness.

- A CPA must maintain integrity and objectivity, must be free of conflicts of interest, and must not knowingly misrepresent facts or subordinate his or her judgment to others.[3] This rule is important when the forensic expert is working with a strong-willed attorney who is advocating for the client. After all, attorneys are duty bound to zealously represent their clients. When providing expert witness services, however, the CPA must be an advocate for the facts, the standards, and the profession, but not for the attorney or underlying client.

- A CPA generally has a duty to keep client information confidential.[4] When serving as an expert witness, the CPA may be required to disclose any factual information learned from the client. This is not true for the CPA who is serving as a consultant.

The AICPA has three standards that may apply to CPAs:

- Statement on Standards for Consulting Services (SSCS) No. 1.

- Statement on Standards for Valuation Services (SSVS) No. 1.

- Statement on Standards for Forensic Services (SSFS) No. 1. This standard was issued to protect the public interest by improving the consistency and quality of practice in the growing forensic services community. The SSFS No. 1 became effective on May 1, 2019.

Some of the important elements in the SSFS No. 1 standard include the following:

- The standard applies to litigation and investigative services.

- Forensic services must be performed with:

  ○ *Professional competence.* Undertake only those professional services that the member or the member's firm can reasonably expect to be completed with professional competence.

  ○ *Due professional care.* Exercise due professional care in the performance of professional services.

- ○ *Planning and supervision.* Adequately plan and supervise the performance of professional services.

- ○ *Sufficient relevant data.* Obtain sufficient relevant data to afford a reasonable basis for conclusions or recommendations in relation to any professional services performed.

- A member may not provide an expert opinion on a contingency fee basis.

- The ultimate decision as to the occurrence of fraud or other legal conclusion is to be determined by the trier-of-fact, and the CPA is prohibited from opining as to the ultimate conclusion of fraud or other legal determinations.

Civil Rules of Procedure

The Federal Rules of Civil Procedure (FRCP) contain an enhanced pleading standard for a plaintiff alleging fraud in its complaint. These rules also provide the framework for civil discovery, including those pertaining to a consultant or expert witness.

- A party alleging fraud in a complaint must meet the higher pleading standard of stating with particularity the circumstances constituting the fraud. For instance, a plaintiff must allege who engaged in the fraud, the fraudulent statement or omission, and how the plaintiff was injured by the fraud. The rule can help protect an innocent individual from being wrongly accused of fraud. It can also stymie a victim of fraud who needs the discovery process to be able to meet the higher standard of pleading the fraud with particularity in the first instance. The net effect of the rule is that victims of fraud may need to enhance their prelitigation investigation efforts to meet this higher burden. See Rule 9(b), FRCP.

- The process of disclosing information among parties during litigation is known as "discovery." The rule states that any nonprivileged matter that is relevant to a party's claim or defense is subject to discovery. The principles behind the FRCP include a liberal discovery process. The idea is that increased transparency may resolve disputes sooner in the legal process. See Rule 26(b)(1) FRCP.

- The attorney work-product doctrine protects from discovery those documents that are prepared in anticipation of litigation. This includes documents of the attorney and other parties who assist the attorney in the litigation, including a consultant. Documents that reflect the mental impressions of these individuals have absolute protection from discovery, and all other documents prepared in anticipation of litigation are also likely shielded from discovery absent a substantial need by an opposing party. See Rule 26(b)(3) FRCP.

- An expert witness has to make the following disclosures during discovery:

  o Written report of opinions and a basis for them.

  o Facts or data the expert relied in forming an opinion.

  o Exhibits that will be used to support an opinion.

  o Expert's qualifications and a list of the publications authored in the past 10 years.

  o List of cases in which the witness testified as an expert in the past 4 years.

  o Compensation to be paid to the expert. See Rule 26(a)(2)(B).

- An expert may be deposed. However, most of the prior communications between the attorney and expert witness are protected from discovery as well as the draft opinions of the expert witness. Also significant, any information pertaining to any consultant (not expert witness) may generally not be discovered. See Rule 26(b)(4) FRCP. These rules may vary under state law.

Daubert

Prior to trial, a party must disclose any expert witness whom it intends to call in its case. The Federal Rules of Evidence Rule 702 provides the criteria a federal judge will use to evaluate a witness's qualifications. Rule 702 states:

> A witness who is qualified as an expert by knowledge, skill, experience, training, or education may testify in the form of an opinion or otherwise if:
>
> (a) The expert's scientific, technical, or other specialized knowledge will help the trier of fact to understand the evidence or to determine a fact in issue
>
> (b) The testimony is based on sufficient facts or data
>
> (c) The testimony is the product of reliable principles and methods
>
> (d) The expert has reliably applied the principles and methods to the facts of the case.

Rule 702 now reflects the amendments that were made after the United States Supreme Court decided the case *Daubert v. Merrell Dow Pharmaceuticals, Inc.*, 509 U.S. 579 (1993). The *Daubert* case involved a scientific expert witness's opinion on the issue of whether the defendant's drug caused a birth defect. The Court held that the trial judge is the gatekeeper for admitting evidence and provided the following factors for trial courts to consider when applying Rule 702:

- Whether the theory can be (and has been) tested
- Whether the theory or technique has been subjected to peer review or publication
- The theory's potential rate of error
- Whether the theory or technique has gained general acceptance

The *Daubert* factors assist a court in assessing whether a witness should be qualified as an expert in a case. The *Daubert* case involved scientific evidence and would not seem to readily apply to financial or fraud-related issues. The United States Supreme Court held in *Kumho Tire Co. v. Carmichael*, 526 U.S. 137 (1999) that *Daubert* does apply to nonscientific expert testimony; however, the method of determining reliability should vary at the discretion of the trial judge. A forensic-accountant expert witness using GAAS or GAAP as the standard being relied upon to analyze an issue should present no problem for a trial judge. A forensic-accounting expert should also have a strong argument when relying on publications like the AICPA's Practice Aids that provide non-authoritative guidance because as they are the product of experts in the field and are published by the AICPA. This type of guidance demonstrates that reliable principles and methods were relied upon by the expert to reach an opinion since they have been peer reviewed by a prominent standard bearer.

The authors of an article appearing in the *Ohio CPA Journal* provide the following guidance for an expert witness in reaching an opinion:[5]

1. Know the relevant professional standards.

2. Apply the relevant professional standards.

3. Know the relevant professional literature.

4. Know the relevant professional organizations.

5. Use generally accepted analytical methods.

6. Use multiple analytical methods.

7. Synthesize the conclusions of multiple analytical methods.

8. Disclose all significant analytical assumptions and variables.

9. Subject the analysis to peer review.

10. Test the analysis—and the conclusions—for reasonableness.

The *Daubert* standard applies in all federal courts. In financial litigation cases in which a CPA serves as the expert witness for the plaintiff or the defendant, the CPA must withstand the *Daubert* challenge to their qualifications, including the nature, scope, and reliability of methods used.[6] Although a significant majority of states now follow the *Daubert* standard, some states still follow the older standard enunciated in *Frye v. United States*, 293 F. 1013 (D.C. Cir 1923). The issue in *Frye* was whether a precursor to the modern-day polygraph could be used by a defendant to demonstrate innocence. The *Frye* court held the standard for the admission of scientific evidence was whether it was "sufficiently established to have gained general acceptance in the particular field in which it belongs." Due to differing standards among courts, the expert witness must work closely with counsel prior to the trial.

Federal Rules of Criminal Procedure

The Federal Rules of Criminal Procedure (FRCrP) control how criminal prosecutions are conducted. Investigators and forensic accountants should have a working knowledge of Rule 6, pertaining to grand juries, and Rule 16, pertaining to discovery.

FRCrP Rule 6

FRCrP Rule 6 provides the details of how a federal grand jury functions. A grand jury meets in secret and is composed of between 16 and 23 jurors. A vote from 12 jurors is required to indict a defendant. In the federal criminal system, a defendant has a constitutional right to be charged by a grand jury indictment for any felony before being required to stand trial. The requirement to be charged by indictment does not apply in a misdemeanor case or one in which the defendant agrees to plead guilty prior to being indicted. In this later circumstance, a cooperating defendant will plead guilty to charges described in a legal document known as an "information" and waive the right to an indictment. This process also signals that the defendant is likely cooperating with the government. Accordingly, when an "information" has been filed by the prosecutor, it can reasonably be inferred that the defendant has cooperated with the government, potentially providing incriminating information against others, before reaching a plea arrangement.

A grand jury also serves as an investigative body with the authority to subpoena documents and witnesses. All matters occurring before a grand jury, known as "grand jury material," are secret. Grand jury material remains secret unless a federal judge takes the unusual step of unsealing the material for a particular purpose. However, the secrecy rule only applies to the government and not to witnesses appearing before the grand jury. The sanction for violating the secrecy rule is punishable by contempt of court. All witness testimony is clearly grand jury material; however, there are divergent viewpoints about whether documents obtained by subpoena are grand jury material. The conservative practice for law enforcement is to consider all such documents as grand jury material and maintain secrecy. This is an important practice to note. Investigators who are conducting parallel civil investigations may want to know what documentary evidence law enforcement has obtained. Due to the grand jury secrecy rules, law enforcement is unlikely to acknowledge the existence of either a grand jury or any document resulting from it.

FRCrP Rule 16

Since broad discovery is required in civil cases, you might think that this principle would be followed in the criminal courts, where an individual's liberty is at stake. This is not the case. First, a defendant has a Fifth Amendment right not to be compelled to be a witness against himself or herself and, therefore, does not have to provide evidence to the government. Further, the government may not have to disclose the entirety of its file to the defense.

The government has to provide any exculpatory information (information tending to exonerate a defendant) that it has in its possession to the defense. This material is known as "*Brady* material."[7] The government also has to disclose any information that it has relating to a prosecution witness, including law enforcement personnel, which the defense could use to impeach or discredit the witness. This is known as "*Giglio* material."[8] An example of *Giglio* material would be the "rap sheet" of an informant whom the government is calling as a witness. It could also include any disciplinary file of law enforcement personnel dealing with untruthfulness or bias of the testifying law enforcement officer.

Under FRCrP Rule 16, the government has to provide to the defense any statement of the defendant and the defendant's prior criminal record. The government also has to provide to the defense any item that is material to preparing a defense, an item that the government intends to use at trial, and any item that has been obtained from or that belongs to the defendant.

Is there a requirement for an expert witness to disclose any information in advance of testifying at a criminal trial? Here again, the criminal rules differ from the civil rules because FRCrP Rule 16 allows the defense to basically control the disclosure of expert witness reports. The rule provides that if the defendant asks for the written summary of the government's expert witness, the government must comply. Otherwise, the government does not have to produce any expert witness reports. Further, if the defendant does make such a request, the request triggers the right for the government to ask for any written summary of the defense's expert witness. Any report that is required to be provided under this rule must include a summary describing "the witness's opinions, the bases and reasons for those opinions, and the witness's qualifications."

Constitutional Guarantees

The United States Constitution provides certain guarantees to criminal defendants. The due process clause requires the government to prove the elements of any criminal charge beyond a reasonable doubt. The Fourth, Fifth, and Sixth Amendments to the Constitution also provide certain guarantees.

Fourth Amendment

The Fourth Amendment guarantees the right to be free from unreasonable searches and seizures, and it also requires the government to obtain a warrant where there is an expectation of privacy. A violation of the Fourth Amendment can result in the exclusion of the evidence from trial. Under the "tainted fruit of the poisonous tree" doctrine, the use of other evidence that was acquired directly or indirectly as a result of the illegal search must also be excluded from evidence.

Fifth Amendment

The Fifth Amendment guarantees the accused the right to be indicted by a grand jury, not to be charged for the same offense twice (double jeopardy), the right against self-incrimination, and the right to the due process of law.

Sixth Amendment

The Sixth Amendment guarantees the right to a speedy trial, to be informed of the nature of the charges, to confront witnesses, and to an attorney.

Federal Rules of Evidence

Evidence is any material from which inferences can be drawn that can resolve a dispute among parties. More specifically, it can be anything presented to the five senses (sight, hearing, smell, taste, and touch), including testimony, documents, and material objects. From this, we can categorize evidence as testimonial, real, and demonstrative. Although the evidentiary rules do not directly address the distinction, evidence can also be described as direct and circumstantial evidence.

Testimonial evidence is oral or written evidence made by a witness to the facts (also known as a "lay witness" or "percipient witness") or an expert witness. Real evidence is the tangible or physical evidence at issue in a case. Demonstrative evidence is not a real item involved in the case. Rather, demonstrative evidence is a tangible item that illustrates or serves as a visual aid, like a map, chart, model, or audiovisual reconstruction.

The distinction between direct and circumstantial evidence can be important in fraud cases. Although the rules of evidence do not distinguish between these concepts, jurors may. Direct evidence proves a fact directly. A video tape of Jane shooting Jack with a gun is direct evidence, and it is compelling. Circumstantial evidence proves a fact by inference. If we go to bed at night and there is no snow on the ground, and the next morning, there is snow on the ground, this is circumstantial evidence that it snowed last night.

Fraud cases often involve circumstantial evidence because intent is typically an element of the pertinent fraud statute. Consider an allegation of insurance fraud resulting from arson. A small-business owner's building that housed all of the inventory burns down. The owner later files a claim with an insurance company for the damage to the building, inventory, and lost profits. The fire department rules that the cause of the fire is arson based on direct evidence that large quantities of gasoline were used as an accelerant, that ignition started in multiple locations in the building, and that burn patterns are irregular. The direct evidence tends to prove that arson is the cause of the fire, but it does not establish who committed the arson. Forensic accountants may be able to establish a circumstantial case that the owner had motive to burn down her business. A review of accounting records, tax records, conversations with employees, and a knowledge of the industry may tend to provide circumstantial evidence that the owner committed arson.

As I described earlier, I want to start with the end in mind. When I am investigating a fraud-related matter, I want to know the elements of the fraud and what evidence it will take to prove it. I also want to ensure that the evidence I collect will be admissible in court. In the content that follows, I have identified many of the rules of evidence that an investigator or forensic accountant should be mindful of when conducting an investigation. Although my discussion involves the Federal Rules of Evidence, a majority of states have adopted an exact or similar version. The material below may only include a summary or a discussion of the rule. The purpose is to create an awareness of evidentiary issues that may be encountered. If considering any of these rules in practice, read the actual rule and consult with an attorney.

Rule 201—Judicial Notice

The court accepts commonly known facts as true without the necessity of evidentiary proof. The purpose is to create judicial efficiency and not burden a party with proving a well-known fact.

Rule 401—Relevance

"Evidence is relevant if it has any tendency to make a fact more or less probable than it would be without the evidence, and the fact is of consequence in determining the action." This is one of the most basic rules of evidence, and the rule itself is self-explanatory.

Rule 402—Admissibility of Relevant Evidence

Unless another rule prevents its admissibility, relevant evidence is admissible and irrelevant evidence is not.

Rule 403—Excluding Relevant Evidence for Other Considerations

Relevant evidence may be excluded if its probative (tendency to prove something) value is substantially outweighed by unfair prejudice, confusing the issues, misleading the jury, undue delay, wasting time, or needlessly presenting cumulative evidence.

Rule 404—Character Evidence

Character evidence is evidence of a general human trait, such as honesty, carefulness, or violence and the propensity of someone to act in conformity with this trait. The general rule is that character evidence is not allowed. Evidence of other crimes or wrongful acts is permitted if it is used for a purpose other than character evidence, such as proving motive, opportunity, intent, preparation, planning, knowledge, identification, absence of mistake, or lack of accident. An exception to the rule applies to a defendant in a criminal case. A defendant may offer character evidence of a defendant's pertinent trait, and if the evidence is admitted, the prosecutor may offer evidence to rebut it. Character evidence may also be used pursuant to Rule 608 by using testimony to show a character of untruthfulness and Rule 609 to attack a character of untruthfulness with a witness's prior criminal conviction.

Rule 406—Habit and Routine Practice

Evidence of a person's habit or an organization's routine practice may be admitted to prove that on a particular occasion, the person or organization acted in accordance with the habit or routine practice.

Rule 408—Negotiations in a Civil Dispute

Evidence that a party paid or offered to pay money in the settlement of a claim in which liability or the amount is in dispute is not admissible. The purpose of this rule is to encourage a settlement between the parties.

Rule 410—Plea Negotiations in a Criminal Case

Statements made to a prosecutor during plea negotiations are not admissible. The purpose of this rule is to encourage a settlement between the parties.

Rule 411—Liability Insurance

Evidence that a person was or was not insured against liability is not admissible to prove whether the person acted negligently or otherwise wrongfully. The purpose of this rule is to prevent prejudice toward a defendant by a jury more readily holding a defendant liable or finding for greater damages just because the defendant is insured.

Rule 501—Privileges

A privilege is a rule of law that protects communication between two parties. Privileged relationships may include attorney–client, accountant–client, physician–patient, psychotherapist–patient, spouses, clergy–penitent, and law enforcement–informant. In federal courts, the court will follow federal common law in deciding which privilege to recognize. Federal courts deciding issues involving state law (known as a "diversity case" because the parties are citizens of different states) will follow the law of privilege in the state involved. Otherwise, federal courts will follow federal common law which generally is more restrictive than state law when recognizing a privilege (e.g. CPA-client privilege is not recognized in federal court). Note that there is also a limited tax practitioner–taxpayer privilege under 26 U.S.C. 7525. This applies to a federally authorized tax practitioner when the tax practitioner is providing tax advice to a taxpayer. The privilege does not apply to criminal cases or matters involving a tax shelter.

Rule 608—Witness Impeachment

A witness's credibility can be attacked or supported by testimony about the witness's reputation for having a character for truthfulness or untruthfulness.

Rule 609—Usage of Prior Criminal Conviction

A prior conviction may be used to attack a witness's character for truthfulness subject to the court's discretion. Misdemeanors and convictions older than 10 years require additional scrutiny.

Rule 615—Sequestering a Witness

A judge may order a witness sequestered from the courtroom while other witnesses are testifying. This rule does not apply to the parties in a case. A judge has discretion when considering whether or not to sequester an expert witness.

Rule 701—Lay Witness

A lay witness testifies to facts observed and is generally not considered an expert witness. A lay witness is also known as a "fact witness" or a "percipient witness."

Rule 702—Expert Witness

See the earlier discussion relating to *Daubert*.

Rule 703—Basis of an Expert's Opinion

An expert may base an opinion on facts or data in the case that the expert has been made aware of or has personally observed. If experts in the particular field reasonably rely on those kinds of facts or data in forming an opinion on the subject, they need not be admissible for the opinion to be admitted.

Rule 704—Opinion on an Ultimate Issue

An opinion is not objectionable just because it embraces an ultimate issue. However, an expert witness cannot reach an opinion about the guilt or innocence of an individual or party.

Rule 705—Expert Witness's Facts and Data

An expert witness can provide an opinion without first disclosing the facts or data used to reach the opinion. The facts or data may have to be disclosed in cross-examination.

Rule 801—Hearsay

Hearsay is the most complicated rule of evidence. Hearsay is defined as, "a statement that the declarant does not make while testifying at the current trial or hearing, and a party offers in evidence to prove the truth of the matter asserted in the statement." For our purposes, statements of individuals made outside the courtroom and any documents may be hearsay. Accordingly, hearsay is not admissible unless the party who made the statement or authored the document testifies in court, or an exception to the hearsay rule applies. A party to the litigation who makes a prior statement (e.g., the CFO who confesses to a forensic accountant) is not defined as hearsay under Rule 801(d)(2), and therefore such an incriminating statement is admissible. The hearsay rule also provides a number of exceptions, including one for documents when certain criteria have been met; see Rule 803(6).

Rule 803(6)—Hearsay Exception for Documents

When the following criteria are met, documents can generally be admitted into evidence as an exception to the hearsay rule:

(a) The record was made at or near the time by—or from information transmitted—someone with knowledge,

(b) The record was kept in the course of a regularly conducted activity of a business, organization, occupation, or calling, whether or not for profit,

(c) Making the record was a regular practice of that activity,

(d) All of these conditions are shown by the testimony of the custodian or another qualified witness, or by a certification that complies with Rule 902(11) or (12) or with a statute permitting certification, and

(e) The opponent does not show that the source of information or the method or circumstances of preparation indicate a lack of trustworthiness.

To admit a document into evidence, a subpoena may have to be issued first to compel a record holder to produce the document. Then, Rule 803(6) must be met to provide an exception to the hearsay rule. This is done by having the custodian of the records certify that the elements of Rule 803(6) are met in what is often known as a "business records affidavit." Further, Rule 902 must be followed to ensure that the document is authenticated.

A bank record is a prime example, because it is probably the most requested document by a forensic accountant. I highly recommend first contacting the bank and developing rapport with the bank official, who may often be a paralegal in the legal department. On a case that I am investigating, I advise the bank representative that I will personally serve the subpoena and business records affidavit. I do this for two reasons: I want to ensure that I get what I want in a timely fashion, and I may learn more about the account holder than I would otherwise have learned.

Rule 902(11)—Evidence That is Self-Authenticating: A document is considered self-authenticating when it meets the requirement of Rule 803(6) (A)-(C) and the opposing party is given notice and an opportunity to inspect the documents.

Rule 1002: Requirement of the Original

The general rule is that the original document, writing, or photograph is required under what is known as the "best evidence rule."

Rule 1003—Admissibility of Duplicates

A duplicate is admissible unless a genuine question is raised about the original's authenticity or the circumstances make it unfair to admit the duplicate.

Testifying

Professionals working on a fraud-related matter may have to later testify in a legal proceeding. In a civil matter, the testimony may be required in a deposition or at a trial. In a criminal matter, the testimony may be required before a grand jury or at a trial. Also, a person may provide testimony as a factual witness or as an expert witness. I have testified in various contexts and have provided training to FBI agents on testifying, including holding mock trials.

One bit of advice I always give witnesses: know what you know, and know what you don't know. When appropriate, this will enable a witness to answer a question more quickly by stating, "I do not know." It will also discourage a witness from trying to answer a question inaccurately. Below is a nonexhaustive list of pointers for those who will be testifying:

- Tell the truth!
- Be prepared.
- Listen carefully to the questioned being asked.
- Think before speaking.
- Maintain confidence.
- Be alert.
- Ask to repeat a question when it is not understood.
- Do not answer in absolutes.
- Have an awareness of nervous habits and mannerisms.
- Have an awareness of body language.
- Look at the attorney asking the question.
- Talk to the jury when answering a question.
- Do not argue with the attorney.

- Do not exaggerate.

- Do not get angry; remain calm and composed.

- Take as much time as is needed to answer a question.

- Lean forward, especially when under attack.

- Educate, and do not advocate.

- Dress professionally and conservatively.

- Answer the question and stop talking.

- Do not volunteer information.

- Stop talking when an objection is made.

- Use plain language.

- Be informative but factual.

- Use examples when possible.

- Know that everyone is watching before, during, and after your testimony.

ACKNOWLEDGMENTS

This book is a compilation of my personal experiences and the knowledge that I have gained from my colleagues as well as those whom I have investigated. Many of my colleagues whom I mention below fall into multiple categories, so I will only mention them once.

I am extremely grateful to the Federal Bureau of Investigation (FBI) for giving me the opportunity to serve the American people. My rich experiences were directly attributable to the many honorable and talented FBI agents and professional staff with whom I proudly served. My use of actual case examples throughout this book required me to obtain a prepublication review by the FBI to ensure compliance with FBI policy and various legal restrictions. Thanks to all of the FBI professionals who assisted Joseph Bender, David Hardy, and Kandi McCullough to ensure that only legally appropriate material is disclosed in this book.

For those individuals whose case I investigated and assisted in their prosecution, I am grateful that many have been rehabilitated, have learned from their experiences, and have now become productive members of society. For the others, I extend hope. From all of these felons, I have gained a tremendous understanding about the mind of a fraudster.

I am most appreciative of the work of my editor for this book and one of my most trusted colleagues, Dr. Sridhar Ramamoorti, ACA, CPA/CITP/CFF/CGMA, CIA, CFE, CFSA, CGAP, CGFM, CRP, CICA, CRMA, MAFF. Sri is a professor and a practitioner and, given his unusual background in accounting and psychology, is an interdisciplinary thought leader in the forensic accounting community. I have been fortunate to coauthor several professional journal articles with him over the last few years. Sri was able to take a manuscript with many shortcomings and bring it to life. I also very much appreciate his graciously writing the Foreword to this book.

I am also very grateful to the sponsors of this book. I would like to thank the law firm of Baker, Donelson, Bearman, Caldwell & Berkowitz, PC and the many professionals at that firm, including Gary A. Barnes, Kathleen "Katy" G. Furr, Kevin A. Stine, and Joe D. Whitley. I would also like to thank the forensic accounting firm, IAG Forensics & Valuation, and the many professionals at that firm, including Laurie Dyke, George Dyke, and Karen Fortune.

I would like to thank fellow partners of the Behavioral Forensics Group, LLC, Jack Bigelow, Dr. Joe Koletar, and Dr. Daven Morrison, for listening to my many theories on fraud and for providing constructive feedback. I have learned much from each one of them.

I have been honored to serve two terms as the President of the Georgia Chapter of the Association of Certified Fraud Examiners. My fellow board members, Nnenneya Anyaebosi, Bill Basket, Kathy Boyd, Lawrence Clark, Michelle Conroy, Chris Grippa, Melanie Handley, Ana Hess, Zane Kinney, Doug Legg, Ron Lepionka, Elliot Long, Debbie McGlaun, Kurt Schulzke, Brandi Steinberg, Kyle Thompson, and Tyler Wright have each been a source of inspiration because of their devotion and commitment to the forensic and investigative community.

Prior to publication, several seasoned professional colleagues reviewed the manuscript. The book is significantly better as the direct result of input from Jay Bienkowski, Scott Hilsen, Stacey Kalberman, Don Kidd, Elliott Lieb, Dr. Bruno Pavlicek, Joe Robuck, David Sawyer, John Schmarkey, Jim Wanserski, and Dennis Williams.

I am very appreciative of the leadership at two universities who have placed their confidence in me and have given me the honor of teaching their students. Thanks to the Georgia State University leadership team, including Kris Clark and Dr. Galen Sevcik, for allowing me to teach all of these years. Thanks to the Fairfield University leadership team, including Dr. Rebecca

Block, Dr. Joan Lee, and Kathi Mettler, for bringing me on campus each year to teach.

Although teaching is supposed to be one of those endeavors in which professors impart their knowledge to students, every semester I find that the reverse is also true. Thanks to all of my former forensic accounting students at Georgia State University and at Fairfield University for making me a better professor. Thanks to the students at the University of Dayton who reviewed an earlier version of the manuscript. A very special thanks goes to Carson-Newman University accounting student Jonny Goss for painstakingly reviewing the footnotes and bibliography.

APPENDIX

Association of Certified Fraud Examiner's Sample Anti-Fraud Policy

SAMPLE ANTI-FRAUD POLICY

BACKGROUND

The corporate anti-fraud policy is established to facilitate the development of controls that will aid in the detection and prevention of fraud against ABC Corporation. It is the intent of ABC Corporation to promote consistent organizational behavior by providing guidelines and assigning responsibility for the development of controls and the conduct of investigations.

SCOPE OF POLICY

This policy applies to any irregularity or suspected irregularity involving employees, as well as shareholders, consultants, vendors, contractors, and outside agencies doing business with employees of such agencies, and/or any other parties with a business relationship with ABC Corporation (also called the Company).

Any investigative activity required will be conducted without regard to the suspected wrongdoer's length of service, position/title, or relationship with the Company.

POLICY

Management is responsible for the detection and prevention of fraud, misappropriations, and other irregularities. *Fraud* is defined as the intentional, false representation, or concealment of a material fact for the purpose of inducing another to act upon it to his injury. Each member of the management team will be familiar with the types of improprieties that might occur within his area of responsibility and be alert for any indication of irregularity.

Any irregularity that is detected or suspected must be reported immediately to the Director of _____, who coordinates all investigations with the Legal Department and other affected areas, both internal and external.

ACTIONS CONSTITUTING FRAUD

The terms *defalcations, misappropriation,* and *other fiscal irregularities* refer to, but are not limited to, the following:

- Any dishonest or fraudulent act
- Misappropriation of funds, securities, supplies, or other assets
- Impropriety in the handling or reporting of money or financial transactions
- Profiteering as a result of insider knowledge of company activities

- Disclosing confidential and proprietary information to outside parties
- Disclosing to other persons securities activities engaged in or contemplated by the Company
- Accepting or seeking anything of material value from contractors, vendors, or persons providing services/materials to the Company (Exception: gifts less than $50 in value)
- Destruction, removal, or inappropriate use of records, furniture, fixtures, and equipment
- Any similar or related irregularity

OTHER IRREGULARITIES	*Irregularities* concerning an employee's moral, ethical, or behavioral conduct should be resolved by departmental management and the Employee Relations Unit of Human Resources rather than the _____ Unit. If there is any question as to whether an action constitutes fraud, contact the Director of _____ _____ for guidance.

INVESTIGATION RESPONSIBILITIES

The _____ Unit has the primary responsibility for the investigation of all suspected fraudulent acts as defined in the policy. If the investigation substantiates that fraudulent activities have occurred, the _____ Unit will issue reports to appropriate designated personnel and, if appropriate, to the Board of Directors through the Audit Committee.

Decisions to prosecute or refer the examination results to the appropriate law enforcement and/or regulatory agencies for independent investigation will be made in conjunction with legal counsel and senior management, as will final decisions on disposition of the case.

CONFIDENTIALITY

The _____ Unit treats all information received confidentially. Any employee who suspects dishonest or fraudulent activity will notify the _____ Unit immediately and *should not attempt to personally conduct investigations or interviews/interrogations* related to any suspected fraudulent act (see REPORTING PROCEDURES section below).

Investigation results will not be disclosed or discussed with anyone other than those who have a legitimate need to know. This is important in order to avoid damaging the reputations of persons suspected but subsequently found innocent of wrongful conduct and to protect the Company from potential civil liability.

AUTHORIZATION FOR INVESTIGATING SUSPECTED FRAUD	Members of the Investigation Unit will have: • Free and unrestricted access to Company records and premises, whether owned or rented • The authority to examine, copy, and/or remove all or any portion of the contents of files, desks, cabinets, and other storage facilities on the premises without prior knowledge or consent of any individual who might use or have custody of any such items or facilities when it is within the scope of their investigation
REPORTING	Great care must be taken in the investigation of suspected improprieties or irregularities so as to avoid mistaken accusations or alerting suspected individuals that an investigation is under way.

An employee who discovers or suspects fraud- ulent activity will *contact the* _____ *Unit immediately.* The employee or other com- plainant may remain anonymous. All inquiries concerning the activity under investigation from the suspected individual, his attorney or representative, or any other inquirer should be directed to the Investigations Unit or the Legal Department. No information concerning the status of an investigation will be given out. The proper response to any inquiries is: "I am not at liberty to discuss this matter." Under no cir- cumstances should any reference be made to "the allegation," "the crime," "the fraud," "the forgery," "the misappropriation," or any other specific reference.

The reporting individual should be instructed to do the following:

- Do not contact the suspected individual in an effort to determine facts or demand restitution.

- Do not discuss the case, facts, suspi- cions, or allegations with anyone unless specifically asked to do so by the Legal Department or _____ Unit.

ACTING IN GOOD FAITH

Anyone reporting any irregularity that is detected or suspected must be acting in good faith and have reasonable grounds for believing the information provided. Allegations made maliciously or with knowledge of their falsity will not be tolerated. People making such allegations may be subject to institutional disciplinary action and/or legal actions by the individuals accused of fraudulent conduct.

WHISTLEBLOWER PROTECTION

Employees of ABC Corporation may not retaliate against a whistleblower for reporting an activity which that person believes to be fraudulent or dishonest with the intent or effect of adversely affecting the terms or conditions of employment (including, but not limited to, threats of physical harm, dismissal, transfers to an undesirable job assignment, demotion, suspension, or impact on salary or wages). A whistleblower is defined as an employee who informs a manager, supervisor, or Director of _____ about an activity which that person believes to be fraudulent or dishonest.

Whistleblowers who believe that they have been retaliated against may file a written complaint with the Director of _____. Any complaint of retaliation will be promptly investigated by the _____, and appropriate remedial measures will be taken if allegations of retaliation are proven. This protection from retaliation is not intended to prohibit managers or supervisors from taking action, including disciplinary action, in the usual scope of their duties and based on valid performance-related factors.

TERMINATION

If an investigation results in a recommendation to terminate an individual, the recommendation will be reviewed for approval by the designated representatives from the Human Resources and the Legal Department and, if the necessary, by outside counsel, before any such action is taken. The _____ Unit does not have the authority to terminate an employee. The decision to terminate an employee is made by the employee's management. Should the _____ Unit believe the management decision is inappropriate for the facts presented, the facts will be presented to executive level management for a decision.

ADMINISTRATION   The Director of _____ is responsible for the administration, revision, interpretation, and application of this policy. The policy will be reviewed annually and revised as needed.

APPROVAL

_____

(CEO/Senior Vice   **Date**
President/Executive)

NOTES

Foreword

1   Theodore Roosevelt, The Man in the Arena. Excerpt from the speech "Citizenship in a Republic," delivered at the Sorbonne, in Paris, France on April 23, 1910.

Preface

1   Willie Sutton and Edward Linn, *Where the Money Was* (New York: Viking Press, 1976).

2   *Where the Money Was*, 160.

Introduction

1   Association of Certified Fraud Examiners, *Report to the Nations: Occupational Fraud and Abuse* (Austin, TX, 2018), 8.

Chapter 1: Fraud Concepts

1   Donald R. Cressey, *Other People's Money* (Montclair, NJ: Patterson Smith, 1973), 30.

2   Steve Albrecht, "Iconic Fraud Triangle Endures," *Fraud Magazine*, July/August 2014.

3   Albrecht, "Iconic Fraud Triangle Endures."

4   Sri Ramamoorti and William Olsen, "Fraud: The Human Factor," *Financial Executive*, July/August 2007, 53–55.

5   Victor Hartman and Sridhar Ramamoorti, "Public Corruption: Causes, Consequences & Countermeasures," *Journal of Government Financial Management* 65, no. 1 (Spring 2016): 43-47.

6   Association of Certified Fraud Examiners, "Who We Are," accessed February 24, 2019, https://www.acfe.com/who-we-are.aspx.

7   Association of Certified Fraud Examiner, "Who We Are.

8   Association of Certified Fraud Examiners, *Report to the Nations*, 11.

9   Mark S. Beasley et al., "An Analysis of U.S. Public Companies," *Committee of Sponsoring Organizations of the Treadway Commission*, May 2010, https://www.coso.org/Documents/COSO-Fraud-Study-2010-001.pdf.

10   Mei Feng et al., *The Role of CFOs in Material Accounting Manipulations*, (The Conference Board, 2010), https://www.conference-board.org/publications/publicationdetail.cfm?publicationid=1938&subtopicid=200.

11   Diane Vaughan, *The Challenger Launch Decision: Risky Technology, Culture, and Deviance at NASA* (Chicago, IL: University of Chicago Press, 1996). In

the sociology literature, Diane Vaughan refers to this as the "normalization of deviance."

12   In this regard, it is interesting to see how artificial intelligence (AI) is being used to fight call-center fraud. See for instance, https://www.pindrop.com.

13   Sridhar Ramamoorti et al., *A.B.C.'s of Behavioral Forensics: Applying Psychology to Financial Fraud Prevention and Detection*, (Hoboken, NJ: Wiley, 2013). An entire chapter is devoted to exploring emotions and fraud.

14   A.B.C.'s, 73.

15   A.B.C.'s.

16   Dr. Daven Morrison advises he learned this term from his father, Dr. David E. Morrison—both are medical doctors and partners in the firm Morrison Associates, Ltd.

17   Silvan S. Tomkins and Robert McCarter, "What and Where are the Primary Affects? Some Evidence for a Theory," Perceptual and Motor Skills 18, no. 1 (1964), doi:10.2466/pms.1964.18.1.119.

18   Ramamoorti, *A.B.C.'s*, 73.

19   Ramamoorti, *A.B.C.'s*, 177–179. This is referred to as "piercing the rationalization."

20   *The New York Times*, "Two Financial Crises Compared: The Savings and Loan Debacle and the Mortgage Mess," The New York Times Web Archive, last modified April 13,2011, https://archive.nytimes.com/www.nytimes.com/interactive/2011/04/14/business/20110414-prosecute.html?_r=0.

21   *Fortune*, "FORTUNE 500: Enron,", accessed January 30, 2019, http://archive.fortune.com/magazines/fortune/fortune500_archive/snapshots/2001/478.html.

22   Third Superseding Indictment, *United States of America v. Bernard J. Ebbers*, (Sept. 15, 2004), https://www.justice.gov/archive/dag/cftf/chargingdocs/ebberss504.pdf

23   Sridhar Ramamoorti and Barry J. Epstein, "Fraud Risk Models Lack Personality." *The CPA Journal*, March 2016, 15–21.

24   Robert B. Cialdini, *Influence: The Psychology of Persuasion*, (New York: Harper Collins, 2007).

25   Cialdini, *Influence* 17.

26   Cialdini, *Influence*, 18.

27   Cf. "The road to hell is paved with good intentions," attributed to Saint Bernard of Clairvaux, ca. twelfth century.

28   Ramamoorti, *A. B.C.'s*, 19.

29   "The Inductees: Sanjay Kumar," Con Artist Hall of Infamy, accessed February 24, 2019. http://archive.pixelettestudios.com/hallofinfamy/inductees.php?action=detail&artist=sanjay_kumar. A real-world case example of this is found in the case of Sri Lankan, Sanjay Kumar, then CEO of Computer Associates, who introduced the "35-day month" to manipulate sales numbers.

Chapter 2: Fraud Defined

1   Henry Campbell Black, *Black's Law Dictionary*, 5th ed., (St. Paul, MN: West Publishing Co., 1979), 594.

2   *Johnson v. McDonald*, 170 Okla.117.

3 The Institute of Internal Auditors, *International Standards for the Professional Practice of Internal Auditing,* 2016, https://na.theiia.org/standards-guidance/Public%20Documents/IPPF-Standards-2017.pdf.

4 Association of Certified Fraud Examiners, *Report to the Nations.*

5 Alan R. Palmiter, *Securities Regulation* (New York: Wolters Kluwer, 2011).

6 Palmiter, *Securities Regulation,* 384.

7 31 U.S.C. §§3729–3733.

8 31 U.S.C §3729(a), (b).

9 These amounts are approximations, since the penalties are adjusted for inflation, see 31 U.S.C. §3729(a)(1).

10 31 U.S.C §3729(a)(1).

11 *Dugdale v. Regina,* 1 El. & Bl. 435, 118 Eng. Rep. 499 (1853).

Chapter 3: Asset Misappropriation

1 Association of Certified Fraud Examiners, *Report to the Nations.*

2 Victor Hartman and Sridhar Ramamoorti, "Procurement Card Fraud," *New Perspectives on Healthcare Risk Management, Control and Governance* 37, no. 4 (Winter 2018): 28.

Chapter 4: Corruption and Conflicts of Interest

1 Department of Justice, Public Corruption, (Federal Bureau of Investigation, 2016), https://www.fbi.gov/investigate/public-corruption.

2 Association of Certified Fraud Examiners, *Fraud Examiners Manual* (2017), 1.601.

3 Association of Certified Fraud Examiners, *Manual,* 2.208.

4 *McNallly v. United States,* 483 U.S. 350, 360 (1987).

5 *McDonnell v. United States,* 579 U.S. __ (2016).

6 *McDonnell v. United States,* 579 U.S. __ (2016).

7 *McDonnell v. United States,* 579 U.S. __ (2016).

8 Transparency International, *Corruption Perceptions Index 2017,* (2017), https://www.transparency.org/news/feature/corruption_perceptions_index_2017#table.

9 15 U.S.C. §§ 78dd-1, *et seq.*

10 15 U.S.C. §§ 78dd-1(a), 78dd-2(a), 78dd-3(a).

11 15 U.S.C. § 78m(b)(2)(A).

12 15 U.S.C. § 78m(b)(2)(B).

13 15 U.S.C. §§ 78dd-1(a), 78dd-2(a), 78dd-3(a).

14 This DOJ and SEC-sponsored resource guide was released in November 2012 and can be found on both the DOJ's and SEC's websites.

15 15 U.S.C. §78m(b)(2)(B).

16 15 U.S.C. §78dd-1(c)(1).

17 15 U.S.C. §78dd-1(c)(2).

18 15 U.S.C. §§ 78dd-1(b), 78dd-2(b), 78dd-3(b).

19 Department of Justice, and Securities and Exchange Commission, *FCPA: A Resource Guide to the U.S. Foreign Corrupt Practices Act,* (DOJ/SEC, 2012), 26.

20 Hartman and Ramamoorti, "Public Corruption," 43–47.

21   Hartman and Ramamoorti, "Public Corruption," 43–47.

22   Hartman and Ramamoorti, "Public Corruption, 43–47.

23   Hartman and Ramamoorti, "Public Corruption, 43–47.

24   John M. Buell, "Ethical Leadership in Uncertain Times," *Healthcare Executive*, May/June 2015, https://www.ache.org/-/media/ache/about-ache/fund-for-healthcare-leadership/ethical_leadership_reprint.pdf?la=en&hash=0CFB2A741B793BB1E7F623A89D90594F55AABBC6. "Ethical erosion" is a term used by Arizona State University clinical professor Jack A. Gilbert, Ed.D., FACHE, and quoted in this article.

25   Hartman and Ramamoorti, "Public Corruption."

Chapter 5: Financial Statement Fraud

1   Cynthia Cooper, *Extraordinary Circumstances: The Journey of a Corporate Whistleblower* (Hoboken, NJ: John Wiley & Sons, 2008), 339.

2   The Securities Investor Protection Corporation (SIPC) trustee estimated actual (cash) losses to investors were only $18 billion.

3   American Institute of Certified Public Accountant, *Consideration of Fraud in a Financial Statement Audit*, AU-C §240.26 and the Public Company Accounting Oversight Board, AS 2401.06. These categories of financial statement fraud can be found in both standards.

4   American Institute of Certified Public Accountant, *Consideration of Fraud*.

5   American Institute of Certified Public Accountant, *Consideration of Fraud*.

6   Financial Accounting Standards Board Accounting Standards Codification No. 606. See section 606-10-55-83 for bill-and-hold arrangements.

7   Financial Accounting Standards Board Accounting Standards Codification No. 606.

8   Financial Accounting Standards Board Accounting Standards Codification No. 606.

9   Financial Accounting Standards Board, *Statement of Financial Accounting Standards No. 5* (Financial Accounting Foundation, 1975).

10   *United States v. Wells*, 102 F.3d 1043, (1996).

11   Financial Accounting Standards Board, *Statement of Financial Accounting Standards No. 86* (Financial Accounting Foundation, 1985).

12   Financial Accounting Standards Board, *Standards No. 5*.

13   See Financial Accounting Standards Board (FASB) Concept Statement No. 2 for a definition of materiality.

14   Larry E. Rittenberg, Karla M. Johnstone, Audrey A. Gramling, *Auditing: A Business Risk Approach*, (Mason, OH: South-Western Cengage Learning, 2010): 132.

15   Rittenberg, Johnstone, and Gramling, *Auditing*, 149.

16   Rittenberg, Johnstone, and Gramling, *Auditing*, 149.

17   Rittenberg, Johnstone, and Gramling, *Auditing*, 149.

18   Rittenberg, Johnstone, and Gramling, *Auditing*, 149.

19   Association of Certified Fraud Examiners, *Report to the Nations*, 17.

20   The Institute of Internal Auditors, *International Professional Practices Framework* (Lake Mary, FL: The Institute of Internal Auditors, 2009), 2.

21   This is the final rule that the SEC adopted pursuant to its rule making under SOX §307.
22   Official Code of Georgia Annotated §43-3-29(b).
23   See Federal Rules of Evidence, Rule 501.
24   Joseph F. Brazel, Keith L. Jones, and Mark F. Zimbelman, "Using Nonfinancial Measures to Assess Fraud Risk," *Journal of Accounting Research* 47, no. 5 (October 2009): 1135–1166.
25   Darrell D. Dorrell and Gregory A. Gadawski, *Financial Forensics Body of Knowledge* (Hoboken, NJ: John Wiley & Sons, 2012). An excellent reference book on this topic.

Chapter 6: Small Organizations: Small Businesses, Local Governments, and Not-for-Profits

1   *United States v. Rita A. Crundwell*, United States District Court, Northern District of Illinois (2012).
2   Rachel Rodgers, "Crundwell Recovery: 5 Years Later," *SaukValley*, April 14, 2017, https://www.saukvalley.com/2017/04/14/crundwell-recovery-5-years-later/a7nasm0/.
3   Securities Exchange Commission, "Municipal Securities Enforcement Actions," last modified February 27, 2017, https://www.sec.gov/municipal/oms-enforcement-actions.html.
4   Financial Accounting Standards Board, *Accounting Standards Update No. 2016-14* (2016), PDF; Financial Accounting Standards Board, *Statement of Financial Accounting Standards No. 117* (1993); American Institute of Certified Public Accountants, *Statement of position 98-2* (AICPA, 1998).
5   Gerard M. Zack, "Not-for-profit Fraud," *FRAUD Magazine*, (September/October 2003).

Chapter 7: Nonoccupational Fraud

1   Michael Cohn, "Informant Blew the Whistle on Price Fixing at ADM," *Accounting Today*, last modified June 21, 2012, https://www.accountingtoday.com/opinion/informant-blew-the-whistle-on-price-fixing-at-adm.
2   Department of Justice, "Romance Scams," Federal Bureau of Investigation, last modified February 13, 2017, https://www.fbi.gov/news/stories/romance-scams.
3   Information, *United States of America v. Bernard L. Madoff*, 09 Crim 213, United States District Court, Southern District of New York, March 10, 2008.
4   Mark C. Knutson, *The Remarkable Criminal Financial Career of Charles Ponzi*, (2011), https://www.mark-knutson.com/blog/wp-content/uploads/2014/06/ponzi.pdf.
5   Knutson, *The Remarkable Criminal*.
6   Knutson, *The Remarkable Criminal*.
7   Mitchell Zuckoff, *Ponzi's Scheme: The True Story of a Financial Legend* (New York, NY: Random House, 2006).
8   Knutson, *The Remarkable Criminal*.
9   *United States v. O'Hagan*, 521 U.S. 642 (1997).
10   *Chiarella v. United States*, 445 U.S. 222 (1980).

11 *Dirks v. SEC*, 463 U.S. 646 (1983).

12 *Salman v. United States*, 580 U.S. ___ (2016).

13 Randall A. Heron and Erik Lie, *What fraction of stock option grants to top executives have been backdated or manipulated?*, (2006), accessed February 11, 2019, https://www.biz.uiowa.edu/faculty/elie/Grants-11-01-2006.pdf.

14 U.S. Securities and Exchange Commission, *"Former UnitedHealth Group CEO/ Chairman Settles Stock Options Backdating Case for $468 Million,"* press release 2007-255, December 6, 2007, https://www.sec.gov/news/press/2007/2007-255.htm

15 See https://www.fedmarket.com/contractors/The-World%5C's-Biggest-Customer.

16 Centers for Medicare & Medicaid Services, Office of the Actuary, "National Health Care Spending in 2016," https://www.cms.gov/Research-Statistics-Data-and-Systems/Statistics-Trends-and-Reports/NationalHealthExpendData/Downloads/NHE-Presentation-Slides.pdf

17 International Monetary Fund, "Report for Selected Countries and Subjects," last modified April 2018, https://www.imf.org/external/pubs/ft/weo/2018/01/weodata/weorept.aspx?pr.x=57&pr.y=14&sy=2017&ey=%20 2018&scsm=1&ssd=1&sort=country&ds=.&br=1&c=111-&s=NGDPD%2CPPPGDP%2CNGDPDPC%2CPPPPC&grp=0&a=.

18 Association of Certified Fraud Examiners, *Report to the Nations*.

19 National Health Care Anti-Fraud Association, "The Challenge of Health Care Fraud," accessed February 13, 2019, https://www.nhcaa.org/resources/health-care-anti-fraud-resources/the-challenge-of-health-care-fraud.aspx.

20 31 U.S.C. §3729(a)(1)(G). These amounts are approximations because the penalties adjust for inflation; see statute.

21 31 U.S.C. §3729(a)(1)(G).

22 U.S. Department of Justice, *Fraud Statistics - Overview*, (2017), https://www.justice.gov/opa/press-release/file/1020126/download.

23 Victor E. Hartman, "Whistleblower Shields and Swords," *New Perspectives on Healthcare Risk Management, Control, and Governance*, (Summer 2018), 49.

24 31 U.S.C §3730(d)(2).

25 Federal Bureau of Investigation, *Insurance Fraud*, https://www.fbi.gov/stats-services/publications/insurance-fraud.

26 U.S. Securities and Exchange Commission, "SEC Defendant Indicted in Money Laundering," last modified September 7, 2011, https://www.sec.gov/litigation/litreleases/2011/lr22084.htm.

27 U.S. Department of the Treasury, SAR Stats, (Financial Crimes Enforcement Network, 2017), https://www.fincen.gov/sites/default/files/sar_report/2017-03-09/SAR%20Stats%203.pdf.

28 Skip Hollandsworth, "The Killing of Alydar," *Texas Monthly*, June 2001, https://www.texasmonthly.com/articles/the-killing-of-alydar/.

29 U.S. Department of Treasury, *FinCEN 2012 SAR Data Reveals Drop in Suspected Mortgage Fraud*, (Financial Crimes Enforcement Network, 2013),

https://www.fincen.gov/sites/default/files/news_release/20130820.pdf

30   Federal Bureau of Investigation, *Financial Institution/Mortgage Fraud,* https://www.fbi.gov/investigate/white-collar-crime/mortgage-fraud.

31   Flangas Law Group, "Piercing the Corporate Veil," last modified September 5, 2012, https://www.fdlawlv.com/blog/BOSVIEW/PIERCING-THE-CORPORATE-VEIL/.

32   Flangas Law Group, "Piercing the Corporate Veil."

33   18 U.S.C. 1839(3).

34   18 U.S.C. 1831.

35   The White House, *IPEC Annual Intellectual Property Report to Congress,* (Executive Branch, March 2018), PDF, https://www.whitehouse.gov/wp-content/uploads/2017/11/2018Annual_IPEC_Report_to_Congress.pdf

36   White House, *IPEC Annual Report,* at 27.

37   White House, *IPEC Annual Report,* at 28.

38   White House, *IPEC Annual Report,* at 28.

39   White House, *IPEC Annual Report,* at 28.

Chapter 8: Cyber Fraud

1   45 C.F.R. §164.304.

2   45 C.F.R. §164.402.

3   This is analogous to "wilding" in a social engineering context. "Wilding" is the activity by a gang of youths of going on a protracted and violent rampage in a public place, attacking people at random.

4   Verizon, *2018 Data Breach Investigations Report,* (2018). https://www.verizonenterprise.com/resources/reports/rp_DBIR_2018_Report_execsummary_en_xg.pdf (September 27, 2018).

5   Verizon, *2018 Data Breach Investigations Report,* at 8.

6   Federal Trade Commission, *Consumer Sentinel Network Data Book,* (2017), https://www.ftc.gov/system/files/documents/reports/consumer-sentinel-network-data-book-2017/consumer_sentinel_data_book_2017.pdf.

7   Federal Trade Commission, *Consumer Sentinel Network Data Book.,* at 3.

8   Equifax, "Equifax Releases Details on Cybersecurity Incident, Announces Personnel Changes," last modified September 15, 2017, https://investor.equifax.com/news-and-events/news/2017/09-15-2017-224018832.

9   Federal Bureau of Investigation, "Business E-mail Compromise, E-mail Account Compromise, the 5 Billion Dollar Scam," last modified May 4, 2017, https://www.ic3.gov/media/2017/170504.aspx#fn3.

10   Federal Bureau of Investigation, "Business E-mail Compromise.

11   Federal Bureau of Investigation, "Business E-Mail Compromise," last modified February 27, 2017, https://www.fbi.gov/news/stories/business-e-mail-compromise-on-the-rise.

12   Stephen Deere, "Confidential Report: Atlanta's Cyber Attack Could Cost Taxpayers $17 Million," *Atlanta Journal Constitution,* last modified August 1, 2018, https://www.ajc.com/news/confidential-report-atlanta-cyber-attack-could-hit-million/GAljmndAF3EQdVWlMcXS0K/?icmp=np_inform_variation-control.

13   Laila Kearney, "Atlanta Officials Reveal Worsening Effects of Cyber Attack," Reuters, last modified June 6, 2018, https://www.reuters.com/article/us-usa-cyber-atlanta-budget/atlanta-officials-reveal-worsening-effects-of-cyber-attack-idUSKCN1J231M.

14   Kearney, "Atlanta Officials Reveal," Reuters.

15   Lily H. Newman, "Atlanta Spent $2.6M to Recover from a $52,000 Ransomware Scare," WIRED, last modified April 23, 2018, https://www.wired.com/story/atlanta-spent-26m-recover-from-ransomware-scare/.

16   Kearney, "Atlanta Officials Reveal," Reuters.

17   Federal Bureau of Investigation, *How to Protect Your Network from Ransomware*, https://www.fbi.gov/file-repository/ransomware-prevention-and-response-for-cisos.pdf/view.

18   Federal Bureau of Investigation, *Protect Your Network*.

19   Federal Bureau of Investigation, *Protect Your Network*.

20   Victor Hartman and Sridhar Ramamoorti, "Ransomware: A Primer," *New Perspectives on Healthcare Risk Management, Control, and Governance*, (Spring 2017), 7.

21   Federal Bureau of Investigation, "Cyber Crime," last modified May 3, 2016, https://www.fbi.gov/investigate/cyber.

22   *U.S. v. Kramer*, 631 F.3d 900 (8thCir. 2011).

Chapter 9: Money Laundering and Tax Fraud

1   International Consortium of Investigative Journalists, "Explore the Panama Papers Key Figures," ICIJ, last modified January 31, 2017, https://www.icij.org/investigations/panama-papers/explore-panama-papers-key-figures/.

2   18 U.S.C. 3292.

3   International Consortium of Investigative Journalists, "About the Investigation," ICIJ, last modified January 31, 2018, https://www.icij.org/investigations/panama-papers/pages/panama-papers-about-the-investigation/.

4   International Consortium of Investigative Journalists, "About the Investigation.

5   International Consortium of Investigative Journalists, "About the Investigation.

6   International Consortium of Investigative Journalists, "About the Investigation.

7   International Consortium of Investigative Journalists, "About the Investigation.

8   International Consortium of Investigative Journalists, "About the Investigation.

9   International Consortium of Investigative Journalists, "About the Investigation.

10   International Consortium of Investigative Journalists, "About the Investigation.

11   International Consortium of Investigative Journalists, "About the Paradise Papers Investigation," ICIJ, last modified November 5, 2017, https://www.icij.org/investigations/paradise-papers/about/.

12   International Consortium of Investigative Journalists, "About the Paradise Papers.

13   International Consortium of Investigative Journalists, "About the Paradise Papers.

14   The first known U.S. indictments resulting from the Panama Papers were filed under seal on September 27, 2018, see *United States of America v. Ramses Owens, et al.*, United States District Court, Southern District of New York, 18 CRIM

693.

15   18 U.S.C. 1956(a)(2)(A).

16   31 U.S.C. 5312(a)(2)(a-z).

17   Justin Scheck and Shane Shifflett, "How Dirty Money Disappears into the Black Hole of Cryptocurrency," *Wall Street Journal*, last modified September 28, 2018, https://www.wsj.com/articles/how-dirty-money-disappears-into-the-black-hole-of-cryptocurrency-1538149743?mod=searchresults&page=1&pos=4.

18   Christian Berthelsen, Matthias Rieker, and Brett Philbin, "HSBC to Pay Record $1.9 Billion Settlement," *Wall Street Journal*, last modified December 11, 2012, https://www.wsj.com/articles/SB10001424127887324478304578173540799215234.

19   Berthelsen, Rieker, and Philbin, "HSBC to Pay."

20   Department of the Treasury, *Tax Gap Estimates for Tax Years 2008–2010* (Internal Service Revenue, 2016), PDF.

21   Department of Treasury, *Tax Gap*.

22   Department of Treasury, *Tax Gap*.

23   I call this the "NatWest Three caper": The NatWest Three, also known as "the Enron Three," refers to three British businessmen: Giles Darby, David Bermingham, and Gary Mulgrew. In 2002, they were indicted in Houston, Texas, on seven counts of wire fraud against their former employer, Greenwich NatWest, which at the time was a division of National Westminster Bank.

24   *United States of American v. Lea W. Fastow*, Indictment, United States District Court, Southern District of Texas.

25   *United States of American v. Lea W. Fastow*.

26   *United States of American v. Lea W. Fastow*.

27   *United States of American v. Lea W. Fastow*.

28   Department of the Treasury, "Audit Techniques Guides (ATGs)," Internal Revenue Service, last modified March 21, 2018, https://www.irs.gov/businesses/small-businesses-self-employed/audit-techniques-guides-atgs.

29   Department of the Treasury, "Audit Techniques Guides.

30   Internal Revenue Service, Internal Revenue Manual §4.10.4.6.2.1.

Chapter 10: Fraud Prevention

1   Sridhar Ramamoorti and Joseph Dupree, "Continuous Controls Monitoring Can Help Deter Fraud," *Financial Executive*, (April 2010). The term "fraud life cycle" may have been first used by Ramamoorti and Dupree in this article, in which they spoke of the fraud life cycle as having both a proactive and a reactive phase.

2   See the Sarbanes-Oxley Act of 2002 §404(b) and PCAOB AS 2201.

3   American Institute of Certified Public Accountants AU-C Section 940.

4   *In Re Caremark International Inc. Derivative Litigation*, 698 A. 2d 959 (Del. Ch. 1996).

5   Brad Dorfman, "Walmart Appoints Anti-bribery Officer," IOL, last modified April 26, 2012, https://www.iol.co.za/business-report/economy/walmart-appoints-anti-bribery-officer-1284162.

6   United States Congress Senate Committee, *The Role of the Board of Directors in*

Enron's Collapse (Washington, D.C.: U.S. Government Printing Office, 2002), https://www.govinfo.gov/content/pkg/CPRT-107SPRT80393/pdf/CPRT-107SPRT80393.pdf.

7   Marianne M. Jennings, *The Seven Signs of Ethical Collapse: How to Spot Moral Meltdowns in Companies... Before It's Too Late* (New York, NY: St. Martin's Press, 2006).

8   Joseph T Wells, "Let Them Know Someone's Watching," *Journal of Accountancy*, (May 1, 2002). https://www.journalofaccountancy.com/issues/2002/may/letthemknowsomeoneswatching.html.

9   Both the Fair Credit Reporting Act, 15 U.S.C. 1681, *et seq.* and the Gramm-Leach-Bliley Act, also known as the Financial Services Modernization Act of 1999 have limitations on the use of certain information.

10   This guide can be found at: https://www.acfe.com/uploadedfiles/acfe_website/content/documents/managing-business-risk.pdf.

11   This guide can be found at: https://www.thecaq.org/sites/default/files/the-fraud-resistant-organization.pdf

12   United States Sentencing Commission, *Guidelines Manual*, §8B2.1(a).

13   United States Sentencing Commission, *Guidelines Manual*, §8B2.1(b)(1-7).

14   The Institute of Internal Auditors, *The Three Lines of Defense in Effective Risk Management and Control*, (IIA, 2013), accessed February 22, 2019, https://na.theiia.org/standards-guidance/Public%20Documents/PP%20The%20Three%20Lines%20of%20Defense%20in%20Effective%20Risk%20Management%20and%20Control.pdf.

Chapter 11: Fraud Detection

1   Mimi Swartz and Sherron Watkins, *Power Failure: The Inside Story of the Collapse of Enron* (New York, NY: Random House, 2003). See Appendix A in her book for a copy of the letter Sherron Watkins wrote to Enron CEO Ken Lay.

2   Ramamoorti, *A.B.C.'s*. An entire chapter is devoted to exploring emotions and fraud.

3   Sridhar Ramamoorti et al., "The Proof of Cash Should Be King Among Forensic Auditing Techniques," *Journal of Forensic & Investigative Accounting* 9, no. 2 (Fall 2017), http://web.nacva.com/JFIA/Issues/JFIA-2017-No2-7.pdf.

4   Mark J. Nigrini, *Benford's Law: Applications for Forensic Accounting, Auditing, and Fraud Detection* (Hoboken, NJ: John Wiley & Sons, 2012), 6.

5   Swartz, *Power Failure*.

6   31 U.S.C. §3729, *et seq.*

7   These amounts are approximations since the penalties adjust for inflation; see 31 U.S.C. §3729(a)(1).

8   31 U.S.C. §3729(a)(1).

9   15 U.S.C. §78u-6(b)(1).

10   15 U.S.C. §78u-6(b)(1)(A-B).

11   15 U.S.C. §78u-6(a)(3).

12   American Institute of Certified Public Accountants, AU-C-240, Appendix A.

13   American Institute of Certified Public Accountants, AU-C-240, Appendix A.

Chapter 12: Investigations

1   29 U.S.C. 2005(a),(c).

2   29 U.S.C. 2006(d).

3   29 U.S.C. 2006(a),(b).

4   *National Labor Relations Board v. J. Weingarten, Inc.*, 420 U.S. 251 (1975).

5   ACFE, *Fraud Examiners Manual* (2017), page 3, 2018.

6   The prohibition of reaching an opinion on the issue of guilt or innocence can be found in the Federal Rules of Evidence 704, American Institute of Certified Public Accountant's Statement on Standards for Forensic Services, and Association of Certified Fraud Examiner's Code of Ethics.

Chapter 13: Fraud Crisis Management

1   *In Re Caremark International Inc. Derivative Litigation*, 698 A. 2d 959 (Del. Ch. 1996)

Chapter 14: The Professionals

1   "Private Investigator License Requirements by State," Private Investigators EDU, accessed February 22, 2019, https://privateinvestigatoredu.org/license-requirements/.

2   Black, *Black's Law Dictionary*.

3   American Institute of Certified Public Accountants, *Statement on Standards for Forensic Services No.1.*

4   Ramamoorti et al. (2013). *A.B.C.'s of Behavioral Forensics.*

5   Public Company Accounting Oversight Board, *AS 1001 Responsibilities and Functions of the Independent Auditor.*

6   Public Company Accounting Oversight Board, *AS 1001 Responsibilities and Functions.*

7   Institute of Internal Auditors, *International Professional Practices Framework*, 2.

Chapter 15: Starting with the End in Mind

1   American Institute of Certified Public Accountants, *AICPA Code of Professional Conduct.* See §1.295.140.04(a)(i).

2   American Institute of Certified Public Accountants, *AICPA Code of Professional Conduct.* See 1.295.140.04(a)(ii)

3   American Institute of Certified Public Accountants, *AICPA Code of Professional Conduct.* See 1.100.001.

4   American Institute of Certified Public Accountants, *AICPA Code of Professional Conduct.* See 1.700.001.

5   R. E. Figlewicz and Hans-Dieter Sprohge, "The CPA's Expert Witness Role in Litigation Services: A Maze of Legal and Accounting Standards," *Ohio CPA Journal* (July-September 2002): 35.

6   See PwC 2018 *Daubert* Study at https://www.pwc.com/us/en/services/forensics/library/daubert-study.html. The PwC 2018 *Daubert* study continues the firm's annual analysis of *Daubert* challenges to financial experts. In the 18 years since the Supreme Court's 1999 ruling in Kumho Tire, PwC has analyzed 2,410 financial expert challenges, including 206 financial expert challenges decided during 2017.

7   *Brady v. Maryland*, 373 U.S. 83 (1963).
8   *Giglio v. United States*, 405 U.S. 150 (1972).

BIBLIOGRAPHY

AICPA. *Statement of position 98–2*. American Institute
of Certified Public Accountants, 1998.

Albrecht, Steve. "Iconic Fraud Triangle endures." *Fraud Magazine*, July/August 2014.

American Institute of Certified Public Accountants. *AICPA Code of
Professional Conduct*. Hoboken, NJ: John Wiley & Sons, 2015.

American Institute of Certified Public Accountant, *Consideration of Fraud in a
Financial Statement Audit*, AU-C §240-26 (New York: AICPA, 2017).

American Institute of Certified Public Accountants. *Statement on Standards for Forensic
Services No.1*. American Institute of Certified Public Accountants, 2007.

Association of Certified Fraud Examiners. *Managing the Business
Risk of Fraud: A Practical Guide*. ACFE, n.d. PDF.

Association of Certified Fraud Examiners. *2018 Report to the Nations:
Occupational Fraud and Abuse*. Austin, TX, 2018.

Association of Certified Fraud Examiners. "Who We Are," accessed
February 24, 2019, https//:www.acfe.com/who-we-are.aspx.

Association of Certified Fraud Examiners. *Fraud Examiners Manual*. Austin, TX, 2017.

Beasley, Mark S., Joseph V. Carello, Dana R. Hermanson, and Terry L.
Neal. "An Analysis of U.S. Public Companies." *Committee of Sponsoring
Organizations of the Treadway Commission*, May 2010, https://www.
coso.org/Documents/COSO-Fraud-Study-2010–001.pdf.

Black, Henry Campbell. *Black's Law Dictionary*, 5th ed. St.
Paul, MN: West Publishing Co., 1979.

Brazel, Joseph F., Keith L. Jones, and Mark F. Zimbelman. "Using
Nonfinancial Measures to Assess Fraud Risk." *Journal of Accounting
Research* 47, no. 5 (October 2009), 1135–1166.

Buell, John M. "Ethical Leadership in Uncertain Times." *Healthcare Executive*,
May/June 2015. https://www.ache.org/-/media/ache/about-ache/

fund-for-healthcare-leadership/ethical_leadership_reprint.pdf?la=en& hash=0CFB2A741B793BB1E7F623A89D90594F55AABBC6.

Cialdini, Robert B. *Influence: The Psychology of Persuasion.* New York: Harper Collins, 2007.

Cohn, Michael. "Informant Blew the Whistle on Price Fixing at ADM." *Accounting Today.* Last modified June 21, 2012. https://www.accountingtoday. com/opinion/informant-blew-the-whistle-on-price-fixing-at-adm.

Cooper, Cynthia. *Extraordinary Circumstances: The Journey of a Corporate Whistleblower.* Hoboken, NJ: John Wiley & Sons, 2008.

Cressey, Donald R. *Other People's Money.* Montclair, NJ: Patterson Smith, 1973.

Department of Justice, Federal Bureau of Investigation, https:// www.fbi.gov/investigate/public-corruption/2016.

Department of Justice, and Securities and Exchange Commission. *FCPA: A Resource Guide to the U.S. Foreign Corrupt Practices Act.* 2012.

Department of the Treasury. "Audit Techniques Guides ATGs." Internal Revenue Service. Last modified March 21, 2018. https://www.irs.gov/ businesses/small-businesses-self-employed/audit-techniques-guides-atgs.

Department of the Treasury. *Tax Gap Estimates for Tax Years 2008–2010.* Internal Service Revenue, 2016. PDF.

Department of Treasury, Internal Revenue Service, *Internal Revenue Manual.*

Dorrell, Darrell D., and Gregory A. Gadawski. *Financial Forensics Body of Knowledge.* Hoboken, NJ: John Wiley & Sons, 2012.

Federal Trade Commission. *Consumer Sentinel Network Data Book.* 2017.

Feng, Mei, Weili Ge, Shuqing Luo, and Terry Shevlin. *The Role of CFOs in Material Accounting Manipulations* (The Conference Board, 2010). https://www.conferenceboard.org/publications/ publicationdetail.cfm?publicationid=1938&subtopicid=200

Figlewicz, R. E., and Hans-Dieter Sprohge. "The CPA's Expert Witness Role in Litigation Services: A Maze of Legal and Accounting Standards." *Ohio CPA Journal,* July–September 2002), 35.

Financial Accounting Standards Board. *Accounting Standards Update No. 2016–10.* 2016. PDF.

Financial Accounting Standards Board. *Accounting Standards Update No. 2016–14.* 2016. PDF.

Financial Accounting Standards Board. *Statement of Financial Accounting Standards No. 117.* 1993.

Financial Accounting Standards Board. *Statement of Financial Accounting Standards No. 5.* Financial Accounting Foundation, 1975.

Financial Accounting Standards Board. *Statement of Financial Accounting Standards No. 86.* Financial Accounting Foundation, 1985.

Flangas Law Group. "Piercing the Corporate Veil." Last modified September 5, 2012, https://www.fdlawlv.com/blog/BOSVIEW/ PIERCING-THE-CORPORATE-VEIL/.

Fortune. "FORTUNE 500: Enron." *Fortune.* Accessed January 30, 2019. http://archive. fortune.com/magazines/fortune/fortune500_archive/snapshots/2001/478.html.

Hartman, Victor E. "Whistleblower Shields and Swords." *New Perspectives on Healthcare Risk Management, Control, and Governance,* Summer 2018, 49.

Hartman, Victor, and Sridhar Ramamoorti. "Procurement Card Fraud." *New Perspectives on Healthcare Risk Management, Control and Governance* 37, no. 4 (Winter 2018), 28.

Hartman, Victor E., and Sridhar Ramamoorti. "Public Corruption: Causes, Consequences & Countermeasures." *The Journal of Government Financial Management* 65, no. 1 (Spring 2016): 43–47.

Hartman, Victor, and Sridhar Ramamoorti. "Ransomware: A Primer." *New Perspectives on Healthcare Risk Management, Control, and Governance,* Spring 2017.

Heron, Randall A., and Erik Lie. *What fraction of stock option grants to top executives have been backdated or manipulated?* 2006.

Hollandsworth, Skip. "The Killing of Alydar." *Texas Monthly.* June 2001. https://www.texasmonthly.com/articles/the-killing-of-alydar/.

The Institute of Internal Auditors. *International Professional Practices Framework.* Lake Mary, FL: The Institute of Internal Auditors, 2009.

The Institute of Internal Auditors. *The Three Lines of Defense in Effective Risk Management and Control.* Altamonte Springs, FL: IIA, 2013.

International Consortium of Investigative Journalists. "about the Investigation." (Website). ICIJ. Accessed March 1, 2019. https://www.icij.org/about/.

Jennings, Marianne M. *The Seven Signs of Ethical Collapse: How to Spot Moral Meltdowns in Companies... Before It's Too Late.* New York, NY: St. Martin's Press, 2006.

Knutson, Mark C. *The Remarkable Criminal Financial Career of Charles Ponzi*. 2011. PDF. https://www.mark-knutson.com/blog/wp-content/uploads/2014/06/ponzi.pdf.

National Health Care Anti-Fraud Association. "The Challenge of Health Care Fraud." Accessed February 13, 2019, https://www.nhcaa.org/resources/health-care-anti-fraud-resources/the-challenge-of-health-care-fraud.aspx.

Nigrini, Mark J. *Benford's Law: Applications for Forensic Accounting, Auditing, and Fraud Detection*. Hoboken, NJ: John Wiley & Sons, 2012.

Palmiter, Alan R. *Securities Regulation*. New York: Wolters Kluwer, 2011.

Public Company Accounting Oversight Board. "AS 1001: Responsibilities and Functions of the Independent Auditor." PCAOB.

Ramamoorti, Sridhar, David E. Morrison III, Joseph W. Koletar, and Kelly R. Pope. *A.B.C.'s of Behavioral Forensics: Applying Psychology to Financial Fraud Prevention and Detection*. Hoboken, NJ: John Wiley & Sons, 2013.

Ramamoorti, Sridhar, and Joseph Dupree. "Continuous Controls Monitoring Can Help Deter Fraud." *Financial Executive*, April 2010.

Ramamoorti, Sridhar, and Barry J. Epstein. "Today's Fraud Risk Models Lack Personality." *The CPA Journal*, March 2016, 15–24.

Ramamoorti, Sridhar, Barry J. Epstein, Darrell D. Dorrell, and Viswanathan Varadarajan. "The Proof of Cash Should be King Among Forensic Auditing Techniques." *Journal of Forensic & Investigative Accounting* 9, no. 2 (Fall 2017). http://web.nacva.com/JFIA/Issues/JFIA-2017-No2–7.pdf.

Ramamoorti, Sri, and William Olsen. "Fraud: The Human Factor." *Financial Executive*, (July/August 2007), 53–55.

Rittenberg, Larry E., Karla M. Johnstone, Audrey A. Gramling. *Auditing: A Business Risk Approach*. Mason, OH: South-Western Cengage Learning, 2010.

Rachel Rodgers, "Crundwell Recovery: 5 Years Later," *SaukValley*, April 14, 2017, https://www.saukvalley.com/2017/04/14/crundwell-recovery-5-years-later/a7nasm0/.

Roosevelt, Theodore. The Man in the Arena. Excerpt from the speech "Citizenship in a Republic." Delivered at the Sorbonne, in Paris, France on Aril 23, 1910.

Securities Exchange Commission. "Municipal Securities Enforcement Actions." Last modified February 27, 2017. https://www.sec.gov/municipal/oms-enforcement-actions.html.

Sutton, Willie, and Edward Linn. *Where the Money Was*. New York: Viking Press, 1976.

Swartz, Mimi, and Sherron Watkins. *Power Failure: The Inside Story of the Collapse of Enron*. New York, NY: Random House, 2003.

Third Superseding Indictment, *United States of America v. Bernard J. Ebbers*, (Sept. 15, 2004), https://www.justice.gov/archive/dag/cftf/chargingdocs/ebberss504.pdf

Tomkins, Silvan S., and Robert McCarter. "What and Where Are the Primary Affects? Some Evidence for a Theory." *Perceptual and Motor Skills* 18, no. 1 (1964), 119–158. doi:10.2466/pms.1964.18.1.119.

Third Superseding Indictment, *United States of America v. Bernard J. Ebbers*, (Sept. 15, 2004),

Transparency International. *Corruption Perceptions Index 2017*, 2017.

United States Congress Senate Committee. *The Role of the Board of Directors in Enron's Collapse*. Washington, D.C.: U.S. Government Printing Office, 2002, https:// www. govinfo.gov/content/pkg/CPRT-107SPRT80393/pdf/CPRT-107SPRT80393.pdf.

Vaughan, Diane. *The Challenger Launch Decision: Risky Technology, Culture, and Deviance at NASA*. Chicago, IL: University of Chicago Press, 1996.

Verizon. *2018 Data Breach Investigations Report*. 2018. https://www. verizonenterprise.com/resources/reports/rp_DBIR_2018_ Report_execsummary_en_xg.pdf (September 27, 2018).

Wells, Joseph T. "Let Them Know Someone's Watching." *Journal of Accountancy*, May 1, 2002.

The White House. *IPEC Annual Intellectual Property Report to Congress*. Executive Branch, March 2018. PDF.

Zack, Gerard M. "Not-for-profit Fraud." *Fraud Magazine* (September/October 2003).

Zuckoff, Mitchell. *Ponzi's Scheme: The True Story of a Financial Legend*. New York, NY: Random House, 2006.

INDEX

405